Tarleton Hoffman Bean

The fishes of Pennsylvania:

With descriptions of the species and notes on their common names, distribution,

habits, reproduction, rate of growth and mode of capture

Tarleton Hoffman Bean

The fishes of Pennsylvania:
With descriptions of the species and notes on their common names, distribution, habits, reproduction, rate of growth and mode of capture

ISBN/EAN: 9783337774967

Printed in Europe, USA, Canada, Australia, Japan

Cover: Foto ©ninafisch / pixelio.de

More available books at www.hansebooks.com

THE FISHES OF PENNSYLVANIA.

With Descriptions of the Species and Notes on their Common
Names, Distribution, Habits, Reproduction, Rate
of Growth and Mode of Capture.

BY

TARLETON H. BEAN, M. D.,

ASSISTANT IN CHARGE DIVISION OF FISH CULTURE, UNITED STATES FISH COMMISSION, HONORARY
CURATOR DEPARTMENT OF FISHES, UNITED STATES NATIONAL MUSEUM, ETC., ETC.

(ii)

INTRODUCTION.

Early in 1891 Mr. Henry C. Ford requested me to prepare a paper upon the fishes of the State of Pennsylvania for the current report of the Fish Commission of which he is president. The scope of the article was, by mutual agreement, to be limited to brief descriptions of the species, with notes upon their common names, distribution, size, habits, reproduction, rate of growth and mode of capture. Inasmuch as the plan of the work involved the illustration of all the important fishes it was not considered essential to introduce keys for the identification of the species.

The descriptions are chiefly original, and are based upon specimens contained in the collection of the United States National Museum at Washington, D. C. The popular notes have been obtained largely from original investigations and, in part, by compilation from the writings of Goode, Gill, Cope, and Jordan. In connection with field work in the service of the United States Fish Commission the writer has derived much information of value, which is here for the first time recorded.

The colored plates were made by Mr. Sherman F. Denton of Wellesley, Mass., from living or fresh specimens. The major portion of the illustrations in black have been reproduced from original drawings belonging to the United States Fish Commission. In addition to these, a number of new illustrations were made by Mr. J. C. Van Hook and Mr. A. H. Baldwin.

Acknowledgments are due to James Thompson of Erie, John W. Hague, Esq., of Pittsburg, A. B. Burns and D. T. Webster, Esq., of Montrose, Ben. L. Hewitt, Esq., Hollidaysburg, Dr. B. H. Warren of West Chester, Hon. Henry C. Ford and John Gay of Philadelphia, and W. L. Powell of Harrisburg, for valuable notes upon the distribution and habits of the species. Mr. Barton A Bean, assistant curator of the department of fishes, United States National Museum, rendered much assistance in preparing the descriptions and drawings of the species.

The scope of this paper does not include statistics of the commercial fisheries, but it may be of interest to remark that, considering the short lake coast of the state, amounting to only forty-seven miles, it is the scene of the most important fisheries of the state. According to the *Review of the Fisheries of the Great Lakes in 1885*, published in the report of the United States Fish Commission, Erie then had nineteen pound-nets and 10,700 gill-nets. Erie fishermen caught nearly two-thirds of all the white fish taken in the lake in that year, their catch amounting to more than 2,000,000 pounds out of a total of 3,500,000 pounds. The wholesale value of the fish products is said to have been

$412,750. The principal commercial fishes were blue pike, lake herring, white fish, suckers and other fish of the same family, sturgeon, perch, pike perch, lake trout, cat fish, saugers, bass, grass pike and muscalonge, these being named in the order of their aggregate in weight. The total catch of these species for the year amounted to 10,793,500 pounds.

Only a few lake trout were taken off Erie and those were large, weighing from twenty five to forty pounds each. White fish are caught in Erie county chiefly in July, August and November. Lake herring and blue pike are taken chiefly in April and the early part of May.

The whole number of species credited to Pennsylvania is one hundred and fifty-seven. The families which are represented by the largest number of species are those including the cat fishes, suckers, minnows, sunfishes and darters.

The following is a provisional statement of the distribution of the species with reference to the Lake Erie basin, the Ohio valley, and the streams of the Atlantic drainage system. The fish fauna of Lake Erie is not sufficiently known to enable me to present it with certainty and completeness.

DISTRIBUTION OF PENNSYLVANIA FISHES.

	Lake Erie.	Ohio valley.	Atlantic basin.
1. Ammocœtes niger,	x	x	
2. Petromyzon marinus,			x
3. Petromyzon concolor,	x	x	
4. Polyodon spathula,	x (?)	x	
5. Scaphirhynchus platyrhynchus,		x	
6. Acipenser sturio,			x
7. Acipenser brevirostrum,			x
8. Acipenser rubicundus,	x	x	
9. Lepisosteus osseus,	x	x	x
10. Lepisosteus platystomus,	x	x	
11. Amia calva,	x	x	x
12. Ictalurus punctatus,	x	x	x
13. Amiurus nigricans,	x	x	
14. Amiurus albidus,			x
15. Amiurus natalis,	x	x	
16. Amiurus vulgaris,	x	x	
17. Amiurus nebulosus,	x	x	x
18. Amiurus melas,	x	x	
19. Gronias nigrilabris,			x
20. Leptops olivaris,		x	
21. Noturus flavus,	x	x	
22. Noturus insignis,			x
23. Noturus gyrinus,			x
24. Ictiobus urus,		x	
25. Ictiobus bubalus,		x	
26. Ictiobus carpio,		x	
27. Ictiobus difformis,		x	
28. Ictiobus velifer,	x	x	
29. Ictiobus cyprinus,		x	x
30. Cycleptus elongatus,		x	
31. Catostomus catostomus,	x	x	x
32. Catostomus teres,	x	x	x
33. Catostomus nigricans,	x	x	x
34. Erimyzon sucetta,	x	x	x
35. Minytrema melanops,	x	x	

Distribution of Pennsylvania Fishes—*Continued*.

	Lake Erie.	Ohio valley.	Atlantic basin.
36. Moxostoma anisurum,	x	x	
37. Moxostoma macrolepidotum,	x	x	x
38. Moxostoma aureolum,	x	x	
39. Moxostoma crassilabre,		x	
40. Placopharynx carinatus,		x	
41. Campostoma anomalum,		x	x
42. Chrosomus erythrogaster,		x	x
43. Hybognathus nuchalis,		x	x
44. Hybognathus regius,			x
45. Pimephales promelas,		x	
46. Pimephales notatus,	x	x	
47. Exoglossum maxillingua,			x
48. Notropis bifrenatus,			x
49. Notropis procne,			x
50. Notropis hudsonius,	x		x
51. Notropis amarus,	x		x
52. Notropis whipplei,	x	x	x
53. Notropis megalops,	x	x	x
54. Notropis chalybaeus,			x
55. Notropis jejunus,		x	
56. Notropis scabriceps,		x	
57. Notropis ardens,		x	
58. Notropis photogenis,			x
59. Notropis dilectus,		x	
60. Notropis atherinoides,	x	x	
61. Ericymba buccata,		x	
62. Phenacobius teretulus,		x	
63. Rhinichthys cataractae,			x
64. Rhinichthys atronasus,		x	x
65. Hybopsis dissimilis,		x	
66. Hybopsis amblops,		x	
67. Hybopsis kentuckiensis,		x	x
68. Semotilus bullaris,			x
69. Semotilus atromaculatus,		x	x
70. Phoxinus elongatus,		x	
71. Phoxinus funduloides,			x
72. Phoxinus margaritus,			x
73. Notemigonus chrysoleucus,			x
74. Carassius auratus,	o	o	*
75. Cyprinus carpio,	o	o	*
76. Hyodon alosoides,	x	x	
77. Hyodon tergisus,	x	x	
78. Clupea vernalis,			x
79. Clupea chrysochloris,	x	x	
80. Clupea sapidissima,			x
81. Brevoortia tyrannus,			x
82. Dorosoma cepedianum,	x	x	x
83. Osmerus mordax,			x
84. Coregonus quadrilateralis,	x		
85. Coregonus clupeiformis,	x		
86. Coregonus artedi,	x		
87. Coregonus tullibee,	x		
88. Thymallus ontariensis,			*
89. Oncorhynchus chouicha,			*
90. Salmo salar,			*
91. Salmo irideus,			*
92. Salmo fario,			*
93. Salvelinus fontinalis,	x	x	x
94. Salvelinus namayeush,	x		
95. Percopsis guttatus,	x	x	x
96. Fundulus majalis,			x
97. Fundulus diaphanus,	x	x	x
98. Fundulus heteroclitus,			x
99. Zygonectes notatus,		x	

* Species so marked have been introduced.

DISTRIBUTION OF PENNSYLVANIA FISHES—*Continued.*

	Lake Erie.	Ohio valley.	Atlantic basin.
100. Zygonectes dispar,		x	
101. Umbra limi,	x	x	
102. Umbra pygmaea,			x
103. Esox americanus,			x
104. Esox vermiculatus,	x	x	
105. Esox reticulatus,	x		x
106. Esox lucius,	x	x	x
107. Esox nobilior,	x	x	
108. Anguilla rostrata,	x	x	x
109. Tylosurus marinus,			x
110. Eucalia inconstans,		x	
111. Gasterosteus aculeatus,			x
112. Apeltes quadracus,			x
113. Menidia beryllina,			x
114. Labidesthes sicculus,		x	
115. Aphredoderus sayanus,	x	x	x
116. Pomoxys sparoides,	x	x	
117. Pomoxys annularis,	x	x	
118. Ambloplites rupestris,	x	x	*
119. Acantharchus pomotis,			x
120. Enneacanthus obesus,			x
121. Enneacanthus simulans,			x
122. Mesogonistius chaetodon,			x
123. Lepomis cyanellus,	x	x	
124. Lepomis macrochirus,		x	
125. Lepomis pallidus,	x	x	x
126. Lepomis auritus,			x
127. Lepomis megalotis,	x	x	
128. Lepomis gibbosus,	x		x
129. Micropterus dolomieu,	x	x	*
130. Micropterus salmoides,	x	x	*
131. Etheostoma pellucida,		x	
132. Etheostoma olmstedi,			x
133. Etheostoma nigrum,	x	x	
134. Etheostoma aesopus,		x	
135. Etheostoma blennioides,		x	
136. Etheostoma caprodes,	x	x	x
137. Etheostoma macrocephalum,		x	
138. Etheostoma peltatum,			x
139. Etheostoma aspro,		x	
140. Etheostoma variatum,		x	
141. Etheostoma zonale,		x	
142. Etheostoma maculatum,		x	
143. Etheostoma flabellare,		x	
144. Etheostoma coeruleum,		x	
145. Perca flavescens,	x	x	x
146. Stizostedion vitreum,	x	x	x
147. Stizostedion salmoneum,	x	x	
148. Stizostedion canadense,	x	x	
149. Roccus lineatus,			x
150. Roccus chrysops,	x	x	
151. Morone americana,			x
152. Morone interrupta,	x	x	*
153. Aplodinotus grunniens,	x	x	
154. Uranidea richardsoni,	x	x	
155. Uranidea viscosa,			x
156. Uranidea gracilis,		x	x
157. Lota maculosa,	x	x	x

*Species so marked have been introduced.

It is hoped that this report will stimulate investigation of the waters of the state with the result of bringing together collections to form the basis of a much more extensive and satisfactory account of the fishes of this great commonwealth. The author will gladly undertake the preparation of a final report provided he can secure the co-operation of collectors in various parts of the state, and particularly in localities wherein the fishes are comparatively little known.

TARLETON H. BEAN.

U. S. FISH COMMISSION, WASHINGTON, D. C.,
November 25, 1892.

FISHES OF PENNSYLVANIA.

Class CYCLOSTOMI. The Myzonts.
Order HYPEROARTIA.
Family **PETROMYZONTIDÆ**. The Lampreys.
Genus **AMMOCŒTES** Duméril.

The genus *Ammocœtes* is best distinguished from *Petromyzon* by the structure of its so-called maxillary tooth, which has the form of a crescent-shaped plate with terminal cusps and sometimes an additional median cusp. In *Petromyzon* this bony plate is short and contains two or three teeth, which are very closely placed.

1. Ammocœtes niger Rafinesque.

The Brook Lamprey. (*Figure 16.*)

The high dorsal fin is divided into two parts by a deep notch. Several of the teeth on the side of the buccal disk are bicuspid and the rest simple. The mandibulary plate is nearly straight and has eight or ten cusps of nearly equal size. The length of the head, including the gills, is contained four and three-fourths times in the total. There are sixty-seven muscular impressions from gills to vent. In the spring a prominent anal papilla is present. The head is longer than the space occupied by the gill-openings and is contained eight and one-third times in the total; the depth, fourteen times. The eyes are large. The mouth is moderately small. The lips are conspicuously fringed with papillae. The teeth change considerably with age; young examples have no median cusp on the maxillary plate. This lamprey is bluish-black above, the lower parts silvery.

The brook lamprey or mud lamprey, also known as the small black lamprey, is found in the Great Lake region, the Ohio valley and the upper Mississippi valley. It occurs also in Cayuga lake, New York. According to Jordan it ranges west to Minnesota and south to Kentucky. It grows to a length of eight inches. Dr. Jordan considers it identical with the common brook lamprey of Europe, *A. branchialis*. The brook lamprey ascends the small streams in the spring to spawn just as the silver lamprey does. It is parasitic, and its spawning habits are similar to those of the sea lamprey. It clings to stones and clogs of earth while depositing its eggs, and is believed by some persons to die after spawning. The probability is that it goes into deep water, where it remains until the spawning season again approaches.

GENUS **PETROMYZON** (ARTEDI) LINNÆUS.

2. Petromyzon marinus LINNÆUS.

The Sea Lamprey. (*Figure 17.*)

Body cylindrical, eel-like, stout, somewhat compressed behind. The mouth is terminal, subcircular in shape and suctorial. It is strongly armed with large conical teeth or cusps mounted on papillae, those of the inner series being bicuspid. Guarding the throat are crescent-shaped plates, bearing pectinate lingual teeth; a pair of these plates on either side and another pair below them. The mandibulary plate has seven cusps. There are seven branchial apertures on each side of the head, the first not far behind the eye; the distance of the last opening from the tip of the snout is contained about five times in the total length. Eye rather small, covered with membrane. The first dorsal originates in about the middle of the length; it is little developed and well separated from the second dorsal, which is confluent with the anal. The anal is very low and only about one-half as long as the second dorsal. The vent is far back, opposite the origin of the second dorsal. The specimen examined is twenty-eight inches long, and is No. 10654 in the United States National Museum collection.

The sea lamprey or lamprey eel inhabits the north Atlantic, ascending streams to spawn and sometimes becoming landlocked. In some interior waters of New York the landlocked form has received the name *unicolor* of DeKay. The species ranges southward on our coast to Virginia. In the Delaware, Susquehanna and their tributaries this is a common fish. Its larval form, which is blind and toothless, is extremely abundant in muddy sand flats near the mouths of small streams, and is a very important bait for hook and line fishing. The sea lamprey grows to a length of three feet. It is dark brown in color, mottled with blackish and whitish. In the breeding season in spring the males have a high fleshy ridge in front of the dorsal. The spawning is believed to take place in May or June. The eels cling to the rocks by means of their suctorial mouths, and the eggs are deposited in shallow water on a rough bottom where the current is swift. Some observers state that they make nests by heaping up stones in a circle and deposit the eggs under the stones. The ovaries are large, but the eggs are very small. The food of the lamprey is chiefly animal matter, and the fish is somewhat of a parasite, burrowing into the side of shad, sturgeon and some other species. The teeth are adapted for this method of feeding. The tooth-bearing bone of the upper side of the mouth contains two teeth which are placed close together. On the bone corresponding with the lower jaw there are seven or nine stout cusps. There are numerous teeth around the disk; the first row on the side of the mouth contains bicuspid teeth; the others are simple. The tooth on the front of the tongue has a deep median groove. The species is adapted for fastening itself to other fishes and extracting from them their blood. The lamprey is considered a good food fish in some localities, but in other places it is rarely eaten. In Connecticut and Massachusetts the species is highly esteemed. It is preserved by salting for several weeks before using. The fish are sometimes caught with the hands and by means of a pole armed with a hook.

in the end. As it is found in shallow water and will not usually relinquish its hold on the bottom, its capture is easily effected.

3. Petromyzon concolor KIRTLAND.

The Silver Lamprey.

The silver lamprey belongs to the sub-genus *Ichthyomyzon* of Girard. It has the tooth on the front of the tongue divided into two portions by a median groove and the dorsal fin continuous but deeply notched. The maxillary tooth is bicuspid; the teeth on the disk are in about four series and all small. The tooth-bearing bone of the lower part of the mouth has seven cusps. The head (from tip of disk to first gill-opening) is two-fifteenths of the total length; with the gill-openings its length is contained four and three-fourths times in the total. There are fifty-one muscular impressions from gills to vent. The body is rather stout, compressed posteriorly. The head is broad and the buccal disk large with its edges not conspicuously fringed. Color bluish-silvery, sometimes with blackish mottlings. Above each gill-opening there is a small bluish blotch.

The silver lamprey or mud eel is found in the Great Lake region and the Ohio and Mississippi valleys. It grows to a length of twelve inches and is usually found in deep water, but runs up the small streams to spawn in the spring. It is a troublesome parasite on the lake sturgeon, the paddle-fish, yellow perch and some other species. It becomes fixed to the skin by means of its suctorial disk, and the irritation of its teeth sometimes causes deep ulcers at the point of attachment. This lamprey has the same peculiarities of development as the sea lamprey and sometimes remains in the larval condition, blind and toothless, until it has reached a length of eight inches.

CLASS PISCES. THE FISHES.

SUBCLASS TELEOSTOMI. THE TRUE FISHES.

ORDER SELACHOSTOMI. THE PADDLE FISHES.

FAMILY POLYODONTIDÆ.

GENUS POLYODON (LACÉPÈDE) BLOCH AND SCHNEIDER.

4. Polyodon spathula WALBAUM.

The Paddle Fish. (*Figure 18.*)

The body of the paddle-fish is fusiform with the snout much produced, spatula-like. Body scaleless, covered with smooth skin. Mouth broad, terminal, somewhat resembling that of a shark. Teeth in jaws very numerous and fine, deciduous. Spiracles with a minute barbel. The operculum is rudimentary, its flap of skin long, reaching almost or quite to the ventral fins. Pseudobranchiæ absent. Gill-arches five, the last rudimentary; gill-rakers long and in a double series on each arch. Gill membranes connected, free from the isthmus. Nostrils double, situated at base of blade. A continuous lateral line from upper portion of head along dorsal outline to tail. Eye small, directed downwards and to the side. Dorsal and anal fins far back, composed of soft rays, nearly opposite. Tail heterocercal, well forked. Upper lobe of caudal, on vertebral column, armed with rhombic plates. The pectoral fins are of moderate size and placed low; ventrals many rayed, abdominal.

The distance from eye to end of snout is about one-third of the total length, including caudal. The depth of the body is contained four and one-half times in distance from eye to base of caudal. The height of the dorsal fin about equals the depth of the body.

This is known as the paddle-fish, spoon-bill or spoon-billed sturgeon, shovel-fish, bill-fish and duck-billed cat; it is called "salmon" in some western hotels.

The names are derived from the remarkable snout, which is produced into a long spatula-shaped process, covered above and below with an intricate network and has very thin flexible edges. The head and snout form nearly half of the entire length of the fish. The fish cannot be confounded with anything else in the waters of the United States. There is in China a similar one, which, however, belongs to a different genus.

Distribution.—The single species of American paddle-fish is confined to the Mississippi valley. It inhabits only the larger streams in Pennsylvania. It is common in the Allegheny and the Monongahela rivers.

Size.—The paddle-fish grows to a length of six feet, and a weight of thirty pounds or more.

Habits.—The species frequents muddy bottoms, but does not feed upon the mud and slime as many persons have supposed. The long snout is useful in procuring its food, which consists chiefly of entomostraca, water worms, aquatic plants, leeches, beetles and insect larvæ.

Prof. S. A. Forbes, director of the Illinois Laboratory of Natural History, has published the first and most satisfactory account of the feeding habits of this shark-like fish. He found very little mud mixed with the food. Prof. Forbes was informed by the fishermen that the paddle-fish plows up the mud in feeding with its spatula-like snout and then swims slowly backward through the water.

"The remarkably developed gill-rakers of this species are very numerous and fine, in a double row on each gill arch, and they are twice as long as the filaments of the gill. By their interlacing they form a strainer scarcely less effective than the fringes of the baleen plates of the whale, and probably allow the passage of the fine silt of the river bed when this is thrown into the water by the shovel of the fish but arrest everything as large as a *Cyclops.*"

I have not found anything recorded as to the spawning habits of the paddle-fish. The young have the jaws and palate filled with minute teeth, which disappear with age.

Mode of capture.—The fish are generally caught by seining.

Edible qualities.—The flesh of the paddle-fish is generally considered tough and shark-like, but individuals of eight or ten pounds are skinned and sold in some of the western markets very freely, and by some persons are thought to be very fair for the table.

ORDER GLANIOSTOMI (THE STURGEONS).

Family ACIPENSERIDÆ.

Genus SCAPHIRHYNCHUS Heckel.

The genus *Scaphirhynchus* is distinguished from the genus of the common sturgeons, *Acipenser*, by the absence of spiracles and by the complete armature of the tail with bony plates. Tail much depressed, wider than deep. Snout depressed, acutely triangular in shape and in the form of a spade. In the young the tail ends in a long filament. Gill rakers fan-shaped. Pseudobranchiæ not developed.

Body elongate with tapering snout and tail. It has rows of bony plates along the top of the back, the median line and near the abdominal outline. Under the dorsal these shields are confluent and are continued over the top of the tail, forming a complete bony covering.

5. Scaphirhynchus platyrhynchus Rafinesque.

The Shovel-nosed Sturgeon.

The body of the shovel-nosed sturgeon is elongate, the tail slender and depressed, the head broad, snout long and flat or shovel-shaped. The tail ends in a filament, which in the young is rather long, often wanting in the adult. The head is contained about three and one-half times in the length to the end of the vertebræ. There is a small spine in front of the eye, another at the posterior edge of the shovel, and in the young there are several spines on the snout. A pair of barbels on the under surface of the snout, situated nearer the eyes than the tip of the snout, their distance from the eye being two-ninths length of the head, while their distance from the snout is more than one-third of the same length. The barbels have rather numerous minute filaments along their edges. The length of the barbels is rather more than one-fourth that of the head. The eye is very small, less than one-seventh the posterior portion of head. The posterior nostril is slightly oblique in position, longer than the eye; anterior nostril about as long as the eye. The height of the body is contained seven and one-half times in the total without caudal, and is nearly half length of head. The length of the snout is contained six and one-half times in total without caudal. The postorbital part of the head is about two-fifths length of head. The pectoral has a very broad base, and its length equals height of body. The distance from the pectoral origin to the ventral origin about equals length of head. The ventral is a little more than one-half as long as the snout. The dorsal and anal fins are small and not so far back as in the lake sturgeon. The dorsal origin is over the twenty-sixth scute of the median series. The length of its base is half length of snout, about equal to its longest ray, which is more than twice the length of its last ray. The anal is under the posterior part of the dorsal; its longest ray nearly one-third length of head, and twice the length of anal base. The least height of caudal peduncle is scarcely more than one-seventh the greatest height of body. The lower lobe of the caudal fin is less than one-third as long as the upper, which is longer than the head. The gill rakers end in several points. Dorsal shields from fifteen to eighteen; median shields, forty-one to forty-six, and ventral shields from eleven to thirteen. The rays of all the fins are slender and numerous. Color very pale yellowish, sometimes whitish.

The shovel-nosed or white sturgeon is found in the Ohio and Mississippi valleys, extending to the upper Missouri and to the Rio Grande. In the large tributaries of the Ohio, in western Pennsylvania, the species is very common. Its maximum length is eight feet, but it is not an important food fish, being but little esteemed. Nothing is recorded of its habits except that it runs up in the small streams in May for the purpose of spawning.

Genus **ACIPENSER** (Artedi) Linnæus.

6. Acipenser sturio Linnæus.

The Common Sturgeon. (*Figure 13.*)

The common or sharp-nosed sturgeon has a stout, roundish and elongate body, its height equalling one-half the length of the head and one-sixth of the total without the caudal. The least depth of the tail equals one-third of the greatest body depth. The head is long, one-third of total without the caudal, and the snout is as long as the rest of the head in the young. The eye is one-sixth as long as the snout. Two pairs of short, slender barbels midway between the mouth and tip of snout. The front of the mouth is nearly under the posterior edge of the pupil. The nostrils are double, the posterior pair more than twice as large as the anterior. The dorsal and anal fins are placed far back and opposite to each other. The distance of the ventral origin from the end of the lower caudal lobe equals the length of the head. The upper caudal lobe is nearly twice as long as the lower. D. 38 to 40; A. 23 to 26; V. 24; lateral plates 27 to 29; dorsal shields 10 to 14; ventral shields 11 and 12.

The color of the upper parts is dark olive-gray, sometimes brownish; the lower parts are light gray or whitish. The pupils are black; the iris golden.

The common sturgeon of the eastern United States is also known as the sharp-nosed sturgeon. It has been considered identical with the European sturgeon, *Acipenser sturio*, and if this theory is correct the range of the species would include the Atlantic ocean southward to Africa and the West Indies. The northern limit on our east coast appears to be Cape Cod. The fish has come up rarely in the Delaware as far as Port Jervis. Dr. Mitchill was the first to call attention to the similarity of the American sharp-nosed sturgeon to the *sturio* of Europe.

This fish attains to a length of twelve feet in American waters and it is stated that European individuals measuring eighteen feet have been taken.

The sturgeon ascends the large rivers from the sea in spring and early summer. It is very common in the lower portion of the Delaware river, where it forms the object of an important fishery. This is the species concerning which so many stories have been related as to its leaping into boats and injuring the occupants.

The mouth of the sturgeon is furnished with a very protractile roundish tube having powerful muscles and intended for withdrawing from the mud the various small shell-fish and crustaceans upon which the animal subsists. The mouth is surrounded also with numerous tentacles, with tactile properties, which are utilized in procuring food.

The reproductive habits of the sturgeon and the embryology of the species have been made the subject of an exhaustive study by Prof. John A. Ryder, of the University of Pennsylvania, whose monograph forms a part of the Bulletin of the United States Fish Commission for 1888, recently published.

The eggs were fertilized and developed artificially by Seth Green and others many years ago, and in some parts of Europe the hatching of the species has been carried on successfully. The United States Fish Commission has also recently taken up the culture both of the marine and the lake sturgeon and these valuable fish will soon be reared on an extensive scale.

The utilization of the flesh, the skin and air bladder and the eggs of the sturgeon is so well known as to require little more than passing mention in this place. The smoking of the flesh and the manufacture of caviare from the eggs are very important industries along our eastern coast.

The sturgeons are easily taken in gill nets and pounds, but the great strength of the fish frequently entails considerable loss of apparatus.

7. Acipenser brevirostrum LE SUEUR.

The Short-nosed Sturgeon.

In the short-nosed sturgeon the snout is very blunt and only about one-fourth to one-third as long as the head. The four short barbels are a little nearer to the end of the snout than to the mouth, and do not reach to the mouth. The head is one-fifth to two-ninths as long as the total to the fork of the tail ; the distance between the eyes slightly greater than length of snout and somewhat more than one-third length of head. The average number of bucklers in the dorsal series is 10 to 11; in the lateral series, 25; in the ventral row, 7 to 8. No preanal scutes. The unarmored portion of the skin, according to recent observations of Prof. John A. Ryder, is almost free from prickles and ossifications. D. 33; A. 19 to 22; V. 17 to 21; P. 30 to 31; C. 60, its lower lobe two-fifths as long as the upper, measuring from the fork. The color of the skin of the upper parts is reddish brown; lower parts nearly white. Peritoneum dark brown viscera almost black.

This little-known sturgeon has not been positively recognized anywhere except in the Delaware and only a few specimens have been obtained in that river. Prof. Ryder collected five examples at Delaware City in the spring of 1888 and has published a description and figures of the species in the Bulletin of the United States Fish Commission for that year.

Size.—The largest specimen known was thirty-three inches long; individuals twenty inches long are capable of reproducing the species.

Uses.—At the present time the short-nosed sturgeon probably never comes into the markets owing to its small size, which prevents its capture in the nets used for taking the common sturgeon. About 1817, however, it was brought in the shad season to Philadelphia and sold for twenty-five to seventy-five cents each.

Reproduction.—Spawning takes place in the Delaware during May. The eggs are deposited in depths of one to five fathoms on hard bottom in brackish or nearly fresh water. Prof. Ryder states that the eggs are extruded by rubbing the belly either against hard places on the river bed or against the rough bodies of the males, two or more of which accompany each female. The gravid roe fish are larger than the males. Prof. Ryder found the ova more or less adhesive immediately after their removal from the abdomen, but the sticky mucus covering is soluble in water. The period of hatching varies from four to six days.

Food.—Up to the third month of its life the young sturgeon has minute conical teeth in its jaws and at this age it is believed to subsist upon "rhizopods, unicellular algæ, infusoria, minute larvæ of insects and worms, crustaceans, etc." Still following the observations of Prof. Ryder, we learn that the sturgeon, when it has reached a length of one inch to one and a half inches, has minute teeth on the floor of the pharynx and feeds upon small water fleas, and probably algæ, worms, embryo fishes, insects and fresh water copepods. Later in life the fish seeks larger crustaceans and the adults occasionally contain fragments of mussel shells. The young fish have been caught under the ice in midwinter and are known to pass most of the year in fresh water.

8. Acipenser rubicundus Le Sueur.

The Lake Sturgeon. (*Figure 20.*)

The body of the lake sturgeon is rather slenderer than that of the common sturgeon. The snout is somewhat blunt; in the young long and slender. The shields of the body are large, about fourteen on the back, thirty or more on the side, and eight or nine along the abdomen, between pectoral and ventral fins. Each shield is surmounted by a strong hooked spine. The head is contained three and one-third times in the length without tail. Barbels four, rather long. Eye small. Dorsal and anal fins small, placed far back as in the pike. D. 35; A. 26.

This is known as the lake sturgeon, Ohio river sturgeon, rock sturgeon, bony sturgeon, red sturgeon and ruddy sturgeon. It inhabits the Mississippi and Ohio rivers and the Great Lakes, and is abundant in the Allegheny. From the lakes it ascends the streams in spring for the purpose of spawning. Dr. Richardson states the northern limit of the sturgeon in North America to be about the fifty-fifth parallel of latitude.

Size.—The lake sturgeon is smaller than the common marine sturgeon, the average adult being less than five feet in length. The average weight of 14,000 mature sturgeon taken at Sandusky, Ohio, was about fifty pounds. It frequently reaches a length of six feet.

In the lakes the species, according to observations of James W. Milner, inhabits comparatively shoal waters.

The food of this sturgeon is made up chiefly of shell-fish, including the genera *Limnæa*, *Melantho*, *Physa*, *Planorbis* and *Valvata*. Eggs of fishes are also to be found in their stomachs.

In lake Erie the species spawns in June, for which purpose it ascends the rivers in large schools until stopped by obstructions or insufficient depth of water. The breaching of the sturgeon is a well-known habit. Instances are recorded of serious injury to persons by sturgeons throwing themselves into boats. The sturgeon will occasionally take a baited hook, but its great strength and unwieldiness make it an undesirable fish for the angler.

Large numbers of sturgeon have been destroyed by fishermen during the whitefish season simply on account of the annoyance caused by their presence in the nets. Now that the flesh is becoming popular for smoking, and the demand for caviare made from the eggs has largely increased, the wanton waste of this fish has been checked. A troublesome parasite of the sturgeon is the lamper eel (*Petromyzon concolor* Kirt.), which attaches itself to the skin, presumably for the purpose of feeding upon the mucus which is exuded from the pores in great abundance, and remains fixed in one position so long as to penetrate to the flesh and produce a deep ulcerous sore.

The lake sturgeon was formerly not very popular, but is rapidly growing into favor. The flesh is eaten in the fresh condition, or after boiling in vinegar or curing by smoking. Smoked sturgeon is now considered almost, if not quite, equal to smoked halibut, and the demand for it is increasing. From the eggs of the sturgeon a very good grade of caviare is produced. "The caviare is made by pressing the ova through sieves, leaving the membranes of the ovaries remaining in the sieve, and the eggs fall through into a tub. This is continued until the eggs are entirely free from particles of membrane, when they are put into salt pickle, and allowed to remain for some time."

ORDER GINGLYMODI. (THE BONY GARS.)

FAMILY **LEPISOSTEIDÆ**. (THE GAR FISHES.)

GENUS **LEPISOSTEUS** LACEPEDE.

9. **Lepisosteus osseus** LINNÆUS.

The Gar Pike.

The gar pike has an elongate, subcylindrical body. Its depth is contained about twelve times in the length; the jaws are greatly produced, the upper being the longer. The length of the head is one-third of the total length, without tail. Teeth in jaws rather fine, sharp and stiff. A single inner row of large teeth, and an outer row of small teeth on each side. The snout is more than twice as long as the rest of the head, its least width being from one-fifteenth to one-twentieth of its length. D. 7 to 8; A. 9; V. 6; P. 10. Scales, 62 to 65. In the young the tail is produced into a filament.

The general color is greenish, the sides silvery, and the belly whitish. Numerous round dark spots on the sides, most distinct posteriorly and most conspicuous in the young, becoming obscure with age. Very young individuals have a black lateral band. The fins are generally plain, with the exception of numerous dark spots.

The specimen described, No. 36,098, United States Nat. Mus., from Stone's R., Tenn., is twenty-four inches long.

This is the common, long-nosed gar pike of the Great Lakes, the Mississippi valley and the eastern states from Pennsylvania to South Carolina. It ranges south to Mexico and west to the plains. Additional names for the species are bill-fish, sword-fish, bony gar, bony pike, alligator, alligator gar and buffalo-fish. Professor Cope recognizes two varieties of this gar in Pennsylvania. One of these abounds in the Susquehanna and the lower Delaware. He distinguishes it by its robust form, short face and gill covers, and the roughened scales of the front part of the body. The other variety occurs in lakes and in the Allegheny river, and is to be known by its slenderer face and gill covers, its smaller size, generally smooth scales, and the absence of dark spots on the body and fins. It should be remembered, however, that the species is extremely variable in these particulars, and all of the names based upon such characters have been generally discarded.

The gar pike attains to a length of five or six feet, of which the head and snout usually form about one-third.

This species is more abundant in the Great Lakes and large streams than in the small rivers. It is emphatically a fish of prey and extremely tenacious of life. It spawns in shoal water, or in the streams, in the late spring and early summer months.

The gar pike is said to be nowhere used for food, because its flesh is tough, and is believed to be unwholesome. I have seen it, however, with the bill cut off and the skin removed, offered for sale in the market at Washington, D. C.

10. Lepisosteus platystomus RAFINESQUE.

The Short-nosed Gar Pike.

The short-nosed gar pike has an elongated body, its depth being contained seven and one-half times in the length; the length of the head is less than one-third length of body to tail. Distance from eye to tip of snout greater than from eye to posterior edge of opercle. Upper jaw slightly longer than the lower; both jaws with many long sharp teeth. Dorsal and anal fins placed far back, near the tail; ventrals in middle of length.

D. 8; A. 9; about fifty-five rows of scales between head and caudal. Fins all more or less black spotted. The specimen described, No. 3241, United States National Museum, from Cleveland, Ohio, is twelve inches long.

The short-nosed gar, because of its shorter snout, which even in young specimens does not much exceed the rest of the head in length, has been considered as representing a separate subgenus, *Cylindrosteus* of Rafinesque.

This fish seldom exceeds three feet in length. Its habits are presumably the same as those of the long-nosed gar and it is equally worthless for food. It may be readily distinguished from the long-nosed species by the shape of its snout, and by its more robust form.

The short-nosed gar inhabits the Great Lakes and the Ohio and Mississippi valleys. It is more abundant in the southern portion of its habitat.

ORDER HALECOMORPHI (THE BOW-FINS).

Family **AMIIDÆ**.

Genus **AMIA** Linnæus.

11. **Amia calva** Linnæus.

The Mud Fish.

The mud-fish has a well-rounded, robust body. Head more or less conical, its top covered with hard bony plates. Body entirely covered with cycloid scales. The mouth is large; maxilla extending far past eye. Depth of body equals three-fourths length of head and is contained slightly more than five times in length of body. Distance from tip of snout to origin of dorsal equals one-third of the total length including tail. Length of dorsal base equal to twice length of head. Anal base very short, nearly one-third of head.

Strong conical teeth in the jaws; in the lower jaw there is a band of finer teeth behind the outer row of large ones. The vomer, palatine and pterygoid bones are finely toothed. A small barbel at anterior nostril. Lateral line continuous, through sixty-two scales. There are seven rows of scales between dorsal and lateral line and eleven or twelve from lateral line to ventral. D. 50; A. 10 or 11.

The color in life is dark olive, the sides with greenish reticulations, the belly whitish. Round dark spots on the lower jaw and gular plate. The male has a roundish black spot with an orange border at the base of the caudal fin.

The bow-fin has various common names, among them mud-fish, dog-fish, lawyer, grindle and John-a-grindle. Its range is as extensive as its character is generally worthless. It is found in the Great Lakes and tributary streams, in the Ohio and Mississippi valleys southward to Texas, and in eastern waters from Pennsylvania to Florida.

The female bow-fin is larger than the male, reaching a length of two feet while the male seldom exceeds eighteen inches. The male is still further distinguished by the presence of large black, margined with orange or yellow, spot or spots at the base of the tail fin. The greatest recorded weight of this fish is twelve pounds.

Habits.—This is one of the most voracious of all fishes. It feeds upon all other fish of suitable size and, also, destroys other animals within reach. The capture of the bow-fin by means of the trolling spoon has recently come into greatly increased favor with anglers because of the game qualities of the fish and its wonderful tenacity of life. The species has been known to live out of the water, exposed to the sunlight, for twelve hours or more. The young may be kept in an aquarium or other receptacle without change of water for months. The spawning season of the bow-fin is in May and June and stagnant sloughs are favorite localities for this purpose. The eggs and young are protected by the parents and the young remain in the pools after the falling waters cause the departure of the adults. Dr. Estes, who has made the best observations upon the reproduction of this species, states that the little ones are protected in the mouth of the parent when suddenly alarmed. The jumping of the bow-fin is one of its most characteristic habits. Dr. Estes saw them turn complete somersaults while in the air.

The bow-fin is not a food fish, its flesh being soft and unsavory, yet Dr. Goode found them to be highly esteemed as a sweet morsel by the negroes of the south. The young are in great demand as bait for pike and pickerel and both these and the adults are interesting for the aquarium because of their colors, the ease with which they endure captivity, the peculiarities of their anatomical structure and their affinities with extinct *Ganoids*.

ORDER NEMATOGNATHI.

Family **SILURIDÆ**. (The Cat-fishes.)

Genus **ICTALURUS** Rafinesque.

12. Ictalurus punctatus Rafinesque.

The Spotted Cat-fish. (*Figure 21.*)

The body of the spotted cat-fish is rather long and slender, its depth being contained five times in the length without caudal and equal to the length of the dorsal spine. The head is moderate, convex above, its length being slightly less than one-fourth total length. The maxillary barbels are very long, longer than head. Eye moderate, five and one-half in head. Pectoral spine two-thirds length of head, humeral process broad, one-half length of pectoral spine. Adipose fin well developed. Caudal deeply forked. The least depth of the caudal peduncle equals one-half depth of body at last dorsal ray. D. I, 6; A. 24; V. I, 8.

Specimen described, No. 27,846, United States National Museum, from Pekin, Illinois.

This species is variously styled the channel cat, white cat, silver cat, blue cat and spotted cat. It is found over a vast extent of country, comprising the Mississippi and Ohio valleys and the Great Lake region. In the eastern states it is absent from streams tributary to the Atlantic, but occurs from Vermont southward to Georgia, westward to Montana and southwestward to Mexico. In Pennsylvania it is limited to the Ohio and its affluents. The adults of this species are bluish silvery and the young are spotted with olive. It is one of the handsomest of the family of cat-fishes, and an excellent food fish. Its introduction into waters in which it is not native has begun and the multiplication of the species is greatly to be desired. The spotted cat grows to a length of three feet and a weight of twenty-five pounds. It is extremely variable in color and in number of fin rays, and has consequently been described under more than twenty different names. It is most abundant in large clear streams. This species is less hardy than most of the other catfishes.

Genus **AMIURUS** Rafinesque.

13. Amiurus nigricans Le Sueur.

The Great Catfish. (*Figure 22.*)

The great catfish has a stout body, a broad and much depressed head and a wide mouth. The depth of the body is contained five times in total length, without caudal; the head equals more than one-fourth of this length. Maxillary barbel as long as anal base, almost as long as the head. Eye rather small. Dorsal base short, one-half height of fin. Adipose fin well developed. Caudal not deeply forked. Pectoral spine as long as dorsal spine, one-half length of head. Least depth of caudal peduncle less than one-half greatest depth of body. D. I, 5 (sometimes 6); A. 25, V. I, 8.

The specimen described, twenty inches long, is No. 36,142, United States National Museum, from Tennessee river, Alabama.

This is the great fork-tailed cat, Mississippi cat, Florida cat, flannel-mouth cat and great blue cat of various writers. It is also called mud cat in the St. John's river, Florida. The species is very variable, as we would expect from its wide distribution. In 1879 Prof. Spencer F. Baird received, from Dr. Steedman, of St. Louis, a Mississippi river catfish weighing one hundred and fifty pounds and measuring five feet in length. The writer described this fish as a new species related to the great black catfish of the Mississippi valley, *Amiurus nigricans*. At the present time it is somewhat doubtful whether or not this is merely an overgrown individual of the species under consideration, and the matter must remain in doubt until smaller examples of *Amiurus ponderosus* have been obtained.

The great fork-tailed cat is a native of the great lakes and the Ohio and Mississippi valleys, and in the southern states its range extends southward to Florida; northward it ranges to Ontario.

This catfish reaches a weight of one hundred pounds or upward, and if it includes the giant form above referred to, we may place the maximum weight at over one hundred and fifty pounds. Dr. Steedman was informed by an old fisherman that the heaviest one he had ever seen weighed one hundred and ninety-eight pounds, but it is doubtful if such large individuals are to be taken at the present time. In Lake Erie this species usually weighs from five to fifteen pounds, and the largest specimens reach forty pounds.

The habits of this fish are presumably about the same as in other species of the family. On account of the great size of the fish it naturally prefers lakes and large rivers. It is a bottom feeder and will take most any kind of bait. This species is wonderfully tenacious of life. It spawns in the spring and protects its young, which follow the parent fish in great schools. Dr. Theodore Gill has reviewed the subject of the catfishes' care of their young in *Forest and Stream* of Nov. 27, 1890.

This is a valued food species, although not a choice fish. In Lake Erie, according to the Review of the Fisheries of the Great Lakes recently published by the United States Fish Commission, the catfish rank next to whitefish in number of pounds taken.

In Lake Erie catfish are taken chiefly by means of set-lines and the fishing is best during the months of June, July and August. The method of fishing is thus described in the review just referred to: "The apparatus consists of from two hundred to four hundred hooks attached by short lines to a main line, which is from five to twenty-seven fathoms long, according to the place in which set, and is held in place by poles or stakes pushed in the mud. The lines are usually set in the lake, but occasionally short ones are fished in the bayous and marshes. Catfish are taken with a bait of herring (*Coregonus artedi*) or grasshoppers, and are mostly used in the families of the fishermen and their neighbors or sold to peddlers. * * * The size of the catfish ranges from five to twenty-five pounds, averaging eight or ten pounds." In some other parts of Lake Erie the set-line fishery for catfish begins April 15. Some of these lines have as many as two thousand hooks. In Toledo these fish bring four and one-half cents a pound. The pound nets also take a good many catfish in the spring and fall. Erie receives its supply of catfish from fishermen who operate in the lake from Erie to Elk creek with set-lines during the summer months. De Kay had the species from Buffalo, where he saw specimens weighing from twenty-five to thirty pounds. He states that it is usually captured by the spear.

14. Amiurus albidus (Le Sueur).

The Channel Catfish. (*Figure 23.*)

The white or channel catfish has a broad stout body; its depth equals the length of the head and is contained four times in the total length to tail. Maxillary barbels reach posterior end of head; mandibulary barbels rather short. Dorsal fin short, adipose well developed, caudal slightly forked, anal long. Humeral process, above pectoral, half length of pectoral spine, rough. D. 1, 6; A. 20.

This is the white cat or channel cat, in Philadelphia distinguished as the Schuylkill cat.

The channel cat ranges from Pennsylvania to North Carolina, and is one of the most abundant of its family in the Potomac river. It is abundant in the Susquehanna and common in the Schuylkill.

This species reaches a length of two feet and a weight of five pounds. It is extremely variable with age. Old examples have the mouth so much wider than in the young that they have been described as a distinct species. The big-mouthed cat of Cope is now considered to be the old form of the white cat. The habits of this species agree with those of other species already mentioned. The name channel cat suggests a favorite haunt of the fish. As a food fish it is highly prized.

15. **Amiurus natalis** (Le Sueur).

The Yellow Catfish.

The yellow catfish is robust and has a rather broad head. The mouth is wide, with the upper jaw usually longer than the lower, sometimes equal to it. The dorsal profile gradually ascends from the snout to dorsal spine. The depth of the body at dorsal spine is contained four and two-thirds times in the total length to base of tail. The length of the head is contained three and two-thirds times in the body length, and equals length of anal base. Eye moderate; maxillary barbel reaching end of head. Humeral process little developed. Dorsal and pectoral spines strong, shorter than soft rays. Height of dorsal equal to twice the length of its base. Adipose fin long as in *Noturus*, opposite to and longer than anal. Caudal rounded. D. I, 6; A. 24; V. I, 8.

Described from specimen No. 36,685, United States National Museum, six inches long, from Huntsville, Alabama.

The yellow cat or chubby cat is found from the Great Lakes to Virginia and Texas. It has many varieties, three of which are mentioned by Prof. Cope as occuring in Pennsylvania, two of them in the Ohio river and its tributaries and the third in Lake Erie. The species is not credited to the region east of the Alleghenies.

The length of the yellow cat sometimes reaches two feet, but averages much less. Nothing special is recorded about the habits of this species. It is most abundant in sluggish streams.

16. **Amiurus vulgaris** (Thompson).

The Long-jawed Catfish. (*Figure 4.*)

This catfish has a stout body; its depth is one-fourth of the total length without caudal. The head is contained about three and three-fourths times in this length. Eye very small. Mouth large; jaws equal or lower jaw sometimes projecting. Barbels long; maxillary barbel as long as head.

The length of the dorsal base is less than one-half that of the anal, while its height is five-sixths of the same length. Adipose fin well developed. The pectoral spine is stout and about two-thirds as long as the fin. Caudal square. Anal rounded. Least depth of caudal peduncle contained two and one-third times in greatest depth of body. D. I, 6; A. 18(20); V. I, 8.

Described from No. 31,946, United States National Museum, twelve inches long, from Winnipeg, Manitoba.

The long-jawed catfish is found in the Great Lake region and westward to Manitoba. It is believed to be very nearly related to the common catfish, *A. nebulosus*, but its projecting lower jaw will serve to distinguish it. This character, however, we know by experience is not so satisfactory as it might be.

This catfish is occasionally taken in the Ohio river, but it is more abundant in Lake Erie. The species reaches a length of eighteen inches and a weight of four pounds.

17. Amiurus nebulosus (Le Sueur).

The Common Catfish. (Figure 25.)

The common catfish has a very stout body, broad head and a short stout caudal peduncle. The depth of body about equals length of head, and is contained from three and one-half to four and one-half times in length. Barbels eight. Maxillary barbels as long as head. Dorsal profile from tip of snout to dorsal fin straight and rather steep. Mouth wide and terminal. Teeth awl-shaped, in broad bands on the inter-maxillaries and dentaries. Dorsal situated in front of middle of body, short and high. Adipose fin stout. Anal large, its base equalling length of head. Caudal square or slightly emarginate. D. I, 6; A. 20 to 22; V. I, 7.

Length of specimen examined seven inches: from Susquehanna river at Havre de Grace, Maryland.

This is known as the common catfish, bull-head, horn-pout, bull-pout and minister. This species has a wider distribution than the white cat, its range including New England and southward to South Carolina, west to Wisconsin and southwest to Texas. It has also been transferred from the Schuylkill to the Sacramento and San Joaquin rivers, California, where it has multiplied so rapidly that is now one of the commonest fishes of those streams. This is the commonest catfish in Lake Erie and its tributaries. The species reaches a maximum length of eighteen inches and a weight of four pounds, but the average size of market specimens is much smaller. In the lower portion of the Susquehanna color varieties of this species are not uncommon. One of them appears to be the same as the *Amiurus marmoratus* of Holbrook; this supposed color variety is found also from Illinois to Florida. The lower Susquehanna has furnished, also, some singularly colored examples of this fish, distinguished by large areas of jet black combined with lemon and white. These freaks are among the most interesting and beautiful observed in this family of fishes.

From Jordan's Manual of the Vertebrates I quote Thoreau's account of the habits of this species: "The horned pout are 'dull and blundering fellows', fond of the mud, and growing best in weedy ponds and rivers without current. They stay near the bottom, moving slowly about with their barbels widely spread, watching for anything eatable. They will take any kind of bait, from an angle-worm to a piece of a tin tomato-can, without coquetry, and they seldom fail to swallow the hook. They are very tenacious of life, 'opening and shutting their mouths for half an hour after their heads have been cut off.' They spawn in spring, and the old fishes lead the young in great schools near the shore, seemingly caring for them as the hen for her chickens."

18. Amiurus melas (Rafinesque).

The Small Black Catfish.

The body of the small black catfish is stout, short and deep. Its depth is contained about three and one-half times in length to tail; in very deep examples only three and one-fifth times. The length of the head is contained three and one-half times in this length. The head is broad, the dorsal profile straight and rather steep from tip of snout to dorsal fin. Eye rather small; barbels long. Caudal peduncle stout. Dorsal I, 6; the spine strong and sharply pointed. The height of the dorsal fin equals one-half length of head. The anal has eighteen rays; its base is two and one-half times as long as dorsal base. The pectoral fin has one sharp spine and seven rays. Tail truncate. Adipose fin well developed. Teeth very fine, awl-shaped and in broad bands.

The small black catfish was known to De Kay as the brown catfish.

It is found in the Ohio and Mississippi valleys, the Great Lake region, also southward to New York. The specific name is derived from its black color. De Kay states that it is very common in Lake Pleasant, Lake Janet and many of the other lakes in the northern districts of the state.

This catfish reaches a length of one foot. Its color is usually blackish or dusky brown, approaching to black, while the lower parts are bluish white. The fins are black, tinged with red, and the barbels are black. The color is subject to considerable variation. The species is too small to be of much value as food and its principal use in northern New York, according to De Kay, was to serve as bait for the lake trout.

Genus Gronias Cope.

"Head broad, depressed. Supraoccipital bone posteriorly free. Branchiostegal membrane with ten rays. Anterior dorsal spine stout; posterior fin separated from caudal. Ventrals with eight rays. Eyes rudimental, covered by the corium. Natatory bladder present.

"The species has the head broader posteriorly, and the anal fin shorter than in the allied species of Amiurus. It may be called *G. nigrilabris*. The muzzle is flat and the jaws equal; the width across the occipital region is equal to the length from the end of the muzzle to the apex of the occipital crest; width below equal to the length from the axilla of the pectoral to the base of the ventral fin.

"From end of muzzle to dorsal spine equal from latter to middle of adipose. Length of head four and one-half times in total length. Maxillary barbels extend three-fourths the distance to the opercular border; outer (longer) mentals scarcely beyond middle branchiostegal angle. Height of body at base of dorsal equal three-fourths length of head. End of pectoral opposite posterior border of first dorsal, its spinous ray serrate; ventrals not reaching anal. Basis of anal terminating a little behind base of adipose; length of caudal peduncle below, equal length of pectoral spine. Rays: D. I-7; P. I-9; V. 8; A. 18; C. 16. Spine of dorsal smooth. Caudal openly emarginate, the emargination much above the middle rays, giving the highest a short lobate outline. Lateral line straight to scapular angle, mouth of axillary mucous duct distinct. Length of head 2 in. 8 l.; width below 2 in. 2 l.; from muzzle to base of ventrals 4 in. 3 l.; to base of caudal 7 in. 9 l.; length of caudal 1 in. 7 l.; another specimen is about ten inches in length. The color of the upper surfaces, tail, fins, barbels and under jaw is black; sides varied with dirty yellow, abdomen and thorax yellowish-white. J. Stauffer informs me that the dark pigment of the skin of this animal comes off upon the hands in handling it."

[Proc. Acad. Nat. Sci., Phila., xvi, 1864, p. 231.]

The cave catfish, as its name suggests, is an inhabitant of subterranean streams; it has been found only in the tributaries of Conestoga creek, in eastern Pennsylvania.

2 Fishes.

This catfish was first discovered by the late Jacob Stauffer, near Lancaster, Pa., and has since been obtained by a number of persons. It has the general appearance of the black catfish previously described, *Amiurus melas*, but the eyes are rudimentary and concealed under thick skin. It is believed to be a recent descendant of the common black catfish or perhaps the common catfish, *A. nebulosus*, and that its condition of blindness is due to its cave life. It is the only blind catfish known. The cave catfish grows to a length of ten inches.

Genus **LEPTOPS** Rafinesque.

20. Leptops olivaris Rafinesque.

The Mud Catfish.

The yellow cat or mud cat has a long slender body, with the head much depressed. The dorsal profile is gradually elevated from tip of snout to origin of dorsal fin; from this point to tail the slope is very slight. The depth of the body at beginning of dorsal is about one-sixth of the total length, without caudal. The length of the head is contained two and two-thirds times in the standard length. The head is very flat. Eye very small. Maxillary barbel almost as long as head. Dorsal rays about equal in length; height of dorsal equal to length of anal base; the spine one-half as long as rays. Fins rounded; caudal emarginate; adipose fin large, its length equal to anal base. Anal and adipose fins opposite. D. I, 6; A. 13; V. I, 8. Described from No. 27,873, United States National Museum, collected in the Illinois river by Prof. S. A. Forbes.

This is known under the name of mud-cat, flat-head cat, Russian cat, yellow cat and goujon.

The mud-cat in Pennsylvania is limited to the Ohio and its tributaries. It is abundant in the Mississippi valley in deep sluggish waters, ranging westward to Iowa and southward to Georgia, but is not found in tributaries of the Atlantic.

This is a very large species reaching a weight of seventy-five pounds, and a maximum length of three feet. The mud-cat prefers muddy bottoms and large sluggish streams. It is a food fish of good qualities and is extensively used notwithstanding its ugliness.

Genus **NOTURUS** Rafinesque.

21. Noturus flavus Rafinesque.

The Stone Catfish.

The stone cat has a moderately elongate body, whose greatest depth and width are nearly equal; the tail is much compressed, and the head flat and broad. The greatest depth of the body is nearly one-fifth of the total length without the caudal; the least depth of the caudal peduncle equals nearly one-half length of head. The mouth is terminal, horizontal, its width equal to postorbital part of head and to length of maxillary barbel. Longer barbel on chin not quite one-half as long as the head. Nasal barbel, when laid back, reaches end of eye. The width of the band of teeth in the upper jaw equals one-third length of head; the backward prolongation is little longer than the eye. The distance between the eyes equals length of snout and eye. The snout is one-half as long as the postorbital part of the head. The dorsal origin is at a distance from tip of snout nearly equal to one-third of total length without caudal. The dorsal base is one-half as long as the head. The spine is very sharp, and as long as the snout. The longest ray is nearly one-half as long as the head. The ventral origin is not far behind the end of the dorsal base; the fin reaches a little beyond the vent, but not to the anal origin. The pectoral reaches to below the third dorsal ray; its spine is about two-fifths as long as the head. The anal origin is a little nearer to base of caudal than to origin of pectoral; the base is as long as the head without the snout, one-fifth of total to base of caudal, and the longest ray equals one-half length of head. The very low adipose dorsal begins over the anal origin and continues into the caudal; in older specimens it is deeply notched. The caudal is rounded. D. I, 6; A. 16; V. 9; P. I, 9. Length of the specimen described, No. 35,877, United States National Museum, six and one-fourth inches. In spirits the upper parts are grayish brown and the lower surface of head and body pale. In life the fish is nearly uniform yellowish brown.

The yellow stone cat is found from Ontario to Virginia and in the Ohio valley. In the Mississippi region it extends west to Nebraska. It inhabits the larger streams. The species has very little value as food on account of its small size. It seldom exceeds twelve inches in length, but it is a very good bait for black bass. The stone cats are much dreaded by fishermen because of the painful wounds sometimes produced by their pectoral spines. There is a minute pore in the axil of the pectoral which is the outlet of a noxious liquid secreted by a poison gland. When this poison is discharged into a wound it causes an extremely painful sore.

22. Noturus insignis Richardson.

The Margined Stone Catfish. (Figure 26.)

The margined stone cat has a moderately elongate and low body, its width greater than its depth, and the least depth of the caudal peduncle about three-fourths greatest depth of body. The head is rather long and depressed, one-fourth of total without caudal, the snout short and rounded. The eye is small, its length one-half width of interorbital space and little more than one-half length of snout. The lower jaw is slightly shorter than the upper; the width of the mouth equals postorbital part of head. The width of the maxillary band of teeth equals one-third length of head; there is no extension backward. The maxillary barbel reaches nearly to the end of the head. Six short gill-rakers below the angle of the the first gill-arch. The dorsal origin is about over the middle of the space between the pectoral and ventral origins; the length of the dorsal base equals the distance between the eyes, and also the length of its spine. The longest ray is one-half as long as the head. The ventral reaches beyond the vent and almost to the anal origin, its length one-half head. The pectoral does not reach to the ventral origin; its spine is one-half as long as the head, rough along its front edge and coarsely serrate behind. The adipose fin is little developed; it begins over the anal origin, and is continuous with the caudal. The anal origin is nearly midway between the pectoral origin and the base of the caudal; the base is scarcely two-ninths of total length without caudal; the posterior and longest rays are scarcely one-half as long as the head. The caudal is rounded. D. I, 7; A. 17; V. 10; P. I, 9. In spirits the upper parts are dark brown, the belly and under surface of head pale. The fins all have a narrow dark margin. The specimen described, No. 18,015, United States National Museum, is four and one-half inches long.

This species, like the others of its genus, is called stone cat, and it is very common in the Susquehanna, where it is highly prized as a live bait for black bass fishing. The species occurs also in the Delaware, but for some reason or other is not so attractive to the black bass as the Susquehanna river race.

This stone cat grows to a length of ten inches; it ranges from Pennsylvania to South Carolina, east of the Alleghenies. The dorsal and caudal fins have a well-defined black margin, from which originated the later name of *Noturus marginatus*.

This is the *Pimelodus livrée* of Cuvier and Valenciennes, and the *P. lemniscatus* of Le Sueur. Cuvier and Valenciennes make the following concluding remarks about the species: "The species is probably viviparous, for the eggs are very large, and contain a well-developed embryo. The ovary contains many eggs of which the diameter exceeds two lines, and moreover they are taken from a small animal, for our example is three inches long."

23. Noturus gyrinus Mitchill.

The Tadpole Stone Catfish.

The tadpole stone cat has a short and stout body, sloping rapidly downward from the dorsal origin to the tip of the snout; its greatest depth contained four and one-third times in total length without caudal; its width contained four and one-half times. The head is short, broad and depressed, its width nearly equal to its length, which is one-fourth of the total without caudal. The width of the mouth equals two-thirds the length of the head; the jaws nearly equal. The width of the maxillary band of teeth equals one-third length of head; there are no lateral backward extensions. The snout is short, two-sevenths as long as the head. The eye is small, one-seventh as long as the head. The maxillary barbel reaches to the base of the pectoral; the outer mandibulary barbel is slightly longer. The nasal barbel is one-half as long as the head. The distance of the dorsal from the tip of snout equals that from origin of ventral to end of anal. The base is as long as the snout and eye combined; the spine is one-third as long as the head, and the longest ray equals length of postorbital part of head. The low adipose fin begins over the anal origin, and is continuous with the caudal. The ventral origin is under the end of the dorsal base; the fin does not reach to anal origin. The pectoral reaches to below the middle of the dorsal. The anal base is one-fifth of total length without caudal; the longest ray equals postorbital part of head. The caudal is rounded. The pectoral spine is one-half as long as the head. The humeral process is one-third as long as the head. D, I, 6; A. 13–15; P. I, 8. Color in spirits dark brown; the belly and under surface of head, paler.

The specimens described, No. 1508, United States National Museum, are from three and one half to four inches long.

This is named the tadpole stone cat. It is the smallest of the genus in Pennsylvania. It occurs in tributaries of the Delaware and also in streams flowing into the Susquehanna. In general it ranges in the Great Lake region, through the Mississippi and Ohio valleys, and in New York, Pennsylvania and New Jersey. Its length does not exceed five inches. The species is too small to be of any value, except for bait, and on account of its tenacity to life, it is greatly in demand for hook and line fishing, especially in the capture of the black bass, for which fish it is one of the best baits known.

ORDER EVENTOGNATHI.

Family **CATOSTOMIDÆ**. The Suckers.

Genus **ICTIOBUS** Rafinesque. Buffalo Fishes.

24. Ictiobus urus Agassiz.

The Big-mouthed Buffalo Fish. (*Figure 25.*)

The big-mouthed buffalo fish has a stout body and head, the back elevated, and a large mouth. The depth of the body is equal to one-third of the total length without tail. The head is contained three and one-fourth times in the standard length. The eye is of moderate size, its length about one-sixth that of the head. Mucus pores well developed. The mouth is somewhat oblique; the maxillary not reaching vertical through eye. The caudal peduncle is broad, its least depth almost half length of head. The rather long dorsal fin commences on middle of body, the length of its base equal to depth of body; the anterior rays high, longest half length of dorsal base; beginning with the ninth the rays are about of equal length, and not much more than one-third length of longest rays.

Caudal forked. Pectoral moderate, its length about equal to that of longest dorsal rays. The anal is short, its base equal to one-half the length of its longest ray, which equals longest dorsal ray. D. 25 or 26; A. 8 or 9. Scales, 7-36-6, large and striated. Lateral line complete and straight. The specimen described, No. 35,882, United States National Museum, from the Missouri river, is fourteen inches long.

The black buffalo, big-mouthed buffalo or mongrel buffalo of authors, occurs in the Mississippi and Ohio valleys, but is less abundant than the other species of the genus. It grows to a length of two and one-half feet, and is extensively used for food. The species is found only in the larger streams, and is distinguished from all the other buffalo fishes by its darker colors, as well as by its large mouth and stout body.

25. Ictiobus bubalus (Rafinesque).

The Red-mouthed Buffalo Fish.

The red-mouthed buffalo fish has the back elevated, body robust more or less compressed, mouth terminal with little developed lips, opercle very large and strong, large scales and a long, low, dorsal fin. The depth of the body equals one-third of its length; the length of the head is contained three and one-half times in the standard length; the dorsal base two and two-thirds in the same length. Diameter of eye equals about one-seventh length of the head. Teeth small and numerous. D. 29; A. 9; V. 10. Scales 7-44-6. The example described, No. 20,774, United States National Museum, from Illinois, is eighteen inches long.

The red-mouthed buffalo fish, also known as the brown buffalo, high-backed buffalo, small-mouthed buffalo, sucker-mouthed buffalo and buffalo fish, is a common inhabitant of the Mississippi and Ohio valleys, but does not occur east of the Alleghenies.

This species reaches a length of two and one-half feet and a weight of fifteen pounds. It frequents large streams. Prof. Forbes has been informed by fishermen that one or more species of buffalo fish have the "peculiar habit of whirling around in shallow water or plowing steadily along, with their heads buried in the mud, and their tails occasionally showing above the surface. These operations have nothing to do with spawning, and it is likely that fishes thus engaged are burrowing for small mollusks and for mud-inhabiting larvæ." The food of this buffalo fish consists of aquatic plants, in the Illinois river chiefly duck weed and *Ceratophyllum*. The animal food includes mollusks, insects and their larvæ and crustaceans. Worms are rarely found in their stomachs. The buffalo is not a choice fish and its flesh is filled with innumerable small bones, yet it is abundant and is eaten in very large quantities. These fish do not take the hook and are usually caught in seines.

26. Ictiobus carpio Rafinesque.

The Carp Sucker. (*Figure 28.*)

The body of the carp sucker is fusiform, back little elevated and sides compressed. The depth of the body at the origin of the dorsal is contained about three and one-fourth times in the length without caudal, the length of the head three and three-fourths times. Muzzle more or less conic, rounded on top; mouth small, horizontal and inferior, with thin lips. Muciferous system on head moderately developed. The eye is of moderate size, its diameter contained five times in length of head. The distance from tip of snout to origin of dorsal equals nearly one-half the distance from tip of snout to caudal base. First and second rays of dorsal partly ossified, first very small, one-third as long as the second which is less than one-half as long as the third or longest ray, which is slightly more than one-half dorsal base. The rays gradually decrease in length from the third to the tenth, which is contained three and one-half times in the third, and are of equal size from this ray back. The pectorals are placed low; ventrals with a broad base and caudal well forked. The scales are large and about equal in size all over the body. D. 28 (to 30); A. 8; V. 10. Scales 7-37-6. The lateral line is well marked and slightly decurved.

Described from No. 36,509, United States National Museum, nine and one-half inches long, from the Rio Colorado, Texas.

The big carp sucker or olive sucker is an inhabitant of the Ohio and Mississippi valleys. It is a common species and grows to a moderately large size, reaching eighteen inches in length, and is the largest of the carp suckers. In the Ohio river and its tributaries it is one of the most abundant fishes. In the Mississippi valley its range extends southward to Texas. The species has not been recorded from Lake Erie.

The food of the carp sucker is similar to that of other species of the genus. It includes soft-shelled mollusks, small crustaceans, worms and aquatic plants.

Although this is not a choice fish it is extensively used for food.

27. Ictiobus difformis (Cope).

The Deformed Carp Sucker.

This species is fusiform, sides compressed, back much elevated, the head conic, rounded on top, with very blunt muzzle. The eye is longer than the snout, one-fourth length of head. Mouth small, horizontal. The greatest depth of the body is at the origin of the dorsal and is contained two and two-thirds times in the total length without caudal; length of head four and one-fourth times. Anterior rays of dorsal much produced, as long as dorsal base and almost equal to depth of body; the posterior rays low. Caudal large, deeply forked. D. 24 (developed rays); A. 8 or 9; V. 9; scales 6-35-7. The scales are large and about equal in size all over the body.

Described from No. 26,274, United States National Museum, nine and one-half inches long, from Alabama.

The deformed carp sucker occurs in the Ohio valley. Prof. Cope records it from the Ohio river. Dr. Jordan reports it from the Wabash and the lower Ohio.

This singular species may be recognized by the great bluntness of its head and by the dorsal fin beginning in front of the middle of the body. It is not a common fish and its size is small, the maximum length being about one foot. It is too rare to be of any commercial importance even if its size were larger. Its habits are similar to those of other members of its genus.

28. Ictiobus velifer (Rafinesque).

The Sail Fish.

The sail-fish has an oblong body with the back much arched; head sub-conic, broad between the eyes. The depth of the body almost equal to one-third of the length with tail; the head is one-fourth of the standard length. The rather large eye is as long as snout, more than one-fourth length of head. The snout projects beyond the mouth, which is small. Lips rather thick, papillose. Gill rakers very numerous, long and slender. The dorsal fin commences over the tenth scale of the lateral line, its first three rays very high, equal to length of dorsal base, or four times length of short rays, which are most numerous. The very short anal is placed opposite end of dorsal, the length of its base less than one-half that of head; its longest ray equal to twice the length of its base. The pectorals are short and placed low on body. The ventrals reach vent. Caudal deeply forked with slender lobes, the upper the longer. Scales large, striated. Lateral line straight, slightly below middle of body. D. 26; A. 8; V. 10. Scales, 6-36-5.

Common names of this species include the following: Quill-back, skim-back, sail fish, spear fish, carp sucker and sailing sucker. In some localities it is called river carp.

In Pennsylvania, according to Prof. Cope, this species of quill-back is found only in the Ohio river and its tributaries. It is extremely common in the Mississippi and Ohio valleys, and occurs, also, in the great lakes and lakes of western New York.

The quill-back reaches a length of one foot, and is not an important food fish. The majority of the common names are bestowed with reference to the very high anterior part of the dorsal fin.

The food of this fish includes small mollusks, insect larvæ, crustaceans and aquatic plants. Prof. Forbes finds that worms and protozoans are rarely present in the stomachs of this species. The amount of vegetation eaten is rather small, and it is much mingled with mud. The mollusk most commonly found is a thin-shelled *Sphærium*.

29. Ictiobus cyprinus (Le Sueur).

The Quill Back.

The quill-back is robust, somewhat compressed, with an arched dorsal profile. The depth of the body equals one third of the length; and the length of the head is contained three and one-half times in the standard body length. Eye slightly more than five times in length of head. Length of dorsal base slightly more than depth of body. This fin originates a little in advance of middle of body. Its first rays very high, the third two-thirds length of longest, thence gradually decreasing in length. D. 25; A. 8; V. 10. Scales, 6-43-5. Described from No. 33,073, United States National Museum, nine inches long, from Havre de Grace, Maryland.

This is called the carp sucker, silvery carp sucker, quill-back, skimback, spear-fish, sail-fish and carp. As now limited, its range is stated to be from Pennsylvania to Virginia, and its center of abundance the region about Chesapeake Bay. Prof. Cope also recognized it as occurring in the Allegheny river and generally throughout the Ohio valley.

The best account of the food of this fish is given by Prof. S. A. Forbes, who records the fish from the large rivers of Illinois and their principal tributaries, also from Lake Michigan and small lakes of northern Illinois. He found it abundant in the lakes and ponds of the river bottoms, and less common than other species of carp suckers in running water. The species consumes less vegetation than the other fishes of its genus, and more mud is mingled with its food. It devours fewer of the large insect larvæ, and no pond snails. "Mollusks made about one-fourth of the food—all the thin-shelled *Sphærium*. Insects averaged about one-third, and *Entomostraca* made nearly one-fourth." No worms or polyzoans were observed, but occasionally protozoa were noticed.

This species reaches a length of one foot.

Genus CYCLEPTUS Rafinesque.

30. Cycleptus elongatus (Le Sueur).

The Black Horse. (*Figure 29.*)

The black horse has an oblong, elongate, somewhat compressed body, very small head, long caudal peduncle and a forked tail. The greatest depth of the body is at the origin of the dorsal fin, and is one-fourth of the standard length; the length of the head is one-seventh length of body. The eye is small, being contained three times in its distance from tip of snout. Mouth small; the upper lip is thick and has several rows of tubercles, the lower lip not so thick and deeply incised behind. The pharyngeal bones are strong, with stout, wide-set teeth, which increase in size downward.

The fins are large; the pectoral falcate; first three rays of dorsal high, the rest low; its base is considerably more than one-third length of body; anal very short. The scales are of moderate size, equal all over the body. D. 30; A. 8; V. 10. Scales, 9-62-9. Lateral line perfect, almost straight. The specimen described is No. 10,790, United States National Museum, from Ohio; length ten and one-half inches.

This is known as the black horse, Missouri sucker, gourd-seed sucker and suckerel. It inhabits the Mississippi valley, is not uncommon in the Ohio river, and Prof. Cope records it as occasional in the Allegheny.

The black horse reaches a length of two and one-half feet and a maximum weight of fifteen pounds. It is the best food fish of the sucker family. The sexes differ in color; the males have the upper parts jet black while the sides are black with coppery luster. The females are olivaceous with coppery shadings. The male has minute tubercles on the snout in the breeding season in spring. Dr. Kirtland noted a migration down stream at the approach of winter. The mouth of this sucker is small and the lips are covered with numerous tubercles.

Genus **CATOSTOMUS** Le Sueur

31. Catostomus catostomus Forster.

The Northern Sucker. (Figure 30.)

The northern sucker has an elongate body, rounded and tapering, with a long and rather slender head. The depth of the body is contained about four and one-half times in the length, and equals length of head. The snout is much longer than in *C. teres*, considerably overhanging the mouth, which is large, with thick coarsely tuberculated lips. D. 10 to 11; A. 7; scales about one hundred in lateral line and about twenty-eight between dorsal and ventral fins.

The northern sucker, long-nosed sucker, or red-sided sucker, as the above species is styled, occurs in the great lakes and northwest to Alaska in clear cold waters. It is very common in Lake Erie. It grows to a length of two feet and is largest and most abundant northward, in Alaska reaching a weight of five pounds. As a food fish the long-nosed sucker is little esteemed; but in cold countries the head and roe are used in making a palatable soup.

The males in the breeding season, in spring, are profusely covered with tubercles on the head and fins and have a broad rosy band along the middle of the body. In the Yukon river, Alaska, Dr. Dall found the fish filled with spawn in April. The eggs are of moderate size and yellow in color. Nelson has seen this species seined by Eskimo in brackish estuaries of streams flowing into Kotzebue Sound. W. J. Fisher has collected specimens on the peninsula of Alaska.

32. Catostomus teres (Mitchill).

The Common Sucker.

The common sucker has a moderately stout body, heavy at the shoulders and tapering to the tail. Its greatest depth is contained four and one-half times in length to tail, slightly more than length of head. Head conical, flattened on top. Mouth rather large and the lips strongly papillose. Dorsal fin situated in middle of length; ventral opposite; anal far back. Second and third branched rays of dorsal highest, two-thirds length of head; third and fourth rays of anal longest, almost equal to length of head. D. 12; A. 7; V. 9. Scales 64; from dorsal to lateral line and from lateral line to ventral 9 or 10. The specimen described, No. 10,548, United States National Museum, from Ecorse, Michigan, is fourteen and one-half inches long.

The common sucker, also known as the pale sucker, white sucker, grey sucker and brook sucker, styled by the Canadian French the *Carpe blanche*, is the commonest member of its genus in waters east of the Rocky mountains. It is found from Canada to Florida and westward to Montana. Covering such a wide range of territory the species is naturally variable and has been described over and over again by many authorities under a great variety of names. The male of this sucker in spring has a faint rosy stripe along the middle of the side. The young are brownish in color and somewhat mottled and have a dark median band or a series of large blotches. The adults are light olive varying to paler and sometimes darker; sides silvery. The species reaches a length of twenty-two inches, and a weight of five pounds. It is a very common inhabitant of ponds and streams of the lowlands, and a small race occurs in certain cold mountain streams of the Adirondack region, where it is dwarfed in size and changed in color, but does not differ in essential characters. Dr. Rothrock, also, obtained a mountain race of this sucker in Twin Lakes, Colorado, at an elevation of 9,500 feet above the sea level.

The common sucker is a very indifferent food fish in the estimation of most people, but when taken from cold waters and in its best condition its flesh is very palatable. It takes the hook readily when baited with common earth worms.

Dr. Richardson says: "It is a common fish in all parts of the fur countries, abounding in the rivers and even in landlocked marshes and ponds, but preferring shallow grassy lakes with mud bottoms. In the beginning of summer it may be seen in numbers forcing its way up rocky streams, and even breasting strong rapids, to arrive at its proper spawning places in stony rivulets; soon afterwards it returns to the lakes. Its food, judging from the contents of the stomachs of those which I opened, is chiefly soft insects; but in one I found the fragments of a fresh-water shell. In the winter and autumn it is common in nets, and in the spawning season (June) may be readily speared, or even taken by the hand, in shallow streams. It is a very soft watery fish, but devoid of any unpleasant flavor, and is considered to be one of the best in the country for making soup. Like its congeners it is singularly tenacious of life, and may be frozen and thawed again without being killed."

33. Catostomus nigricans Le Sueur.

The Stone Toter. (Figure 31.)

The stone toter has a peculiar physiognomy; the head is flattened on top, the interorbital space concave and the frontal bone short, broad and thick. The body is sub-terete, its depth being contained four and one-third times in the length without caudal or equal to length of head. The eye is rather small, being contained three times in length of snout. Mouth large, lips well developed and strongly papillose.

Fins all large; the dorsal base equals two-thirds length of head, while the pectoral is considerably longer than dorsal. Caudal moderately forked. Lateral line fully developed, on median line of body. Scales moderate, equal. D. 11; A. 7; V. 9; Scales, 7-52-7. Specimen examined, No. 8446, United States National Museum, from Cayuga lake, New York.

The stone roller has a wide distribution and a wonderful variety of common names. Among them are hammer head, stone lugger, stone toter, crawl-a-bottom, hog molly, hog mullet, mud sucker, hog sucker, banded sucker, large-scaled sucker and black sucker. The name shoemaker was formerly applied to this species in Lake Erie, perhaps on account of the resemblance of its color to that of shoemaker's pitch.

Prof. Cope says that this species in Pennsylvania is most abundant in tributaries of the Ohio and in the Susquehanna, while in the Delaware it is uncommon. It ranges from western New York to North Carolina and westward to Kansas. It is the most remarkable looking of all the suckers in Pennsylvania, and may always easily be distinguished by the shape of its head. The species grows very large, reaching a length of two feet. It delights in rapid streams of cold, clear water. Its habit is to rest quietly on the bottom, where its color protects it from observation. It is sometimes found in small schools. The spawning season is in spring and the young are found abundantly in small creeks as well as in the rivers. The food consists of insect larvæ and small shells, and it is especially fitted for securing its prey under stones in the rapids.

As a food fish this sucker has little value.

Genus **ERIMYZON** Jordan.

34. Erimyzon sucetta (Lacépède).

The Chub Sucker.

The body of the chub sucker is oblong, rather deep and compressed, its depth one-third of the standard length. The head is rather short, broad above, its length one-fourth of total length to caudal. The mouth is rather small and but slightly inferior, protractile. The eye is contained five times in length of head, and slightly less than twice in its distance from tip of snout. Dorsal short, rather high, placed in middle of length; ventrals directly underneath dorsal. Highest dorsal ray (fourth), not quite equal to second anal ray; about two-thirds length of head. Caudal slightly forked. No lateral line. D. 11; A. 7; V. 7. Scales, 37; transverse, 13. Described from No. 27,867, United States National Museum, from Illinois; length, nine inches.

This is known as the chub sucker, sweet sucker, rounded sucker, creek fish and mullet. It has a wide range, practically including all the waters of the United States east of the Rocky mountains. In Pennsylvania it inhabits slow muddy streams in all parts of the state, especially the eastern. From the other Pennsylvania suckers it may be readily distinguished by the absence of the lateral line. In the South, notably in Florida, the variety *oblongus*, to which the Pennsylvania form belongs, is replaced by the variety *sucetta*, which is a handsomer fish, with larger dorsal fin, and beautiful striated scales. The chub sucker grows to a length of about one foot. It is very tenacious of life, and is a ready biter, but has little value for food. The young, up to the length of several inches, have a very distinct black lateral band. They are often found in the shelter of water lillies and other aquatic plants close to brackish waters.

In the market of New York, according to De Kay, the chub sucker makes its appearance in October, November and December. Its food consists of minute crustaceans, insect larvæ and aquatic plants.

Genus **MINYTREMA** Jordan.

35. Minytrema melanops Rafinesque.

The Striped Sucker. (*Figure 35.*)

The striped sucker is robust; the greatest depth of its body is contained four times in the length without caudal; length of head four and one-half times. Eye moderate, its diameter contained five times in length of head. The caudal peduncle is stout, its least depth a little more than twice in length of head.

The mouth is of moderate size, and horizontal in position. D. 12 to 14. Scales, 46-13. The lateral line is almost complete in adults, but absent in the young. "Color dusky, coppery below, a dusky blotch behind dorsal; each scale with a dark spot at its base, most distinct in adult, these forming longitudinal stripes; male tuberculate in spring."

The striped sucker, also called soft sucker, sand sucker and black-nosed sucker, is found in the great lakes, and south to South Carolina and Texas. In Pennsylvania it is limited to Lake Erie and the Ohio valley.

The striped sucker grows to a length of eighteen inches. Old males have the head tuberculate in the breeding season in the spring. The species is very readily distinguished by the dark stripes along the sides produced by spots at the base of each scale. In the young of this sucker there is no lateral line, but in adults it is almost entire.

This species prefers clear, sluggish waters and grassy ponds. It readily adapts itself to life in the aquarium. It feeds almost entirely on mollusks, insects and insect larvæ. The species is not much esteemed as a food fish, although it is sold in large numbers.

Genus **MOXOSTOMA** Rafinesque.

36. Moxostoma anisurum (Rafinesque).

The White-nosed Sucker.

The body of the white-nosed sucker is elongate, little compressed, slightly arched anteriorly. Its depth is contained three and one-third times in the length to end of scales. The head is moderately large, its length being contained less than four times in total length without tail-fin. Eye large, nearly twice in its distance from tip of snout. The mouth is moderate, with well-developed lips. Snout rather blunt and scarcely projecting beyond the mouth. Fins all well developed. The dorsal fin is large; its first ray is as long as the dorsal base, or about seven-eighths length of head. D. 15; A. 7; scales, 5-43-4. The specimen described, No. 10,793, United States National Museum, from Ohio, is sixteen inches long.

The white-nosed sucker is known also as the carp mullet, small-mouthed red horse and long-tailed red horse. This sucker has a wide distribution, occurring in the Great Lake region and northward, the Ohio valley and the eastern states south to North Carolina. It is not, however, an abundant species. In Pennsylvania Prof. Cope records it as common in Lake Erie and the Allegheny river, and generally confounded by fishermen with the red horse (*M. macrolepidotum*). The white-nosed sucker is a small species, seldom exceeding one foot in length. It is not a valuable food fish, and there is nothing on record concerning its habits.

In some North Carolina streams this is the commonest species of sucker.

37. Moxostoma macrolepidotum (Le Sueur).

The Red Horse. (*Figure 33.*)

The red horse has a stout and more or less rounded body, whose depth is one-fourth of the total length without the caudal. The least depth of the caudal peduncle is equal to almost half length of head. The head is broad, flattened above; snout blunt, overpassing mouth. The length of the head is contained four and two-thirds times in the total length without caudal. The eye equals about one-fourth length of head. The mouth is large, with full lips, the lower being especially well developed. A line of muciferous pores connects the lateral line of one side with that of the other across the nape, and from this line there extends on either side of the head a line which branches back of the eye, and is continued forward by two lines, one above the eye, ending at nostrils, and one under eye, passing nostrils to tip of snout; there is still another line of these pores on lower margin of cheeks.

The dorsal fin is short, its highest ray but slightly longer than dorsal base. Anal fin very short, with long rays, the longest two and a half times as long as the base of the fin, or equalling length of longest dorsal ray. Caudal forked.

D. 13 to 14; A. 8. Scales, 6–45–6. Described from No. 12,316, United States National Museum, a specimen fourteen inches long, from the Potomac river.

The common red horse, known also as the white sucker, mullet and large-scaled sucker, is an extremely variable species occurring in the Great Lake region, Chesapeake Bay region, south to Georgia and Alabama, and west to Dakota. It is a large species and reaches a length of two feet. The principal varieties are noted in Pennsylvania; one of them, *duquesnei*, is found in the Ohio river, the other, *macrolepidotum*, is common in the Susquehanna, and less abundant in the Delaware. It is abundant in Lake Erie. DeKay described the fish from Oneida lake, where it is called mullet and sucker.

The red horse inhabits clear waters and ascends small streams in May to spawn. As a food fish it ranks low, but the species is freely sold. Its food consists principally of mollusks and a small percentage of plants and insects. Minute crustaceans also form a small portion of its food.

38. Moxostoma aureolum (Le Sueur).

The Golden Sucker.

The body of the golden sucker is oblong, the back in front of the dorsal elevated and compressed, head short, conic, broad between eyes. The eye is rather large, one-fourth length of head, which is contained five times in total length without caudal. The depth of the body is contained three and one-half times in this length. Caudal peduncle deep, compressed, its least depth equal to one-half length of head. Mouth small, the snout somewhat projecting.

Fins all well developed. The anterior rays of dorsal longest, as long as dorsal base; pectoral and longest anal rays equalling length of head. Caudal forked. Scales large, about equal in size all over body and finely striated. D. 15; A. 8; scales, 6-46-6. Lateral line complete.

Described from a specimen fifteen and one-half inches long, No. 31,942, United States National Museum, obtained in Lake Winnipeg, Manitoba.

The golden sucker has the additional names of lake mullet, lake red horse and golden red horse. It inhabits the great lakes and the region northward, also the Ohio valley. It is common in Lake Erie, but not in the Ohio.

This species grows to a length of eighteen inches, and is one of the handsomest of the suckers. Prof. Forbes records it from lakes of northern Illinois, also abundantly in the central part of that state. Its food, according to this author, consists chiefly of mollusks and insects. Although freely eaten it has little to recommend it for the table.

39. Moxostoma crassilabre (Cope).

The Long-tailed Red Horse.

The long-tailed red horse has a moderately elongated body, its depth contained three and one-fourth to three and one-half times in the total length without caudal. The head is short, forming one-fifth or nearly one-fifth of the standard length. The snout is pointed, and overhangs the mouth, which is very small. The small eye is one-fifth as long as the head. The dorsal is high, the longest rays one and one-third to one and one-half times the base of the fin. The margin is concave, making the fin falcate. The anal is large, shaped like the dorsal, its tip reaching beyond the base of the caudal. The lobes of the caudal are unequal, the upper produced. D. 12 to 14; A. 7. Scales, 5-44-5. The dorsal and caudal fins are bright red, the sides silvery tinged with dusky above, some dark spots at the bases of the scales and the lower fins white.

The long-tailed red horse is an inhabitant of the Ohio valley, and ranges southward to North Carolina. It is described as having the form of a white-fish, the body deep, the head small and with a sharply conic and projecting snout; the lobes of the tail are unequal, the upper one being much the longer. This is a handsome species, the sides silvery with copper reflections. The dorsal and caudal fins bright are red. Prof. Cope found it in western Pennsylvania. Its habits are doubtless similar to those of other species of the genus, but there is nothing on record about this subject, so far as we know.

Genus **PLACOPHARYNX** Cope.

40. Placopharynx carinatus Cope.

The Big-jawed Sucker. (*Figure 34.*)

The big-jawed sucker has the body moderately long, heavy forwards, particularly at the shoulders, and the tail comparatively slender. The greatest depth equals one-fourth of the total length without the caudal, and the least depth of the caudal peduncle is two-fifths of the greatest depth. The head is short, thick, with a deep and nearly vertical snout; its length is contained about four and one-half times in the standard length. The snout is about twice as long as the eye, and more than one-third as long as the head. The eye is moderate in size, one-fifth as long as the head, placed high; the interorbital width one-half length of head. The mouth is large, inferior, with strongly plicate lips, the maxilla reaching to below the posterior nostril. The sickle-shaped pharyngeal bone has about ten of its teeth enlarged, increasing rapidly in size to the lowermost, the crowns of the large teeth with a concave grinding surface. The dorsal origin is above the thirteenth, and the ventral origin below the seventeenth scale of the lateral line. The dorsal base is as long as the head without the snout, and the longest ray is three-fourths as long as the head; the last ray is one-half as long as the longest. The ventral does not reach nearly to the vent; its length equals two-thirds that of the head. The anal origin is under the thirty-first scale of the lateral line; the anal base is one-third as long as the head; the longest anal ray is four-fifths as long as the head, and nearly three times as long as the last ray. The caudal is large and deeply forked, the middle rays about two-fifths as long as the external rays. The pectoral is large, its length six-sevenths that of the head. D. ii, 12; A. iii, 7; V. 9; P. 16; scales, 6-42-5. Color in spirits pale yellowish brown, the fins paler; in life brassy green above, the lower fins red. Length of the specimen described, No. 36,090, United States National Museum, from the Black Warrior river, 13½ inches.

The big-jawed sucker was, until recently, considered a very rare fish, but has been rediscovered in numerous localities, and its range is now known to extend from Ohio to Georgia and Arkansas. It is a large-scaled fish with a remarkably large mouth. Its color is brassy green, paler below, and the ventral and anal fins are red. Externally there is very little to distinguish this sucker from some species of buffalo fish, but the teeth in the pharynx are very different from those of all other suckers. The lower seven to twelve teeth on each side are very large, scarcely compressed, truncate and resembling in this respect the teeth of some of the minnows rather than suckers. Recent collectors in western streams have found this curious large sucker to be a very common fish in numerous localities. It grows to a length of two feet, and is extensively used for food. According to Prof. S. A. Forbes it is probable that the enlarged teeth of the pharynx are related to a preference for molluscan food. In large individuals taken from the Illinois river, Prof. Forbes found the food to consist of small shells and insects, the latter consisting chiefly of the larvae of water beetles. Aquatic plants are occasionally mixed with the food, but probably by accident.

Family CYPRINIDÆ. The Minnows.

Genus CAMPOSTOMA Agassiz.

41. Campostoma anomalum (Rafinesque).

The Stone Roller.

In the stone roller the body is moderately stout and not greatly compressed; the caudal peduncle is long and deep. The greatest depth of the body is contained four to four and one-half times in the total length without the caudal; the depth of the caudal peduncle, eight and one-half to nine times in the same length. The snout is obtuse, twice as long as the eye, and two-fifths as long as the head. The maxilla reaches to the vertical from the posterior nostril, which is more than twice as far from tip of snout as from eye. The dorsal origin is over the twentieth scale of the lateral line, and the ventral origin under the nineteenth. The dorsal base is one-half, and its longest ray two-thirds as long as the head. The ventral reaches nearly to vent. The pectoral is one-sixth of total length without caudal. The anal origin is under the thirty-second scale of the lateral line; the anal base is as long as the snout, and the longest ray equals the head, not including the snout. The caudal is moderately forked. D. 8; A. 7 or 8; scales, 8-52 to 53-8; teeth, 4-4. Color in spirits brownish above, lower parts pale. In living examples the scales are somewhat mottled with blackish, and there is a dusky vertical bar behind the opercle; dorsal and anal fins olivaceous in females and with a nearly median dusky cross-bar. Breeding males have the iris orange, the dorsal and anal fins crimson, and the head, and sometimes the body, covered with large roundish tubercles.

The stone roller is likewise called stone toter, stone lugger and steelback minnow. It is a fish of very wide distribution, ranging from western New York to North Carolina and throughout the Ohio and Mississippi valleys west to Minnesota and southwest to Texas. It is an extremely variable species, and everywhere common. It is, moreover, one of the most singular of American fishes, in having the air bladder surrounded by numerous turns of the long intestine. In this respect it is unique among fishes. The stone roller grows to a length of eight inches, but has no importance as food. It feeds upon aquatic plants. The young are hardy in the aquarium, where they feed upon confervæ and diatoms. The sexes are very unlike. The males in the breeding season have the head, and frequently the entire body covered with large tubercles, and the upper half of the dorsal and anal fins fiery orange and with a dark cross-bar about the middle of these fins.

The species is rather sluggish, but when frightened its movements are very rapid. It is a bottom feeder.

Genus CHROSOMUS Rafinesque.

42. Chrosomus erythrogaster Rafinesque.

The Red-bellied Dace. (Figure 55.)

The red-bellied dace has a fusiform, moderately elongate and thick body, whose greatest height is contained from four and one-fifth to five times, and the least depth of its caudal peduncle eight and one-half times in the total length to the caudal base. The head is conical, with pointed snout as long as the eye, which is about one-fourth as long as the head. The head equals one-fourth of total length to caudal base. The maxilla reaches nearly to below the front of the eye. The lateral line varies in development, sometimes reaching to above the origin of the ventrals, and continued backward even farther at intervals, but usually not extending to ventrals. The dorsal origin is over the space between the ventral origin and the vent; about thirty-nine rows of scales between it and the nape. The dorsal base is one-half as long as the head, the longest ray equals head without snout. The pectoral reaches nearly to ventral origin, and the ventral reaches vent. The anal base is two-fifths as long as the head; the longest ray equal to longest of the dorsal. The caudal is moderately forked, its middle rays two-thirds as long as the outer. D. 8; A. 7; V. 8; P. 12; scales, 18-80 to 85-10; teeth, 5-5. Length of specimens described, from Yellow creek, three inches. A narrow, dusky line along the top of the back. Two narrow, dark bands on the sides, the lower one passing forward on the head to tip of snout. The space between the bands and below bright silvery. Breeding males have the bases of the dorsal, anal and caudal fins, and the area between the dark bands scarlet, while the body is covered with minute tubercles, and the fins generally are vivid yellow.

The red-bellied minnow or dace is found from Pennsylvania to Dakota and Tennessee. It is abundant in small streams and is a strikingly beautiful fish. Along the sides are two blackish bands, one beginning above the eye and extending to the tail; another traverses the eye and follows the lateral line to the base of the caudal, where it ends in a black spot. The belly and the space between the bands are bright silvery, replaced by scarlet red in breeding males, which have the same color at the bases of the dorsal, caudal and anal fins. In the height of the breeding season the fins are bright yellow, and the body is covered with small tubercles. According to Prof. Cope the red-bellied minnow is not found in the Delaware, but it occurs in the Susquehanna, and is common in the streams of western Pennsylvania. It reaches a length of three inches, and is similar in its habits to the stone roller, with which it associates. It prefers clear streams, which have their origin in springs. As an aquarium fish this is scarcely excelled in beauty and hardiness, and as a bait for the black bass it has few superiors.

GENUS **HYBOGNATHUS** AGASSIZ.

43. Hybognathus nuchalis AGASSIZ.

The Silvery Minnow.

The silvery minnow has a moderately stout and short body as compared with its eastern representative (*H. regius*), the greatest height equalling one-fourth of the total length without the caudal, and the least depth of the short caudal peduncle equalling nearly one-half of the greatest depth of the body. The body is compressed, its greatest width less than one-half its height. The head is short, its upper and lower profiles tapering equally into the short and not very obtuse snout, which is as long as the eye, and three-elevenths as long as the head. The mouth is small, slightly oblique, with jaws nearly equal, or, the lower slightly included, the maxilla without a barbel, and reaching to below the anterior nostril. The dorsal origin is over,

3 FISHES.

and the ventral origin under, the twelfth scale of the lateral line. The base of the dorsal is two-thirds as long as the head; the longest ray equals the distance from the nostrils to the end of the operculum, and the last ray is less than one-half as long as the longest. The ventral does not reach to the vent; its length two-thirds that of the head. The anal origin is under the twenty-fourth scale of the lateral line; the base of the fin is scarcely as long as the postorbital part of the head; the last ray is one-third, and the longest ray two-thirds as long as the head. The pectoral is four-fifths as long as the head, and reaches to below the eleventh scale of the lateral line. The caudal is moderate in size and deeply forked, the middle rays less than one-half as long as the external rays. D. ii, 7; A. ii, 7; V. 8; P. 15; scales, 6-38 to 39-4; teeth, 4-4, long, much compressed, and with a long oblique grinding surface. The lateral line is gently decurved on about the first six scales, thence straight and median to the root of the caudal fin. Color in spirits light brown with a broad silvery band, the fins all pale. The specimens described, No. 36,451, United States National Museum, from the Saline river, Benton, Ark., are three and one-half to three and three-fourths inches long.

The silvery minnow, or blunt jaw, according to the present interpretation of the species, occurs from New Jersey to South Carolina, west to Dakota, and southwest to Texas. In the Potomac river there is a large variety, described by Girard as *H. regius*, which reaches a length of seven inches. This variety has the body deeper and the eye larger than in the western form. The largest individuals recorded were nine inches long.

This species spawns in the early spring, and is extensively used for food along with the *Notropis hudsonius*, spawn-eater, or so-called smelt or gudgeon.

44. Hybognathus regius Girard.

The Smelt Minnow.

The smelt minnow has a rather elongate body, with the head small and the snout short and blunt. The greatest depth is contained from four to four and one-third times, and the least depth of the caudal peduncle nearly ten times in the total length to base of caudal. The snout is as long as the eye, and two-sevenths as long as the head. The width of the space between the eyes is nearly one and one-half times the length of the eye. The maxilla reaches to the vertical through the hind edge of the posterior nostril. The lower jaw is received within the upper. No barbel. The head is two-ninths of total length to base of caudal. The dorsal origin is above the fourteenth scale of the lateral line, and immediately over the ventral origin. The anal origin is under the twenty-sixth scale of the lateral line. The length of the dorsal base equals that of the snout and eye combined; the longest dorsal ray equals nearly one-fifth of total to base of caudal. The pectoral reaches to below the eleventh, and the ventral to the twenty-third scale of the lateral line. The anal base is as long as the postorbital part of the head; the longest anal ray equals head without snout. The caudal is large and deeply forked, its middle rays less than one-half as long as the outer. D. 8; A. 8; V. 9; P. 15; scales, 8-40-6; teeth, 4-4. Length of specimen described, from the Potomac river, five and five-eighths inches. Color in life greenish above, paler below, the sides with a broad silvery band; in spirits the upper parts become light brown. The fins are uniformly pale.

This large variety of the silvery minnow is sometimes called smelt minnow. It occurs in Maryland and Virginia, and its probable occurrence in the Susquehanna is mentioned by Prof. Cope. It reaches a length of seven inches, and is highly prized as a food fish. This minnow takes the hook very freely early in the spring, when gravid females are extremely common.

I have placed this as a variety of *H. nuchalis* in deference to the views of Dr. Jordan, although it appears to me sufficiently distinct to retain the name applied to it by Girard. It is highly probable that the silvery minnow which Prof. Cope describes in the report for 1879-80 is the variety just mentioned. It has been found in the Raritan by Dr. Abbott, in the spring, associated with the smelt, and Prof. Cope justly believes that it will be found in the Delaware.

Genus **PIMEPHALES** Rafinesque.

45. Pimephales promelas Rafinesque.

The Fat-head Minnow.

The fat-head minnow has a short, deep and moderately thick body, and the head short with a very obtuse snout. The greatest depth of the body is equal to or slightly greater than length of head, and is contained from three and two-thirds to four and one-fourth times in total length without caudal. The least depth of the caudal peduncle equals the length of the postorbital part of the head. The head forms about one-fourth of the total length to base of caudal; the width of the head equals two-thirds of its length. The eye is as long as the snout and two-ninths as long as the head. The mouth is very small, terminal, slightly oblique, the maxilla not reaching vertical through hinder nostril. The dorsal origin is above, and the ventral origin below the twenty-first scale of the lateral line. The dorsal base is two-thirds as long as the head; the first ray is about as long as the eye, and the longest as long as the head without the snout. The ventral reaches a little beyond the anal origin; its length equal to dorsal base. The anal base equals nearly one-half length of head, and the longest ray is as long as the dorsal base. The caudal is moderate and not deeply forked. The lateral line is continuous on about twenty to twenty-eight scales, and in one specimen continued with interruptions almost to the caudal base. D. i, 8; A. i, 7; V. 8; P. 18; scales, 9-45 to 49-6; teeth, 4-4. Length of specimens described, three inches. Color in spirits light brown, top and sides of head darker. A broad dark band on the base of the dorsal, most distinct anteriorly and sometimes absent behind. Males in spring are dusky, with black head, and the snout and chin with numerous coarse tubercles.

The fat-head or black-head is an inhabitant of the Ohio valley and the Great Lake region west to Dakota and southwest to Texas. It is common in sluggish brooks, and instances have been known of its distribution by the action of cyclones. In Pennsylvania it is common in tributaries of the Ohio.

The fat-head grows to a length of two and one-half inches. The sexes differ in color, the females being olivaceous, while the males are dusky, and in the spring have the head black and the snout covered with numerous large tubercles. The species has no value as food, but it is an interesting one for the aquarium. Its food consists of mud and algæ, and it seems to prefer a muddy bottom.

46. Pimephales notatus RAFINESQUE.

The Blunt-nosed Minnow.

The blunt-nosed minnow has a moderately elongate body and a slender caudal peduncle. The head is somewhat conical with a short and blunt snout. The greatest depth of the body nearly equals length of head, and is two-ninths of total length without caudal. The least depth of the caudal peduncle equals about one-half of the greatest depth of body. The snout is as long as the eye, and one-fourth as long as the head. The mouth is very small, inferior, nearly horizontal, the maxilla reaching to below the anterior nostril and provided with a short, thick, somewhat club-shaped barbel. The dorsal origin is slightly behind the ventral origin and over the seventeenth scale of the lateral line. The dorsal base is two-thirds as long as the head, and about equal to the longest dorsal ray. The ventral origin is under the sixteenth scale of the lateral line ; the fin does not reach to the vent. The anal origin is under the twenty-seventh scale of the lateral line ; the base of the anal is two-fifths as long as the head, and the longest ray is equal to postorbital part of the head. The caudal is moderately large and forked. The lateral line curves very slightly downward as far as the ventral origin, and then follows straight along the median line ; it is complete. D. i, 8; A. i, 7; V. 8; P. 15; scales, 6-42 to 45-5; teeth, 4-4. Length of specimens described, three inches. Color in spirits light brown ; the fins, except the dorsal, paler. A black spot about as large as the eye on the front of the dorsal. In life the sides are bluish. Breeding males have the black on the dorsal continued backward on the membrane covering the rays and the head black, while the snout has about fourteen to seventeen large pointed tubercles. A dusky shade sometimes present at base of caudal.

The blunt-nosed minnow is a larger species than the fat-head, reaching a length of four inches, and its range extends from Quebec to Delaware, west to Kansas and south to Mississippi. It differs from the fat-head in having a complete lateral line, but the sexual differences in this species are similar to those in the fat-head. The males in spring have the head black and the snout with many large tubercles. The species is extremely variable and changes greatly with age. It frequents small and muddy streams, and its food consists of decaying vegetable matter.

GENUS **EXOGLOSSUM** RAFINESQUE.

47. Exoglossum maxillingua (LE SUEUR).

The Cut-lips or Chub. (*Figure 35.*)

The cut-lips has a stout, short and thick body, its greatest height nearly equal to the length of the head, and one-fourth of the total without caudal. The caudal peduncle is short and deep, its least depth about one-half head. The snout is short and obtusely conical, its length somewhat greater than the eye, and nearly equal to one-third of the head. The maxilla reaches to below the nostrils, its length equalling that of the snout. Head four and one-fifth in total to base of caudal. The dorsal origin is nearly over the anal origin, and in the vertical through the twenty-third scale of the lateral line. The dorsal base is about one-half as long as the head, and its longest ray equals twice the distance from the dorsal origin to middle of eye. The pectoral is about as long as the longest dorsal ray, and the ventral reaches to the anal origin. The base of the anal is one-half as long as the longest anal ray. The caudal is moderately forked. D. 8; A. 7; scales, 9-54-6; teeth, 1, 4-4, 1. Length of specimen described, four and three-fourths inches, from Tacoma, D. C. Color brown or olivaceous, darker above; a short and narrow dark bar above root of pectoral; young with a dusky bar at the caudal base. Fins dusky, their extremities pale.

The cut-lips may be readily distinguished by the three-lobed lower jaw, the dentary bones being closely united and the lower lip represented by a fleshy lobe on each side of the mandible.

The chub is known as cut lips, butter chub, nigger chub and day chub. It is a very common species in the Susquehanna and its tributaries, and is considered a good pan fish. Its range is not extensive, reaching only from western New York to Virginia. It grows to a length of six inches, and may be at once distinguished from all of the other minnows by its three-lobed lower jaw. It is believed that this singular structure of the mouth enables the fish to scrape mollusks from their hold on rocks, as its stomach usually contains small shell fish. The chub bites readily at a baited hook, and is therefore highly prized by boys.

Genus NOTROPIS Rafinesque.

48. Notropis bifrenatus (Cope).

The Bridled Minnow.

[Hybopsis bifrenatus Cope, Cypr. Pennsylvania, 1866, page 384.]

"Color above straw, the scales delicately brown-edged, below impure white, with a narrow black line along base of anal fin to caudal. Along each side from caudal fin around the end of muzzle, including the end of the mandible, a shining black band one and one-half scales in width. This is bordered above on the muzzle, forming an arc from orbit to orbit, by an orange band, which is strongly margined above by the brown of the top of the front. Opercular and suborbital regions below the black band, pure silvery.

Front convex between the orbits; length of muzzle equal diameter of iris band and pupil, sometimes nearly equal orbit. Iris colored in continuation of the lateral band. The lateral line rarely extends half way to the dorsal fin, while the pores of the same may be observed at the bases of the scales for half the remaining length of the animal. Length of the largest specimen, nineteen lines; breadth of muzzle at nares one and five-tenth lines. Radii of the scales strong."

This little minnow has no common name, and it attains to a length of only two inches. It is found from Massachusetts to Maryland, and in the tributaries of the Delaware it is abundant. The body is light olive or sometimes straw-colored, and there is a jet black band along the side, making this a very conspicuous little fish. It is a useful bait for game fishes, particularly the black bass.

49. Notropis procne (Cope).

The Shiner.

This little minnow has a short, slender and compressed body and a very slender caudal peduncle. The greatest depth at the dorsal origin equals the length of the head, which is about one-fourth of the total without caudal. In some described specimens the head is contained four and three-fourths times and the depth of the body five and one-fourth times in the total length without caudal. The snout is short and obtuse, shorter than the eye, which is two-fifths as long as the head. The mouth is terminal and small, the maxilla not reaching to front of eye, and the jaws equal. The lateral line is gently curved downward over the pectoral, and, in the specimen examined, becomes interrupted in its posterior half. The dorsal origin is over the twelfth scale of the lateral line, and nearly over the ventral origin. The dorsal base is a little more than one-half as long as the head, and the longest ray is as long as the head. The ventral reaches to the anal origin. The anal base is one-half as long as the head, and the longest anal ray is four-fifths as long as the head. The caudal is moderately forked. D. 8; A. 7; V. 8; P. 13; scales, 5-32 to 34-3; teeth, 4-4. Length of specimen described, from Havre de Grace, Md., two and one-fourth inches. Color in spirits light brown, the belly pale and lower half of head silvery. A narrow dark line along the top of the back, and a narrow dark median band continued forward on the nose. Fins all pale.

The shiner is found from western New York to Maryland. Prof. Cope found it abundant in the tributaries of the Delaware and Susquehanna, in slow moving streams. It reaches a length of two and one-half inches.

This minnow is olivaceous, with a dark lateral band. The tail is long, which suggests the specific name *procne*, a kind of swallow. This little fish is suitable for the aquarium, and is an excellent bait for game fishes.

50. Notropis hudsonius (CLINTON).

The Spawn Eater.

The spawn-eater has a moderately elongate and compressed body, its greatest height contained four and one-half times in the total length without caudal, and about equal to length of head. The head is conical, with short, blunt snout equal to the diameter of the eye, which is contained three and one-half times in the length of the head. The space between the eyes equals length of postorbital part of head. Mouth small, nearly horizontal, the lower jaw very slightly the shorter, the maxilla reaching the vertical through the posterior nostril. The lateral line is slightly curved downward over the pectoral, straight and median for the rest of its course. The origin of the dorsal is over, and of the ventral under the thirteenth scale of the lateral line. The dorsal base is two-thirds as long as the head, and the longest ray as long as the head. The ventral reaches nearly or quite to the vent. The anal origin is under the twenty-fourth scale of the lateral line; the anal base is one-half, and the longest anal ray four-fifths as long as the head. The caudal is large and deeply forked, its middle rays one-half as long as the outer. D. 8; A. 8 or 9; V. 8; P. 14; scales, 7-38-5; teeth 2, 4-4, 1 or 2, with a narrow grinding surface on at least two. Length of specimens described, from Washington, D. C., three and one-half to four and one-fourth inches. Color in spirits pale brown, the fins and all of head except upper surface pale; a broad median silvery band, its greatest width about equal to diameter of eye; a dusky spot at the root of the caudal in the young.

The spawn-eater is said to occur from Lake Superior to New York and southward. In Pennsylvania begins a form elsewhere described as *N. amarus*, which differs in the structure of the pharyngeal teeth. The spawn-eater attains a length of ten inches; it is olivaceous and sometimes has a band along the side. The young have a round black spot at the base of the caudal fin. The teeth of this minnow are usually four in the principal row, and two in the inner row.

This minnow does not much frequent small streams, but is abundant in the Delaware river and also in Lake Erie.

51. Notropis amarus Girard.

The Gudgeon or Smelt.   (*Figure 47.*)

The gudgeon has a moderately elongate and compressed body and a slender caudal peduncle. The greatest depth equals one-fourth of the total length to base of caudal, and the least depth of the peduncle equals the length of the postorbital part of head. The head is rather short, with an obtuse short snout; the length of the head is nearly one-fourth of the total to base of caudal. The snout is one-fourth, and the eye one-third as long as the head. The maxilla extends to the vertical through the front of the eye; the lower jaw is slightly included; the mouth is slightly oblique. The width of the head equals nearly two-thirds of its length. The distance between the eyes equals the length of the orbit. The dorsal origin is over, and the ventral origin under the tenth scale of the lateral line. The length of the dorsal base equals two-thirds that of the head, and the longest dorsal ray is four-fifths as long as the head. The anal base is as long as the postorbital part of the head, and the longest ray is about two-thirds as long as the head. The ventral reaches nearly to the vent and the pectoral to below the eighth scale of the lateral line. The lateral line is very slightly bent downward over the pectoral. The caudal is moderate in size and deeply forked. D. ii, 7; A. ii, 7; V. 8; P. 15; scales, 6-36 to 39-4; teeth, 1, 4-1, 1 or 1, 4-4, 0 in the example described, from the Susquehanna river, length four and one-fourth inches. The teeth are slightly hooked, and two or three on each side have a developed grinding surface. The color in spirits is light brown, the sides of body and lower half of head silvery; the young have a dusky median lateral band, which is sometimes continued on the snout, and a more or less distinct small dark blotch at the base of the caudal. The fins are all pale.

The gudgeon or smelt of Pennsylvania is a variety of *N. hudsonius* of Clinton, which ranges from Lake Superior to New York, and south in streams east of the Alleghenies to Georgia. The southern form is the variety *amarus* of Girard, which exhibits some difference in its pharyngeal teeth. The species is an extremely variable one. It grows to a length of about eight inches. Prof. Cope records it as abundant in the Susquehanna, especially in the lower part of the river.

This is a handsome silvery fish, and is as much used for food as its associate, the silvery minnow. The name spawn-eater, sometimes applied to it, indicates that the species is destructive to the eggs of other fishes.

The *N. amarus* is abundant in lake Erie, and grows to a large size, and is known there as the lake minnow. It is not common in small streams.

52. Notropis whipplei Girard.

The Silver Fin.

The silver-fin has a moderately elongate body, which is fusiform in the adult. The caudal peduncle is short and stout. The depth of the body at the ventral fin equals nearly one-fourth of the total length to the caudal base. The head is conical, compressed and with a pointed snout a little longer than the eye, which is two-ninths as long as the head. The mouth is moderate, terminal, slightly oblique, the jaws nearly equal, the maxilla reaching to vertical through front of eye. The head is two-ninths of total length without caudal. The dorsal origin is a little behind the ventral origin, and over the fifteenth scale of the lateral line. The length of the dorsal base equals one-seventh of the total without caudal, and the longest ray is as long as the head without the snout. The ventral reaches nearly to the anal. The anal begins under the twenty-first scale of the lateral line; its base is as long as the dorsal base, and its longest ray is about two-thirds as long as the head. The caudal is large and moderately forked. The lateral line curves downward over the pectoral. D. 8; A. 9; V. 8; P. 14; scales, 6-38 to 41-4; teeth, 1, 4-4, 1, with more or less serrate edges. Length of specimen described, from the Susquehanna river, four inches. In spirits the back is brown, the sides dull silvery, the scales with a dusky margin, and the lower parts are whitish. A narrow and long black blotch on the membrane between the sixth and seventh, and another between the seventh and eighth dorsal rays. Lower fins pale. Males in spring have the fins partly or wholly charged with white pigment, and in the height of the breeding season the pigment in the dorsal has a greenish tint, and the top of the head and snout is covered with minute tubercles.

The silver-fin ranges from western New York to Virginia and west to Minnesota and Arkansas. It is a common species and a variable one. It reaches a length of four inches. In Pennsylvania it occurs in all the rivers and creeks, but, according to Prof. Cope, is least common in tributaries of the Delaware.

It is one of our finest minnows for the aquarium, and is useful as food and bait for larger fishes.

53. Notropis megalops Rafinesque.

The Rough Head.

The rough-head when young has the body moderately elongate, but it becomes deeper with age, and much compressed. The caudal peduncle is short, and its depth equals length of postorbital part of head. The depth of the body at the ventral is contained three and one-third to four times in the total length without the caudal. The head is short, deep and thin, its length one-fourth of the total without caudal, its width about one-half its length. The eye is as long as the snout, and two-sevenths as long as the head. Mouth moderate, terminal, oblique, the maxilla reaching about to vertical through front of eye. The dorsal origin is over, and the ventral origin under the twelfth scale of the lateral line. The length of the dorsal base equals one-seventh of the total without the caudal, and its longest ray one-fifth of the same length. The ventral reaches nearly or quite to vent. The anal origin is under the twenty-third scale of the lateral line. The anal base is one-half, and the longest ray two-thirds as long as the head. The caudal is large and deeply forked. The lateral line descends in a long curve, becoming straight and median over the anal origin. D. 8; A. 9; V. 8; P. 15; scales, 7-40 to 41-4; teeth, 2, 4-4, 2, with narrow grinding surface. Length of specimens described, from four to four and one-half inches.

This is the common shiner, and has received the additional names of red-fin, dace and rough-head. The species is very widely distributed, and is extremely variable, and as a consequence some geographical races have received distinct names. It extends from Maine to the Rocky Mountains, but is absent from the Carolinas and Texas. It grows to a length of eight inches.

The upper parts of this fish are steel blue, and the scales are dusky at the edge and base. The sides are silvery, overlaid with a gilt line; there is another gilt band along the back. The belly is silvery, except in spring males, in which it is a bright rosy color. The male, in the breeding season, has the lower jaw and the top of the head and nape covered with small tubercles. In the breeding condition this is a very handsome species, although the females and young lack the bright colors of the adult male. In Pennsylvania the species is common everywhere, and is best known under the name of red-fin. It reaches a very large size in Lake Erie. It has no value except as food and bait for more valuable fishes, especially the black bass and pike-perch. The flesh is very soft and cannot be kept long after death.

The shiner runs into small brooks, and is most abundant in eddies and other quiet portions of the streams.

54. Notropis chalybæus (Cope).

The Pigmy Minnow.

[Hybopsis chalybæus Cope. Cyprinidæ of Pennsylvania, 1866, page 383.]

"Head three and eight-tenths (sometimes four) times in length to base of caudal; length of latter equal from opercular margin to nares. Muzzle shorter than diameter of orbit, slightly acuminate, and exceeded by tip of mandible when viewed from above; head flat above, less angulate on temporal regions than many species, the superior plane narrower there than between the orbits; supraopercular region oblique. Teeth slightly hooked, masticatory surface well marked, upper tooth nearly opposite angle of the ala. Dorsal fin elevated, with eight rays, a very little behind above ventrals; latter pointed, reaching anal. Anal slightly elongate, exceptionally with nine rays; pectorals pointed, not reaching ventrals. Superior outline rising to dorsal fin, then immediately descending, forming with the nearly parallel ventral line, the elongate caudal peduncle. Caudal peduncle deeply forked.

"The broad, burnished, black lateral band does not descend below the lateral line on the middle of the body; it occupies one and two half rows of scales. Above it on head and body the color is fulvous brown, excepting a straw-colored crescent from orbit to orbit round the nose; terminal half of mandible black; sides of head below, silvery; of body, straw-colored; no distinct vertebral stripe, or spots on fins.

"This is a very small species, nearly the smallest of the Cyprinidæ; a specimen before me, apparently full grown, measures only one inch, eight and five-tenths lines in total."

The pigmy minnow inhabits the Delaware river, and grows to a length of only two inches. The Latin name signifies steel-colored. The fish is brown with a jet black lateral band, and in the male the lower parts are orange.

Prof. Cope found this species in tributaries of the Delaware, especially in dams and ponds. The shining black lateral band makes this a conspicuous little fish.

55. Notropis jejunus Forbes.

The Hungry Minnow.

This minnow has a stoutish and not very long body, with a short and rather heavy caudal peduncle. The greatest depth equals two-ninths of the total length to the caudal base; the least depth of the peduncle equals length of postorbital part of head. The head is moderate; the snout very short and blunt, its length about two-thirds that of the eye. The eye is nearly one-third as long as the head. The mouth is moderate in size, oblique, the lower jaw slightly included, and the maxilla reaching to below the front of the eye. The head is one-fourth of total length to base of caudal; its width equals one-half of its length, and the width of the space between the eyes equals two-fifths length of head. The dorsal origin is over, and the ventral origin under the thirteenth scale of the lateral line. The dorsal base is as long as the postorbital part of the head, and the longest ray is as long as the head without the snout. The ventral reaches nearly to the vent, which is under the twenty-first scale of the lateral line. The pectoral reaches to below the ninth or tenth scale of the lateral line. The anal base is nearly one-half as long as the head, and its longest ray is a little more than one-half length of head. The caudal is moderate and well forked. The lateral line has a very shallow downward curve over the pectoral. D. ii, 7; A. ii, 6 or 7; V. 8; P. 14; scales, 5-36 to 37-3½; teeth, 2, 4-4, 1 (according to Forbes, 1, 4-4, 1, in a specimen studied), all hooked. In spirits the body is pale yellowish brown; a broad, silvery median band, and a faint dusky line along the edge of the back; a triangular or spear-shaped dark spot on the vertex; fins all pale, but the dorsal is sometimes finely spotted. The specimens described are two and one-fourth inches long.

This small minnow, attaining to a length of three inches, is recorded by Dr. Jordan from Pennsylvania to Kansas. In Pennsylvania it occurs only in the Ohio river basin. The species is too small to be important, except as food for larger fishes.

56. Notropis scabriceps Cope.

The Rough-headed Shiner.

The rough-headed shiner has a stout body, its greatest height contained four and one-fourth times in the total length without the caudal, and its thickness one-half the length of the head. The least depth of the caudal peduncle is two-fifths of the greatest depth. The head, one-fourth of total without caudal, is short and thick, with a short, obtuse snout, the latter being two-thirds as long as the eye, which is two-fifths to one-third as long as the head. The mouth is obliquely placed, moderate in size, the maxilla reaching nearly to below the front of the eye, the jaws equal. The origin of the dorsal is over, and of the ventral under the twelfth scale of the lateral line. The dorsal base is as long as the postorbital part of the head; the longest ray is more than twice as long as the last ray, and as long as the head without the snout. The ventral reaches nearly to the vent, its length nearly two-thirds that of the head. The anal origin is under the twenty-first scale of the lateral line; the anal base is as long as the eye, the longest anal ray is two-thirds as long as the head. The pectoral is as long as the head without the snout. The caudal is rather large and well forked. The lateral line is gently decurved in the first half of its length. D. ii, 7; A. ii, 7; V. 8; P. 15; scales, 6-38-4; teeth, 2, 4-4, 2, strongly hooked. Color pale brown with a broad silvery area on sides, and a lateral band made up of dusky specks, this continued on the snout. The name *scabriceps* (rough-headed) refers to the tuberculate condition of the head in breeding males.

The length of the specimen described, No. 36,655, United States National Museum, from Rolling Fork, New Haven, Ky., is two and one-half inches.

The rough-headed shiner has been found in the Kanawha, and will probably be found in other tributaries of the Ohio. The name is in allusion to the prickles developed on the head of males in the breeding season in spring.

57. Notropis ardens Cope.

The Red-fin. (*Figure 38.*)

The red-fin has a moderately elongate and compressed body, with a slender caudal peduncle. The greatest depth equals two-ninths of the total length to base of caudal, and the least depth of the caudal peduncle is equal to or less than one-half of greatest depth of body. The head is moderate in size, its length contained four to four and one-fourth times in the total to base of caudal. The snout is pointed, its length about one-third that of the head. The lower jaw projects slightly beyond the upper. The maxilla reaches beyond the front of the eye, and in one example nearly to the front of the pupil. The eye is nearly one-third as long as the head, and is equal to the distance between the eyes. The mouth is moderately oblique. The dorsal origin is over the eighteenth and the ventral origin under the fifteenth scale of the lateral line. The dorsal base is one-half as long as the head, and the longest dorsal ray is as long as the head without the snout. The ventral reaches to the vent, and the pectoral to below the sixteenth scale of the lateral line. The length of the anal base equals one-seventh of total length to base of caudal, and the longest anal ray is two-thirds as long as the head. The caudal is moderate in size and deeply forked. The lateral line curves moderately downward in the first half of its length. D. ii, 7; A. ii, 9; V. 8; P. 13; scales, 9-46 to 50-5; teeth, 2, 4-4, 2, the two middle ones with a small hook and narrow grinding surface. Length of the specimens described, two and one-half inches. In spirits the body is light brown; a broad silvery median band; abdomen golden; a small black blotch at the origin of the dorsal; fins all pale. Breeding males are steel blue with the belly and lower fins brick red, whence the Latin name *ardens*, burning. In a male two and one-half inches long the top of the head and snout is covered with small, pointed tubercles.

The red-fin is found from Minnesota to Tennessee; east of the Alleghenies its southern limit is Virginia. In Pennsylvania it is limited to the tributaries of the Ohio. The red-fin attains to a length of three and one-half inches. The sexes are conspicuously different in color, especially in the breeding season. The male has the fins brick red in spring, and the upper surface of its head is covered with many whitish tubercles. The species has a large black spot at the base of the front portion of the dorsal fin.

The red-fin delights in small clear streams.

58. Notropis photogenis Cope.

The White-eyed Shiner.

The white-eyed shiner has a slender and rather thick body, with a long and low caudal peduncle. The greatest depth is contained five to five and one-half times in the total length to the caudal base, and the least height of the caudal peduncle equals one-half of greatest depth of body. The head is moderate in size, with short conical snout and the mouth oblique. The jaws are equal in length; the slender maxilla reaches to below the front of the eye, and the margin of the upper jaw is provided with minute tooth-like asperities. The snout is nearly as long as the eye, and two-sevenths as long as the head. The eye is three-tenths as long as the head. The width of the head equals one-half its length. The distance between the eyes equals one of their diameters. The dorsal origin is over the sixteenth scale of the lateral line, and the ventral origin under the twelfth. The dorsal base is one-half, and the longest ray nearly three-fourths as long as the head. The anal origin is slightly behind the end of the dorsal base and under the twentieth scale of the lateral line; the base is two-thirds as long as the head, and the longest ray equals the combined length of snout and eye. The ventral reaches nearly to the vent, and the pectoral to the eleventh scale of the lateral line. The caudal is rather small and deeply forked. The lateral line curves deeply over the pectoral, and does not become median until near the base of the caudal. D. ii, 7; A. iii, 10; V. 8; P. 14; scales, 7-41-4; teeth, 2, 4-4, 2, three of those in the principal row hooked. Color in spirits pale yellowish brown; a silvery lateral band as wide as the eye is long; cheeks silvery; fins all pale; a faint dark line along the outline of the back. The specimens described are two and three-fourths inches long, No. 30,447, United States National Museum. The eye is large and white, whence the name white-eyed shiner. Breeding males in spring have the head covered with minute prickles.

The white-eyed shiner occurs in the Allegheny region from Pennsylvania to North Carolina. It is a very common fish, and varies with locality. The species reaches a length of only three inches.

59. Notropis dilectus GIRARD.

The Rosy-faced Minnow.

The rosy-faced minnow has the body moderately long and thin, with a short and deep caudal peduncle. The greatest depth of the body equals one-fourth, and the least depth of the peduncle one-eighth of the total length to base of caudal. The head is moderate in size; its width one-half of its length, which is one-fourth of the total to base of caudal. The snout is pointed and shorter than the eye, which is one-fourth to two-sevenths as long as the head, and equal to the distance between the eyes. The mouth is oblique and the lower jaw projects slightly; the maxilla reaches nearly to below the front of the pupil. The dorsal origin is over the fifteenth, and the ventral origin under the twelfth scale of the lateral line. The base of the dorsal is one-half as long as the head, and the longest dorsal ray equals the length of the head without the snout. The ventral reaches to the vent, which is under the eighteenth scale of the lateral line. The anal base is as long as the snout and eye combined, and the longest anal ray is two-thirds as long as the head. The caudal is moderate in size, and deeply forked. The lateral line curves gently downward over the pectoral. D. ii, 7; A. ii, 8; V, 8; P. 13; scales, 6-36-4; teeth, 2, 4-4, 2, hooked. The specimens described are two inches long. In spirits the body is pale brown; a silvery shade along the median line; the head silvery except above; belly golden; fins all pale. In life the upper parts are olive green and the sides silvery. Males in the breeding condition in spring have prickles on the snout and the forehead, gill covers and dorsal base with a rosy flush. The name *dilectus* means delightful.

The rosy-faced minnow, although reaching a length of only three inches or less, is a very beautiful fish. It is abundant in the Ohio valley and extends westward to Nebraska. This is the *Alburnellus rubrifrons* of Cope.

60. Notropis atherinoides RAFINESQUE.

The Emerald Minnow.

The emerald minnow or rosy minnow has a long and thin body and the caudal peduncle moderately short and deep. The greatest depth of the body is contained four and three-fourths to five and one-half times in the total length to caudal base; the least depth of the caudal peduncle is contained eleven and one-half times in the same length. The greatest width of the body is one-half its height. The head is of moderate size, its length two-ninths of the total to caudal base. The snout is short and somewhat pointed, its length one-fourth that of the head. Eye large, about three and one-fourth times in length of head. Mouth oblique, moderate, the maxilla reaching front of eye. The dorsal origin is midway between the eye and the base of the caudal, over the seventeenth scale of the lateral line. The base of the fin is two-fifths as long as the head, and the longest ray equals the length of the head without the snout. The ventral origin is under the thirteenth scale of the lateral line, and the fin scarcely reaches to below the end of the dorsal base. The pectoral reaches to below the eighth or ninth scale of the lateral line. The anal origin is under the twenty-fourth scale of the lateral line; the base is one-half as long as the head, and the longest ray equals the snout and eye combined. The caudal is rather large and deeply forked. The lateral line sweeps downward in a long and shallow curve, becoming nearly median over the anal base. D. ii, 7; A. ii, 9; V. 9; P. 11; scales, 6-39-4; teeth, 2, 4-4, 2 or 1, some of them with a slight hook and narrow grinding surface. The specimens described, No. 8735, United States National Museum, are four to four and one-half inches long. In spirits the upper parts are light brown, the sides and cheeks silvery, and the belly golden brown; the fins all pale; the width of the silvery stripe is equal to diameter of eye. In life the upper parts are greenish; breeding males have the snout rosy.

The emerald minnow is found in the Great Lake region, the Ohio valley and south to Tennessee, being abundant in lakes and in rapids of rivers. The variety found in Pennsylvania has a shorter snout and a smaller eye than the typical *atherinoides* and has received the specific name *dinemus;* but the differences are not supposed to be constant. The emerald minnow reaches a length of five inches; it is gregarious like other minnows, and its golden lateral stripe on a clear green ground makes it a handsome species.

GENUS **ERICYMBA** COPE.

61. Ericymba buccata COPE.

The Silver-mouthed Dace.

The body is moderately elongate, and its width is about two-thirds of its height, which is contained four and two-thirds times in the total length without caudal. The peduncle of the tail is rather short, its least depth equal to one-half greatest depth of body. The head is comparatively long, its length contained three and one-half times in the total without caudal. The snout is long and pointed, its length nearly one-third that of head. The mouth is small, slightly oblique, and the maxilla reaches to the vertical through the anterior nostril. The lower jaw is included within the upper. The eye is one-fourth to one-third as long as the head, and longer than the interorbital space. The bones of the lower part of the head are remarkably cavernous. The dorsal origin is over the ventral, over the tenth scale of the lateral line, and nearly midway between tip of snout and base of caudal. The dorsal base is as long as the postorbital part of the head, and the longest ray equals the head without the snout. The ventral reaches to the vent; the pectoral nearly to ventral origin. The anal origin is under the twenty-first scale of the lateral line. The anal base is one-third as long as the head, and the longest ray equals the length of snout and eye combined. The caudal is moderate in size and well forked. The lateral line is only slightly bent downward over the pectoral. D. ii, 7; A. ii, 7; V. 7; P. 15; scales, 5-33 to 36-4; teeth, 1, 4-4, 0, the inner row frequently absent, some of the teeth with a slight hook. In spirits the color is light brown; a broad silvery band on the sides and cheeks; fins all pale. In life the sides show bluish reflections, and there is a dark dorsal streak. Breeding males have neither tubercles nor bright colors.

Length of the specimens, No. 36,803, United States National Museum, three inches.

This singular and interesting little fish is found in the Ohio and Mississippi valleys, and has recently been taken in the Mississippi and in west Florida. Northward it ranges to Michigan and west to Kansas. It is extremely common in the Ohio valley in small clear brooks and in ponds.

This dace reaches a length of five inches, and it is one of the most remarkable of the members of the minnow family, because of the depressions in the bones of the lower part of the head. The color is olivaceous, with silvery sides. There is a lateral chain of brown dots and a narrow vertebral line.

This species has no importance except as food for black bass and other valuable species.

Genus PHENACOBIUS Cope.

62. Phenacobius teretulus Cope.

The Sucker Minnow.

This species was first described by Professor Cope in the Proceedings of the Academy of Natural Sciences, Philadelphia, 1867, page 96, as follows:

"Head stout, four and two-thirds in total length, exclusive of caudal fin, equal depth at dorsal fin; orbit three-fifths in length of former, its superior rim on frontal plane. Preorbital bone elongate parallelogrammic. Muzzle elongate, decurved obtuse, heavy. Canthus of mouth opposite middle of o. preorbitale; supra opercular region rounded; isthmus wide; form moderate, caudal peduncle not attenuated. Scales with coarse concentric lines and radii; 6-43-5; thoracic region scaled. Pectoral fin not reaching ventrals, nor ventrals the anal. Dorsal narrow, elevated; caudal deeply forked; radii D. 1, 8; C.+18½; A. 7; V. 1, 8; P. 17. Total length of specimen, 3 in. 6. 5 l. Above pale olive yellow, the scales faintly edged with black; below silvery; end of muzzle and band on each side to orbit blackish; a leaden band on each side on middle line from behind ventrals to base of caudal, which is occasionally broken into spots.

"The affinities of this fish appear to be to *Ceratichthys*; its habits and food are probably similar; as in that genus the natatory bladder is well developed. Its habitat appears to be in the rapid parts of the river; I have not seen it in the tributary creeks, though I have examined them carefully. Several specimens procured."

The sucker minnow has been found in tributaries of the Kanawha river, in West Virginia, and doubtless inhabits other tributaries of the Ohio in western Pennsylvania.

The lips of this minnow have transverse ridges resembling those found in some of the suckers. The species has a dusky lateral band. The general color is yellowish, darker above.

This species reaches a length of three and one-half inches.

Genus RHINICHTHYS Agassiz.

63. Rhinichthys cataractæ C. & V.

The Long-nosed Dace.

The long-nosed dace has a moderately elongate body, with short and stout caudal peduncle and a moderate-sized head. The greatest depth is contained four and two-thirds times in the total length without caudal; the least depth of the caudal peduncle eight and one-half times. The width of the body equals the combined length of snout and eye. The length of the head is one-fourth of the total without caudal and three times the length of the snout. The eye is placed high, one-fifth to one-fourth as long as the head and about two-thirds as long as the interorbital width. The mouth is horizontal, small, placed under the snout, the lower jaw the shorter, the upper lip thick and provided with a small barbel at each end. The maxilla reaches to below the posterior nostril. The dorsal origin is above the twenty-third scale of the lateral line and the ventral origin is under the twentieth. The dorsal base is one-half, and the longest ray four-fifths as long as the head. The ventral reaches a little beyond the vent and almost to the anal origin. The pectoral reaches nearly or quite to the origin of the ventral, being longer in males. The anal origin is under the thirty-fourth scale of the lateral line and a little behind the end of the dorsal. The anal base is one-half, and the longest ray three-fourths as long as the head. The caudal is comparatively large and well forked. The lateral line drops gently downward in a short curve over the pectoral and becomes median over that fin. D. ii, 7; A. ii, 6; V. 8; P. 12; scales, 13-57 to 65-10; teeth 2, 4-4, 2; three of the principal row hooked. Length of the specimens described, No. 8505, United States National Museum, three and one-half inches. In spirits the color is brown mottled with grayish; the under surface of head sharply defined and pale; the fins all pale. Breeding males in spring have the lips, cheeks and lower fins crimson. There is no distinct lateral band.

The long-nose dace or Niagara gudgeon is found in New England and the Middle States, and in the Great Lake region, in clear cold water. In Pennsylvania, according to Cope, it is limited to the rapids and swift waters of the eastern part of the state. It grows to a length of five inches. The sides are without the black lateral band, which is characteristic of the black-nosed species. The general color is olivaceous or dark green with the lower parts paler. The back is nearly black. Some of the scales are mottled with dark and olivaceous. The young have a trace of a dusky lateral band. The spring males have the fins, lips and cheeks crimson. The long-nosed dace frequents rapids and rocky pools, and is associated in mountain regions of eastern Pennsylvania with the brook trout. Its movements are swift and powerful and it is a very shapely little fish. As a bait for the black bass it is scarcely surpassed.

64. Rhinichthys atronasus MITCHILL.

The Black-nosed Dace. (*Figure 28.*)

The black-nosed dace has a moderately long and stout body, with a broad back, and rather small conical head. The greatest depth of the body is contained four and one-fourth to four and one-half times in the total length without caudal. The least depth of the caudal peduncle equals one-half greatest depth of body. The head is one-fourth as long as the fish to caudal base; its width is about one-half its length and the snout nearly one-third to two-sevenths. The eye is as long as the snout and much less than width of interorbital space. The mouth is small, slightly oblique and with nearly equal jaws; the maxillary barbel small or wanting; the maxilla reaches to below the front edge of the posterior nostril. The dorsal origin is nearer to root of caudal than to tip of snout, over the twenty-sixth scale of the lateral line. The length of the base is contained two and one-third times in that of the head, and the longest ray equals length of head without snout. The ventral origin is slightly in advance of the dorsal origin and the fin extends to the vent. The pectoral reaches to the sixteenth scale of the lateral line. In breeding males it is greatly thickened. The anal origin is behind the end of the dorsal base, under the thirty-fourth scale of the lateral line; the fin is variable in length with sex and age, sometimes five-sixths as long as the head. The caudal is small and not deeply forked. The lateral line curves downward over the pectoral, soon becoming median. D. ii, 6 or 7; A. ii, 6; V. 8; P. 11; scales 10-56 to 63-10; teeth 2, 4-4, 2, three of the principal row strongly hooked. Length of the specimens described, No. 33,984, United

States National Museum, two and five-eighths to three inches. In spirits the upper parts are brown and are separated from the silvery lower parts by a dark lateral band, as wide as the short diameter of the eye and continued on the snout. Breeding males in spring have the lateral band and the lower fins crimson, running into orange in summer. In the young the dark median band extends on the tail fin.

The black-nosed dace or "rock fish" is represented in our waters by two forms, one of which is found in the eastern portion of the Great Lake region and from Maine to Virginia; this is replaced in the upper lake region and in the Ohio valley, southward to Georgia and Alabama by the blunt-nosed variety, *Rhinichthys obtusus* of Agassiz. In Pennsylvania both forms occur, the blunt-nose being limited to the Ohio valley. This is the brown-nosed dace of Professor Cope. It is stouter than the black-nosed dace of the eastern portion of Pennsylvania and paler in color. The black-nosed dace reaches a length of three inches. This fish prefers clear small brooks. Swift and active in its movements and beautiful in colors, it is one of the most interesting inhabitants of the waters in which it lives.

Genus **HYBOPSIS** Agassiz

65. Hybopsis dissimilis (Kirtland).

The Spotted Shiner.

The spotted shiner has a long and slender body, its greatest depth being nearly one-fifth of the total length without the caudal. The caudal peduncle is long and low, its least depth two-fifths of greatest depth of body. The width of the body equals two-thirds of its depth. The head is moderately large, its length one-fourth of the total without the caudal. The snout is long, but obtusely rounded at the point, its length one and one-half times the diameter of the eye, which is two-sevenths the length of the head. The mouth is small, inferior, horizontal, the maxilla reaching to below the anterior nostril and with a small barbel at its hind end. The gill-openings are separated by a very broad isthmus. The dorsal begins over the sixteenth scale of the lateral line and slightly in advance of the ventral; the dorsal base is one-half as long as the head; the longest ray is as long as the head without the snout; the last ray is as long as the snout. The ventral reaches to the vent, its length one-seventh of the total without the caudal. The pectoral reaches to below the thirteenth scale of the lateral line. The anal origin is under the twenty-seventh scale of the lateral line; the anal base is short, equalling the diameter of the eye; the longest ray is as long as the ventral; the last ray is one-third as long as the head. The caudal is moderately large and deeply forked, the middle rays one-half as long as the external rays. The lateral line is nearly straight and median. D. ii, 8; A. ii, 6; V. 7; P. 15; scales, 6-43-5; teeth, 4-4, hooked and with a short grinding surface. In spirits the back is brown, the lower parts are whitish and the sides are broadly striped with silvery. In life the lateral stripe is bluish and overlaid with dusky spots, and is continued forward through the eye around the snout. The fins are pale. The specimen described, No. 36,746, United States National Museum, from White river, Indiana, is three and one-half inches long.

The spotted shiner occurs in the Great Lake region and Ohio valley, southward to Kentucky, and west to Iowa. It is abundant in creeks of western Pennsylvania. This species grows to a length of six inches, and derives its name of spotted shiner from the bluish band along the sides which is interrupted so as to form spots. The sides are bright silvery in color, and the fins unspotted. The body is long and slender.

This fish is most common in the Great Lakes and in the channels of large streams, and does not run into small brooks. It is a ready biter, and is caught in large numbers by hook fishing. It is useful as bait.

66. Hybopsis amblops (RAFINESQUE).

The Silver Chub.

The silver chub has a moderately elongate, but thick body, whose greatest depth equals one-fifth of the total length without the caudal, and is not much less than the length of the head. The caudal peduncle is slender, its least depth one-half of the greatest depth of body. The head is short, its length two-ninths of the total without the caudal. The snout is short, blunt, nearly vertical, rounded, its length three-fourths diameter of eye. The eye is large, placed high, its long diameter three-eighths length of head. The mouth is small, terminal, placed low, nearly horizontal, the maxilla reaching to below front of eye and provided with a slender barbel one-third as long as the eye. The dorsal origin is over the twelfth scale of the lateral line; the base of the fin is one-half as long as the head; the longest ray is one-fifth of the total without caudal, and nearly as long as the head; the last ray is one-half as long as the longest. The ventral origin is under the dorsal origin; the fin reaches almost to the vent. The anal origin is under the twenty-third scale of the lateral line; the anal base is one-half as long as the head; the longest ray is as long as the head without the snout, and the last ray is a little more than one-half as long as the longest. The caudal is large and well forked. The pectoral base is below the median line of the body; the fin is as long as the head without the snout. The lateral line has a very short downward curve near its origin and is straight and median in the rest of its course. D. iii, 7; A. ii, 7; V. 8; P. 13; scales, 6-38-4; teeth, 1, 4-4, 1 (sometimes 1, 4-4, 0). In spirits the upper parts are pale brown, the lower parts lighter, the belly yellowish. A plumbeous lateral stripe, continued on the head and around the snout. The fins are all pale. In life the upper parts are greenish, and the silvery median band overlies dark pigment. Males without tubercles and red coloration in breeding season. The specimen described, No. 36,769 United States National Museum, from French Broad river, Tennessee, is about three inches long.

The silver chub or big-eyed chub inhabits the Ohio and Mississippi valleys, and is common southward to Alabama. It reaches a length of four inches. The color is greenish; sides with a dark band, overlaid by silver, extending forward around the snout.

The big-eyed chub, as its name implies, has a very large eye, which is one of its distinguishing features. It is said that the male has not the red fins and the tubercles which are found in the males of so many of the minnows. In the tributaries of the Ohio river this chub prefers sandy or gravelly bottoms and river channels. It is not common in the small streams.

67. Hybopsis kentuckiensis RAFINESQUE.

The Horned Chub (Figure 30.)

The horned chub has a stout and rather short body, its greatest depth nearly equal to length of head and one-fourth of total length without caudal. The snout is long and obtuse, its length rather more than one-third length of head, and nearly twice

4 FISHES.

diameter of eye. The mouth is large and placed low; the maxilla reaches to below front of eye; the lower jaw shorter than upper. The dorsal fin is slightly nearer to root of caudal than to tip of snout; its base is one-half as long as the head, and two-thirds as long as its longest ray. The ventral is under the front part of the dorsal; its length equals dorsal base. The anal begins under the twenty-fourth scale of the lateral line; its longest ray about one-seventh of total to base of caudal. The pectoral is two-thirds as long as the head, and reaches to below the thirteenth scale of the lateral line. The caudal is moderately forked. D. iii, 7; A. iii, 6; scales, 6–40 to 45–5. The ground color is bluish olive, the head darker; green and coppery reflections on the sides. The fins are pale orange, pinkish in the spring, the lower parts white. Breeding males have the top of the head swollen into a crest and covered with coarse tubercles, from which arises the name horned chub; they also have sometimes a red spot on each side of the head. The young have a broad dark median band and a dusky spot at the base of the tail.

Names.—The horned chub is known in some localities as nigger chub, river chub and jerker; occasionally it is called horned dace or hornyhead.

Distribution.—The species ranges from Pennsylvania westward to Dakota and south to Alabama. In Pennsylvania it is common in the Susquehanna and the Ohio basin, but absent from the Delaware. It abounds in large rivers, and is rarely seen in small brooks.

Size, etc.—This fish grows to a length of ten inches and is good for the table. As a bait for the black bass the young horned chub cannot be excelled, because of its endurance on a hook.

Genus **SEMOTILUS** Rafinesque.

68. Semotilus bullaris Rafinesque.

The Fall Fish. (*Figure 41.*)

The fall fish has a moderately deep, elongate and compressed body and a stout caudal peduncle. The greatest depth is one-fourth of the total length without caudal, and the least depth of the peduncle equals three-eighths length of head. The head is rather large, one-fourth of total without caudal, with pointed snout, which is two-sevenths of the head's length. The mouth is oblique; the jaws nearly equal, the maxilla extending to below front of eye. The eye is placed high, and is about one-fourth as long as the head. The dorsal origin is over the sixteenth or seventeenth scale of the lateral line; the base of the fin is one-half, and the longest ray two-thirds as long as the head. The ventral origin is under the fifteenth scale of the lateral line; the fin does not reach to the vent, its length one-seventh of total without caudal. The anal origin is under the twenty-seventh scale of the lateral line; the base of the fin is one-third as long as the head, and the longest ray is as long as the ventral. The caudal is large and deeply forked. The lateral line curves downward abruptly over the pectoral, becoming median over the end of that fin. D. ii, 7; A. ii, 7; V. 8; P. 18; scales, 7–46–5, teeth, 2, 5–4, 2, or 2, 4–4, 2, all more or less strongly hooked. In spirits the upper parts are grayish brown, the sides and cheeks silvery, the lower parts whitish, the fins all pale. In life the upper parts are steel blue, the sides and belly silvery; breeding males in spring have the belly and lower fins rosy. The specimens described, No. 9202, United States National Museum, are from five and one-half to six and one-fourth inches long.

The fall fish or dace is one of the largest of the minnow family in Pennsylvania, reaching a length of eighteen inches, and it is one of the most beautiful species, as well as game in its qualities. As a food fish, however, it is not greatly esteemed. It is extremely common in the Delaware river and its tributaries, and moderately abundant in the Susquehanna.

The fall fish is found from Quebec to Virginia. The fish delights in rapid, rocky portions of large streams, and in the deep channels. Upon being hooked it fights with desperation for a short time, but its resistance is soon overcome. Thoreau describes it as a soft fish with a taste like brown paper salted, yet the boy fishermen of Pennsylvania will still continue to covet and admire this handsome and ubiquitous representative of the minnows.

69. Semotilus atromaculatus MITCHILL.

The Horned Dace or Chub.

The chub has a slender and moderately elongate body, its greatest height immediately in front of the ventrals about equal to the length of the head without the snout and contained from four to nearly five times in the total length without the caudal. The greatest thickness of the body is about two-thirds of its greatest height. The head is thicker than the body and rather short with an obtuse and moderately declivous snout, whose length is about two-sevenths that of the head and considerably greater than the diameter of the eye. The eye is rather small, placed high, its diameter nearly one-fifth the length of the head and scarcely more than one-half of the space between the eyes. The mouth is moderate, very slightly oblique, the jaws subequal or the lower slightly included; the end of the maxilla reaches very slightly past the vertical through the front of the eye. Maxillary barbel not evident in this example, although usually present in large individuals. The lateral line is abruptly bent downward over the first half of the pectoral, straight and nearly median during the rest of its course. The origin of the dorsal is over the twenty-seventh scale of the lateral line, and the ventral origin is under the twenty-fourth scale. The length of the dorsal base equals the combined length of the eye and snout. The first divided ray is the longest, its length two-thirds that of the head. The last ray is one-half as long as the longest. The ventral does not reach to the vent; its length scarcely greater than the post-orbital part of the head. The anal origin is under the thirty-seventh scale of the lateral line; the length of the anal base is a little more than one-third that of the head, and the longest anal ray equals the post-orbital part of head. The tail is rather slender, the least depth of caudal peduncle equalling one-half the greatest depth, and the distance of the anal from the origin of the middle caudal rays nearly equal to the length of the head. The pectoral when extended, reaches to below the sixteenth scale of the lateral line. The caudal is moderate in size and not very deeply forked, its rays being about two-thirds as long as the external rays. D. ii, 7; A. iii, 8; V. 8; P. 15. Scales, 9-58-6. Teeth of right side 2—5; of left side 2—4. Those of the left side strongly, and those of the right side less strongly hooked. Teeth of the upper row with a well developed grinding surface.

The length of the specimen described, No. 21,661, United States National Museum, from the Susquehanna river at Bainbridge, Pennsylvania, is four and one-fourth inches.

The color is bluish-brown above; sides with a distinct dusky band, not so wide as the eye and becoming obsolete in the adult. Young specimens have the end of this band more pronounced, forming a black spot at the base of the caudal. A small black spot always present on the front of the base of the dorsal, its size in the specimen described being about two-thirds that of the eye. In life the belly is whitish. Breeding males have the belly rose-tinted and the black dorsal spot bordered with red; they have, also, rather large tubercles on the snout.

The common chub, creek chub, smaller fall fish or horned dace has a wider distribution than *S. bullaris*, but it does not grow quite so large, seldom exceeding one foot in length. Its range extends from New England to Missouri, southward to Georgia and Alabama. It is extremely common and ascends the small streams. In Pennsylvania it is the commonest minnow in the Allegheny and Susquehanna basins, and is sufficiently common in the Delaware. According to Professor Cope, it reaches four pounds in weight and is a fair food fish. This species is more characteristic of the small streams and clear ponds, and it takes the hook very freely.

GENUS **PHOXINUS** AGASSIZ.

70. Phoxinus elongatus (KIRTLAND).

The Red-sided Shiner.

The red-sided shiner has an elongate fusiform body, its greatest depth two-ninths of the total length without the caudal, its greatest width nearly one-half of its depth. The caudal peduncle is long and slender, its least depth two-fifths of greatest depth of body. The head is large, two-sevenths of total length without the caudal, with long pointed snout and wide mouth. The snout is as long as the eye, and two-sevenths as long as the head. The width of the interorbital space is about equal to the diameter of the eye. The lower jaw projects strongly. The maxilla reaches to below the middle of the eye. The gill-openings are wide, the membranes separated by a very narrow isthmus. The dorsal origin is over the twenty-fifth scale of the lateral line; the base of the fin is two-fifths as long as the head; the longest ray is as long as the head without the snout; the last ray is about one-half as long as the longest. The ventral origin is under the twenty-third scale of the lateral line; the fin extends to the vent, equalling length of eye and snout combined. The anal origin is under the thirty-seventh scale of the lateral line; the anal base is two-fifths as long as the head; the longest ray twice as long as the last ray, and one-fourth of its distance from the tip of the snout. The caudal is large and deeply forked. The pectoral is two-thirds as long as the head, extending to below the seventeenth scale of the lateral line. The lateral line is abruptly decurved over the anterior half of the pectoral. D. iii, 7; A. iii, 7; V. 8; P. 14; scales, 12-63-7 (sometimes 10-70-5); teeth, 2, 5-5, 2, hooked, some of them with a narrow, grinding surface. In spirits the color is dark brown; a narrow dark stripe along the middle of the side, extending on the head and around the snout; the fins are pale. In life the back is dark bluish, the belly silvery; breeding males have the first half of the lateral stripe crimson and the belly and lower fins rosy. The specimen described, No. 8467, United States National Museum, from Meadville, Pa., is three inches long.

The red-sided minnow is found from Pennsylvania to Minnesota. In this state it occurs only in the Ohio basin. It reaches a length of four inches.

71. Phoxinus funduloides (GIRARD).

The Black-striped Dace.

The black-striped dace has a moderately elongate body with a short and deep caudal peduncle. The greatest depth is contained four times in the total length without the caudal, and the least depth of the peduncle eight times. The head is rather short, the snout short and obtuse, the lower jaw slightly projecting. The eye is large, placed high, a little longer than the snout, and one-third as long as the head. The mouth is large and oblique, the maxilla reaching to below the front edge of the pupil. The dorsal origin is slightly behind the ventral origin, and immediately over the nineteenth scale of the lateral line. The dorsal base is one-half as long as the head; the longest ray is five-sixths as long as the head and twice as long as the last ray. The ventral reaches to the anal origin, its length equalling the head without the snout. The pectoral almost reaches the ventral origin. The caudal is moderate in size and deeply forked. The lateral line begins on the level of the top of the eye, and is abruptly decurved on the first eleven scales, after which it runs straight to the root of the caudal, being far below the median line above the ventral origin. D. iii, 7; A. iii, 7; V. 8, P. 15; scales, 10–10–5; "teeth, 2, 5-4, 2," slightly hooked. Color in spirits brown above, yellowish brown below; a broad, dusky lateral band, not running through the eye, but continued on the snout. In life the dusky lateral stripe is bounded above by a narrow pale streak. Breeding males have the belly and under surface of head red. The specimen described, No. 39,293, United States National Museum, from Four Mile Run, Va., is three and one-third inches long.

The rosy dace is found from Pennsylvania to North Carolina. It is common in the Susquehanna basin, but less so in tributaries of the Delaware. Prof. Cope described this as the most brilliantly colored fish found in Pennsylvania.

72. Phoxinus margaritus (COPE).

The Pearl Minnow.

[*Clinostomus margarita* COPE. Cypr. of Pennsylvania, 1866, page 377.]

"The muzzle obtuse, mouth oblique, scarcely attaining the line of the anterior margin of the orbit. Head four times in body to base of caudal fin, equal to greatest depth. Eye three-fourths its diameter from end of muzzle, and equal postero-inferior margin of operculum. Scales less exposed on anterior than on posterior regions; 11-58-8 to 9. The lateral line is discontinued 5-8 scales anterior to the caudal fin. Pharyngeal teeth slender, 2, 5-4, 2. Dorsal originating behind origin of ventrals, 1.8. C. 19. A. 1.8. V. 8, extending three-fourths from their origin to the anus; P. 17, reaching two-thirds way to ventrals.

"From origin caudal to that of first dorsal ray, 12 l.; from latter to opposite posterior margin orbit, 9.5 l.; from same to end of muzzle, 13.5 l.; base first anal ray to base of caudal, 8 l.; end muzzle to base ventrals, 12 l.; total length, 2 in. 6 lin.

"Coloration above light olive, without dorsal line, but darker shade at origin dorsal fin, with a minute slaty dusting, and a few lateral speckles of the same. Sides to half-way above the lateral line with opercula, plumbeous silvery; below bright crimson (in midsummer) to lower margins of pectoral and ventral fins; median line below, straw-colored. Muzzle blackish; fins unspotted."

The pearl minnow is limited to the Susquehanna river and its tributaries. It is a stout-bodied little species, growing to a length of only three inches.

GENUS **NOTEMIGONUS** RAFINESQUE.

73. Notemigonus chrysoleucus (MITCHILL).

The Roach. (*Figure 45*).

The body of the roach is compressed, the back elevated and the head depressed and very small. The depth of the body is one-third of the total length without the tail; the head is contained four and two-thirds times in this length. The eye is contained three and one-half times in the length of the head. The mouth is small, oblique, the maxillary not reaching to vertical through front of eye.

The dorsal fin is much higher than long, its base is equal to the least depth of the caudal peduncle or twice the diameter of the eye, situated on middle of body opposite the space between the ventral and anal fins. Anal longer than dorsal, its longest ray slightly exceeding the length of the base. Caudal forked. Lateral line much decurved on lower half of body behind pectorals.

D. 8; A. 13; scales, 10-53-3; teeth, 5-5, hooked and with grinding surface.

The roach, shiner, golden shiner or bream is one of the commonest fishes of Pennsylvania. It is found from New England to Minnesota and southward. A variety of the roach replaces the common northern form from North Carolina to Texas.

The roach grows to a length of one foot and a weight of one and one-half pounds. It frequents sluggish waters, abounding in bayous and weedy ponds, as well as in tidal waters. According to Jordan its favorite shelter is the yellow pond lily. It may be readily distinguished by its shape, which resembles that of the shad, and by the very long anal fin, which contains from fourteen to seventeen rays. The colors of this fish are greenish above, and the sides silvery with golden reflections. Fins usually yellowish; lower fins scarlet in breeding males. Although the roach is not a good food fish, it is taken by the hook in large numbers, and is a very useful species for bait.

Genus **CARASSIUS** Nilsson.

74. Carassius auratus (Linnæus).

The Gold Fish. (*Figure 45.*)

The body of the gold fish is oblong in shape, stout, with the back elevated and compressed. Its depth at dorsal origin is contained about two and one-half times in the total length without the tail; the head is contained three and one-third times in this length. The head is small in front of eye, being depressed on snout and the dorsal profile from tip of snout to dorsal fin is very steep. The rather small eye equals one-fifth or less length of head. The mouth is rather small, the maxilla not reaching vertical from front of eye, oblique and terminal. No barbels. Teeth compressed, 4-4. The dorsal fin is high and long, commencing over the seventh scale of the lateral line and running back to near the caudal. Its longest rays, first and second, a little longer than the spine, equal to one-half depth of body, or length of head from pupil to its posterior end. From the third to the last the rays gradually decrease in size, the last being less than one-half the length of the longest. The first dorsal spine is minute, one-fourth length of second, which is strongly and coarsely serrated. The anal is short, the length of its base being but two-thirds length of its longest rays; first spine small, one-third length of second, which is stout and serrated. Pectoral fin broad and rounded, its length three-fifths that of head, or equal to longest anal ray. It reaches to ventral, which is placed well forward. Caudal fin large. Scales large, deeper than long; lateral line median, complete, almost straight. D. II, 18; A. II, 7; V. 9. Scales, 5-30-6. The specimen described, No. 22,107 U. S. Nat. Mus., from the carp ponds at Washington, D. C., is eight inches long.

The common gold fish or silver fish is a native of Asia, from whence it was introduced into Europe, and from there into America, where it is now one of the commonest aquarium fishes, and is extremely abundant in many of our streams. In Pennsylvania it abounds in the Delaware and Schuylkill rivers. It is extremely variable in color and form, usually orange, or mottled with black and orange, but in some streams silvery individuals are more common than any of the mottled varieties. It grows to a length of twelve inches and is an indifferent food fish. It spawns early in the spring, and in pond culture it is subject to many dangers and attacked by numerous enemies. The species, however, is extremely hardy, prolific and tenacious of life.

Genus **CYPRINUS** Linnæus.

75. Cyprinus carpio Linnæus.

The Carp. (*Figure 1.*)

The carp has a stout and moderately elongate body and a small head. The greatest depth equals one-third of the length without the caudal fin. The length of the head is nearly one-fourth of the total to the base of the tail. The caudal peduncle is about two-fifths as deep as the body, and the caudal fin is strongly forked. The eye diameter is contained six and one-half times in the length of the head. The mouth is moderate, the upper jaw not extending to front of eye. The dorsal begins at a distance from tip of snout equal to twice length of head; the length of its base equals twice length of pectoral; the longest ray equals length of head without the snout; the last ray is two-fifths as long as the head. The anal begins under the fifteenth ray of the dorsal; its longest ray is two-thirds as long as the head, and more than twice as long as the last ray; the length of its base is about two-fifths length of head. The ventral begins under the second ray of the dorsal; its length nearly equals longest dorsal ray. The pectoral is nearly one-fifth of total length without the caudal. The long spines of the dorsal and anal are strongly serrate along their hinder edges. A barbel on the upper lip and another at the angle of the mouth on each side; the longest barbel about equal to diameter of eye. Three varieties are recognized—the scale, mirror and leather carp—based chiefly on the scaling of the body. The leather carp is nearly naked and is said to be the best variety; the mirror carp has a few large scales, irregularly placed, and the scale variety has the body completely scaled. The color is olivaceous, varying into dusky and blue. In the leather carp the lower parts are more or less suffused with yellowish. D. III, 20; A. III, 5; V. 1, 7; P. 15; scales, 5-38-5.

The carp is a native of Asia and has been introduced into Europe and America as a food fish, chiefly for pond culture; it thrives in all warm and temperate parts of the United States and reaches its best condition in open waters. In Texas it has grown to a length of twenty-three inches in eleven months after planting. The leather variety is most hardy for transportation. Mr. Hessel has taken the carp in the Black and Caspian seas; salt water seems not to be objectionable to it, and it will live in stagnant pools, although its flesh will be decidedly inferior in such waters. The carp hibernates in winter, except in warm latitudes, takes no food and does not grow; its increase in size in temperate latitudes occurs only from May to August.

Reproduction.—The spawning season begins in May and continues in some localities until August. A carp weighing four to five pounds, according to Mr. Hessel, yields from four hundred thousand to five hundred thousand eggs; the scale carp contains rather more than the other varieties. During the spawning the fish frequently rise to the surface, the female accompanied by two or three males. The female drops the eggs at intervals during a period of some days or weeks in shallow water on aquatic plants. The eggs adhere in lumps to plants, twigs and stones. The hatching period varies from twelve to sixteen days.

Size.—According to Hessel the average weight of a carp at three years is from three to three and one-fourth pounds; with abundance of food it will increase more rapidly in weight. The carp continues to add to its circumference until its thirty-fifth year, and in the southern parts of Europe Mr. Hessel has seen individuals weighing forty pounds and measuring three and one-half feet in length and two and three-fourths feet in circumference. A carp weighing sixty-seven pounds and with scales two and one-half inches in diameter was killed in the Danube in 1853. There is a record of a giant specimen of ninety pounds from lake Zug in Switzerland. Examples weighing twenty-four pounds have been caught recently in the Potomac river at Washington, D. C.

Food.—The carp lives principally on vegetable food, preferably the seeds of water plants, such as the water lilies, wild rice and water oats. It will eat lettuce, cabbage, soaked barley, wheat, rice, corn, insects and their larvæ, worms and meats of various kinds. It can readily be caught with dough, grains of barley or wheat, worms, maggots, wasp larvæ and sometimes with pieces of beef or fish.

ORDER ISOSPONDYLI.

Family **HIODONTIDÆ**. (The Moon-eyes).

Genus **HIODON** Le Sueur.

In the moon-eyes the body is oblong, compressed, covered with cycloid silvery scales of moderate size. Head short, naked, with obtuse snout and no barbels. The mouth is terminal, of moderate size; jaws subequal. The margin of the upper jaw is formed by the non-protractile intermaxillaries and the slender maxillaries, which are articulated to the end of the intermaxillaries. The opercular apparatus is complete. Intermaxillary and mandible with small cardiform teeth, wide set. Feeble teeth on the maxillaries. A row of marginal teeth on the tongue; those in front very strong canines. A band of short close-set teeth on middle of tongue. Vomerine teeth small, close set, in a long double series. Teeth on the palatine, sphenoid and pterygoid bones. The lower jaw is received within the upper, so that the mandibulary teeth are opposite to those on the palatine bone. The very large eye has a little-developed adipose eyelid. Nostrils large, close together, with a flap between them. Gill membranes deeply cleft, free from isthmus, their base covered by a fold of skin. Branchiostegals eight to ten. No pseudobranchiæ. Gill rakers short, thick

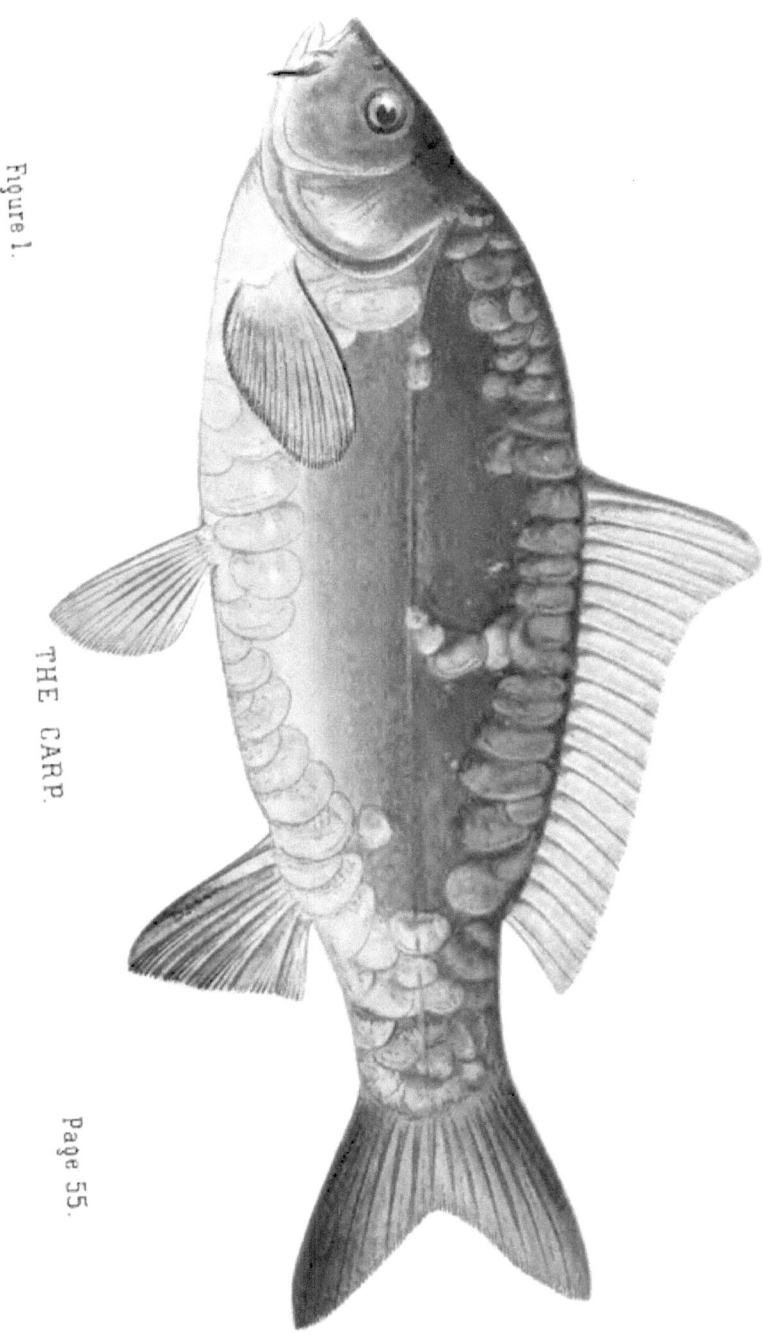

Figure 1.

THE CARP.

page 55.

and few in number. A straight and well-developed lateral line. Belly without scutes. No adipose fin. Dorsal fin over the caudal part of the vertebral column. Anal long and low. Ventrals large. Caudal deeply forked. Stomach horseshoe-shaped, with blind sac. Intestine short. One pyloric appendage. Air bladder large and simple. The eggs fall into the abdominal cavity before exclusion.

76. Hiodon alosoides RAFINESQUE.

The Northern Moon-eye. (Figure 44.)

Body deep, much compressed, its greatest depth equalling two-sevenths of the total without caudal. The head is short, containing the length of the eye about three and one-half times, and equalling a little more than one-fifth of the total without caudal. The snout is very blunt, the mouth large and oblique, the maxilla reaching beyond the middle of the eye. There is a well-developed keel along the entire length of the belly. D. 9; A. 32; scales, 6-57-7. The general color is bluish, silvery on the sides, with golden reflections.

The northern moon-eye is found from the Ohio river throughout the Great Lake region to the Saskatchewan. It is very common in Manitoba and other parts of British America. In Pennsylvania it is limited to the western region. It is very readily distinguished from the other species of the genus by its short dorsal fin, which contains only nine rays. It grows to a length of about one foot. The flesh is not greatly esteemed, but it is a beautiful fish, and has excellent game qualities.

77. Hiodon tergisus LE SUEUR.

The Moon-eye.

The shape of the body is similar to that of the northern moon-eye. The belly has a slight, but obtuse keel in front of the ventrals and is compressed to a rather sharp edge behind the ventrals. Head short, its length two-ninths of total without caudal; the eye much longer, about one-third length of head. The greatest depth of the body is nearly one-third of total length. The pectoral is as long as the head without the snout; the ventral not much more than two-thirds length of head; its origin is under the eighteenth scale of the lateral line. The anal origin is under the seventh developed ray of the dorsal. The longest anal ray is less than one-half head. The anal base is as long as the head; its last ray is less than one-half longest ray. The anal has a deep notch. The longest dorsal ray is little more than length of dorsal base. The last ray is not much more than one-half longest. The caudal is deeply forked.

D. 12; A. 28 to 32. Scales 6-58-8.

Upper parts greenish in life, the sides and abdomen brilliant silvery.

This species is called moon-eye, toothed herring and silver bass. It is found in Canada, the Great Lake region and the upper part of the Mississippi valley, being very common in large streams and lakes. It abounds in Lake Erie and the Ohio, and is seined in large numbers.

This species grows to a length of one foot and, like the other, although a beautiful fish and possessed of excellent game qualities, its flesh is full of small bones. It is a good fish for the aquarium. It will take a minnow or the artificial fly very readily and the utmost skill is required in its capture. Its food consists of insects, small fishes and crustaceans.

Dr. Richardson describes this fish as a member of the minnow family, which, he says, is known to the Canadians under the name La Quesche. The fish is described as having the back brilliant green, sides and abdomen with a silvery lustre. The specimens which were taken in the Richelieu, where it falls into the St. Lawrence, were about nine or ten inches long.

Family **CLUPEIDÆ**. The Herrings.

Genus **CLUPEA** (Artedi) Linnæus.

The genus *Clupea*, which includes the shad, river alewife or herring and the Ohio golden shad or skip-jack, admits of division into several subgenera, one of which includes the common sea herring and other marine species, another the shad and still another the river alewives. The latter have the suborbital bone longer than deep and are supplied with teeth on the tongue and in some species in the jaws.

78. Clupea vernalis Mitchill.

The Branch Herring. (*Figure 45.*)

Body deep and heavy forwards, much compressed. Its greatest depth at dorsal origin, equals one-third of total length to base of tail. The least depth of caudal peduncle equals but one-half length of head. The head is short, being almost as deep as long, about one-fifth of the standard length. The eye is large, deeper than long, its length slightly greater than its distance from tip of snout, about three and one-half in head. Maxillary broad, extending to the vertical through pupil; upper jaw emarginate, lower jaw slightly projecting. Length of dorsal base almost equal to that of head; its highest ray about two-thirds as long as the base or equal to anal base. The anal is low, its longest ray being equal to length of eye. Caudal deeply forked partially scaled near base. Length of pectoral less than that of dorsal base.

D. 16; A. 17 to 19; scales 50 to 54; transverse 15.

In the male the dorsal is higher, its longest ray about equal to length of dorsal base, or about two-thirds length of head. Color on back blue, silvery and paler on sides and underneath. A black spot behind head. Dusky lines on body, which are only visible on large examples.

Described from No. 27,197, United States National Museum, from Potomac River; length eleven inches.

The branch herring, river herring, or alewife, has a variety of additional names. It is the ellwife or ellwhop of Connecticut River, the spring herring of New York, the big-eyed and wall-eyed herring of the Albemarle, the saw-belly of Maine, the gray-back of Massachusetts, the gaspereau of Canada, little shad of certain localities, and the Cayuga Lake shad of New York.

Distribution.—The recorded range of the branch herring is from the Neuse river, North Carolina, to the Miramichi river, in New Brunswick, ascending streams to their headwaters for the purpose of spawning. The fish is found abundant in Cayuga and Seneca lakes, N. Y., where it has probably made its way naturally. In Lake Ontario, since the introduction there of shad, the alewife has become so plentiful as to cause great difficulty to fishermen, and its periodical mortality is a serious menace to the health of people living in the vicinity. The belief is that the fish were unintentionally introduced with the shad. In Pennsylvania the branch alewife occurs in the Delaware and the Susquehanna in great numbers in early spring.

Size.—This alewife seldom exceeds one foot in length, the average market examples being about ten inches. The weight of the largest is about one-half pound, and the average weight is about five or six ounces.

Habits.—The fish enter the rivers earlier than the shad and return to the sea, or to estuaries adjacent to the river mouths at some undetermined date in the fall. During the summer months, enormous schools of full grown, but sexually immature alewives migrate along the coast, feeding upon small crustaceans, and themselves furnishing food for bluefish, sharks, porpoises and other predaceous animals; but none of them are known to enter fresh waters. In the rivers the alewives appear to eat nothing, but they can be captured with small artificial flies of various colors. Their eggs are somewhat adhesive and number from sixty thousand to one hundred thousand to the individual. They are deposited in shoal water; spawning begins when the river water is at 55 to 60 degrees Fahrenheit. The period of hatching is not definitely known, but is believed to exceed four days.

Growth.—During the spring and summer the young grow to a length of two or three inches; after their departure from the streams nothing is known of their progress, but it is believed that they reach maturity in four years. We have no means of learning the age of the immature fish seen in great schools off shore, and thus far the rate of growth is unsettled.

Uses and capture.—The branch alewife, although full of small bones, is a very valuable food fish, and is consumed in the fresh condition as well as dry salted, pickled and smoked. The fry can be reared in ponds by placing adults in the waters to be stocked a little before their spawning season, and they make excellent food for bass, rock fish, trout, salmon and other choice fishes. The proper utilization of the immense over-supply of these fish in Lake Ontario has become a serious economic problem. Seines, gill-nets, traps and pounds are used in the capture of alewives, and anglers often take them in large numbers with artificial flies.

79. Clupea chrysochloris Rafinesque.

The Golden Shad.

This species has a few strong and distinct teeth in the jaws, the lower jaw strongly projecting, the caudal peduncle stout and the belly strongly serrated. In shape the body resembles that of the sea herring; it is compressed, rather low, its depth slightly more than one-fourth of the total length without caudal and about equal to the length of the head. The eye is large, nearly one-fourth length of head; the maxilla extends nearly to the hind margin of the eye; the length of the upper jaw is more than one-half length of head. The origin of the dorsal is over the ninth series of scales, and the length of its base corresponds with ten rows of scales. The ventral origin is under the middle of the dorsal; the fin is one-half as long as the head. The pectoral reaches the fourteenth series of scales of the lateral line; its length is two-thirds that of the head. The anal is moderately long and low; its longest ray about twice length of eye and one-half length of its base. The longest dorsal ray equals postorbital part of head. The caudal is deeply forked. There are twenty-three gill rakers below the angle of the first arch. D. iii, 15; A. iii, 16. Scales 15-52 to 58. Scutes 20 + 13 to 14. The body is blue with reflections of green and gold; the lower parts silvery.

The golden shad or skip-jack is a common inhabitant of the Ohio and Mississippi valleys and the Gulf of Mexico. In Pennsylvania this fish is confined to the Ohio and its tributaries. It prefers large streams. It has made its way into the Great Lakes through canals. The presence of the golden shad in the salt water of the Gulf Mexico was discovered by Mr. Silas Stearns, near Pensacola, Florida. This species grows to a length of eighteen inches.

Unlike most other species of *Clupea* this one, according to observations of Professor S. A. Forbes, in Illinois, is predaceous, feeding upon other fishes. Two examples examined by him had eaten gizzard shad (*Dorosoma*), and another one individuals of some unidentified fish. The young of the golden shad, two and one-fourth inches long, had consumed nothing but terrestrial insects including flies, small spiders, etc.

As far as we can learn, it never ascends small streams. In the lower part of the Mississippi valley it migrates into salt water; in the upper portion of this region its permanent residence is in fresh water. The name skip-jack is given in allusion to its habit of skipping along the surface of the water. Having many small bones and its flesh being tasteless this fish has no value for food.

80. Clupea sapidissima Wilson.

The Shad. (*Figure 4.*)

The shad is now referred to the genus *Clupea*, but differs from the typical sea herring in the shape of the cheek bone, which is somewhat deeper than long. The adult is toothless, but the young has well-developed, though small, teeth in the jaws, which sometimes persist until the fish has reached a length of fifteen inches. To this subgenus the name *Alosa* was given by Cuvier.

The shad has a deep body and a large mouth, with the jaws about equal. The gill rakers are very long and slender, varying with age from forty to sixty below the angle of the first arch. In the female the dorsal originates a little in front of the middle of the length, in the male somewhat farther in front. The dorsal of the male is rather higher than that of the female, while the body is not so deep. In the female the greatest depth is one-third of the total without caudal, and the length of the head two-ninths. In the male the length of the head is one-fourth of the total without caudal.

The dorsal has thirteen divided rays and four simple ones; anal, nineteen divided and three simple. Scales, 16–60 to 65. Scutes, 22 + 16.

The color is bluish or greenish with much silvery. A dusky blotch close behind the head, two-thirds as large as the eye, and frequently from several to many in one or two rows behind this. The lining of the belly walls is pale.

Figure 2.

THE SHAD

The shad is known also as the white shad, and in the colonial days it was known to the negroes on the lower Potomac river as the white fish. It is found naturally along the Atlantic coast of the United States from the Gulf of St. Lawrence to the Gulf of Mexico, ascending streams at various dates from January, in its extreme southern limit, to June, in far northern waters. In the Delaware and Susquehanna it makes its appearance in April and departs after spawning; but remains sometimes as late as July 18, and many die in the streams.

The original distribution of the shad has been widely extended by artificial introduction. In certain rivers flowing into the Gulf of Mexico the fish has been established by planting. In the Ohio river a fishery has been created by the same method, and in the Sacramento river, Cal., the shad was successfully introduced and has colonized not only this river, but all suitable rivers from San Francisco to southern Alaska. It is now one of the common market species in San Francisco and other west coast cities.

In the Susquehanna the shad was formerly one of the most important native food fishes, but its range is now very limited on account of obstruction by dams. Twenty years ago the Fish Commissioners reported that a few shad were taken yearly above the Clark's Ferry dam, none, or at most a few dozen, above the Shamokin dam, none above Nanticoke dam and none above Williamsport. The largest run of shad that has been known to pass the Columbia dam was that of 1867. "In 1871 the finest Columbia shad were hawked in the market at Harrisburg, thirty miles from the fisheries, at considerably less than a dollar a pair. The catch at Columbia exceeded one hundred thousand."

The obstructions in the Delaware have been almost entirely overcome. In 1891 shad were caught higher up the Delaware than for many years, and spawned in the upper reaches of the river, beyond the New York state line. In 1891 the Delaware, for the first time since 1823, was restored to its normal condition by means of the fishway at Lackawaxen and, according to Col. Gay, it is at present the best shad river in the country. The number of eggs obtained for artificial propagation in the lower river was unusually small, but the number naturally deposited in the upper waters was greater than for many years. Col. Gay observed a large number of big female shad at Gloucester city, but a great scarcity of males. This involved a long run up the river before spawning. The cause is believed to be the low temperature of the water during May, the lack of rain cutting off the usual supply of warm surface water, and the tributaries of the upper river brought down nothing but cold spring water, keeping the temperature of the river below the normal for spawning purposes, consequently the shad ascended more than three hundred miles. Mr. Ford noticed that every pool in the upper river was full of shad, and he saw them playing in the water by hundreds. Mr. Van Gordon saw them above Port Jervis, and they were observed as far up as Deposit, N. Y.

The shad reaches a length of two feet. It is claimed that fifty years ago shad weighing from eight to thirteen pounds were not uncommon in the Susquehanna. It is stated that even larger individuals were taken. In California the shad reaches a larger size than it does in the East; specimens weighing from thirteen to fourteen pounds being often seen in the markets. The average weight of females is four or five pounds. The male is much smaller.

The young shad remain in the rivers until the approach of cold weather, when they descend to the sea and are usually seen no more until they return as mature fish ready for reproduction. They are known to feed upon small flies, crustaceans and insect larvæ. They have been fed with fresh water copepods and kept alive in this way until they had obtained a length of more than one inch. In the carp ponds, at Washington, Dr. Hessel succeeded in rearing shad upon the *Daphnia* and *Cyclops* to a length of three or four inches, and one time when they had access surreptitiously to an abundant supply of young carp, well fed individuals reached a length of six inches by the first of November. Shad have been kept at the Central Station of the United States Fish Commission over the winter, but at the age of one year, doubtless for lack of sufficient food, the largest was less than four inches long. At this age they were seen to capture smaller shad of the season of 1891, which were an inch or more in length. The Commissioner of Fisheries detected young shad also in the act of eating young California salmon, and upon one occasion found an undigested minnow, two or three inches long, in the stomach of a large shad; adults have been caught with minnows for bait. The principal growth of the shad takes place at sea and when the species enters the fresh waters for the purpose of spawning it ceases to feed, but will sometimes take the artificial fly and live minnows.

The migratory habit of the shad has already been referred to. The spawning habits have been thus described by Marshall McDonald: "The favorite spawning grounds are on sandy flats, bordering streams and on sand bars. The fish appear to associate in pairs, usually between sundown and eleven p. m. When in the act of spawning they swim close together near the surface, their dorsal fins projecting above the water and their movements producing a sound which fishermen call 'washing.' The eggs are expressed by the female while in rapid motion; the male following close and ejecting his milt at the same time. Such of the eggs as come in contact with the milt are impregnated, but the greater portion of them are carried away by the current or destroyed by spawn-eating fishes. After impregnation the eggs sink to the bottom and, under favorable conditions, develop in from three to eight days." According to Seth Green, the embryo shad swim as soon they break the shell and make their way to the middle of the stream where they are comparatively safe from the predaceous fishes. A mature female shad of four or five pounds contains about 25,000 eggs on the average, but as many as 60,000 have been obtained from a six-pound fish and 100,000 were obtained from a single female on the Potomac. There is great mortality among the shad after spawning. Dead fish of both sexes are frequently seen floating in the water in the late months of summer.

Genus **BREVOORTIA** Gill.

81. Brevoortia tyrannus (Latrobe.)
The Menhaden.

The menhaden is a fish of the herring family. The exposed surfaces of its scales are very narrow and deep. The body is similar in shape to that of the shad, the depth one-third of length, without caudal, and somewhat greater than the length of the head. The mouth is large; the jaws are toothless. The upper jaw extends to below the hind margin of the eye. The eye is about as long as the snout, one-fifth length of head. The fins are small, the pectoral not much more than one-half the length of head and twice as long as the ventral. The dorsal base is equal in length to the pectoral; longest dorsal ray more than twice as long as the last ray and about two-fifths length of head. The anal rays are shorter than those of the dorsal; length of anal base little more than one-half length of head. The origin of the dorsal is about midway between tip of snout and end of middle caudal rays. The sides and fins are silvery, yellowish, the upper parts bluish. Behind the head there is a large dark spot, larger than the pupil, followed by numerous smaller dark spots.

The menhaden has received more than thirty common names, among which the one here employed is the best known and most suitable. In New Jersey it is frequently called bunker or moss bunker and in some other localities it is the bony fish. It is also called bugfish, because of a crustacean parasite which is found in the mouth.

The menhaden reaches a length of fifteen inches or more. Its average size is about one foot. It is found along our east coast from Maine to Florida, swimming in immense schools and fluctuating greatly in abundance. In certain localities its movements are affected chiefly by temperature.

The use of the menhaden as a source of oil and a material for fertilizers is so well known as scarcely to need mention here. As a food fish it is not esteemed in Pennsylvania and is seldom eaten in most localities, although in other places it is considered a good food fish. Since the mackerel are becoming scarce, menhaden are often salted in barrels as a substitute for that fish.

Genus **DOROSOMA** Rafinesque.

82. Dorosoma cepedianum (Le Sueur).
The Mud Shad.

The genus *Dorosoma* has a herring-like body, with a short and obtuse snout. The body is much compressed and is covered with moderately large, thin, cycloid scales. The head is scaleless, short and small; the eye large and provided with an adipose eyelid. The belly is compressed to an edge, which is armed with sharp serratures.

Mouth small, transverse; the lower jaw the shorter. Jaws toothless. The maxilla does not extend to the middle of the eye. Gill rakers numerous, moderately long and slender. Gill membranes deeply cleft and free from the isthmus. Pseudobranchiæ well developed. Lateral line wanting. The dorsal fin is placed nearly over the middle of the body, slightly behind the origin of the ventral. Its last ray is produced into a long filament. The pectorals and ventrals are rather long and each is provided with an appendage formed of several elongate overlapping accessory scales. The caudal is deeply forked; anal very long, its last rays low. The stomach is stout and short, resembling the gizzard of a hen. The depth of the body is contained two and two-thirds times in the total without caudal, the length of the head four and one-third times. Eye longer than snout, one-fourth length of head. The third ray of the dorsal is two-thirds as long as the head, and the filamentous ray nearly equals the head in length. Length of dorsal base about one-half that of head; anal base two-sevenths of total length of body without tail, its longest ray two-thirds length of ventral or one-third that of head. Pectoral three-fourths as long as head. Lower caudal lobe longer than upper, its length equal to that of the head.

D. iii, 10; A. ii, 31. Scales 56 to 64, about 20 in a transverse series. Scutes in front of ventrals 17, and from ventrals to vent 12.

Upper parts bluish; sides silvery, sometimes with golden reflections. In young individuals there is a large dark blotch on each side not far behind the head; this disappears with age.

The mud shad, also known as gizzard shad, winter shad, stink snad, white-eyed shad, hickory shad, hairy back and thread herring, is found in brackish waters along the coast from New York southward to Mexico, ascending streams and frequently becoming land-locked in ponds. A variety of this fish is also common in the Ohio and Mississippi valleys, from whence it has spread through canals into Lakes Erie and Michigan. This fish grows to a length of fifteen inches and a weight of two pounds. It spawns in summer and its food consists of algæ, confervæ, desmids and diatoms. With its food it takes large quantities of mud from which it separates the organic substances after swallowing. This is a beautiful species, somewhat resembling the shad in general appearance and has been very successfully kept in the aquarium, where its bright colors and graceful movements make it attractive, but its flesh is soft, tasteless and seldom eaten when any better can be obtained. In most regions fishermen consider it a great nuisance and throw away their entire catch. Negroes eat the mud shad from tributaries of the Chesapeake, and in Florida the fish has been utilized to some extent in making guano. The name gizzard shad alludes to the form of the stomach, which is very much like that of a hen.

FAMILY **ARGENTINIDÆ** (THE SMELTS).

GENUS **OSMERUS** (ARTEDI) LINNÆUS.

83. Osmerus mordax (MITCHILL).

The Smelt. (Figure 56.)

The smelt has an elongate and somewhat compressed body, and a long, pointed head, with the lower jaw projecting. The mouth is large, the maxilla extending slightly behind the eye. Small teeth on the intermaxillaries and maxillaries and the front of the lower jaw. Posteriorly the teeth of the mandible are larger. The tongue is armed with a few large, fang-like teeth and there are widely set teeth on the vomer, palate and pterygoid bones and at the root of the tongue. Gill rakers long and slender. Branchiostegals 8. The dorsal is small, nearly median, over the ventrals. Anal moderately long. Scales large, thin, easily deciduous, in about seventy-five rows along the sides. Lateral line short, not extending much beyond the end of the pectoral. A few small pyloric caeca. The height of the body is nearly one-fifth of the total length without caudal and nearly equal to the length of the head. The eye is nearly one-fifth as long as the head. The pectoral equals the longest dorsal ray in length and also length of anal base. The ventral is one-half as long as the head. Longest anal ray not much more than one-half anal base.

D. ii, 8; A. iii, 14; V. ii, 7.

The upper parts are greenish; a broad silvery band along the sides; body and fins with numerous minute, dusky points.

The smelt is known along our east coast from Labrador to Virginia. It probably extends still farther north, but the record of Mr. W. A. Stearns, published in the Proceedings of the National Museum for 1883, p. 124, fixes the most northern locality known at present. He found the smelt common in August in shoal water off the wharves of Cape Britain. In Pennsylvania the fish is common in the spring in the Delaware and Schuylkill rivers. In numerous lakes of Maine, New Hampshire, and other New England states, the smelt is common, land-locked, and thrives as well as in the salt water. Its range has been widely extended by artificial introduction, which is very easily effected by transporting the fertilized eggs from the small brooks in which the species spawns. The eggs are adhesive and attach themselves to stones, and their transportation is accomplished very readily.

The smelt grows to a length of one foot. The average size as found in the markets is about seven inches. It enters the rivers for the purpose of spawning and is most abundant in the winter and early spring months. Spawning takes place in the Raritan river, N. J., in March.

The eggs of the smelt have been artificially hatched by Mr. Ricardo, Fred. Mather and other fish culturists. The food of this species consists mainly of shrimps and other small crustaceans.

The smelt is an excellent food fish and is also used for bait, and still more extensively as food for land-locked salmon, lake and brook trout and other important *Salmonoids*, which are artificially reared in lakes. It has proved to be one of the best fishes for this purpose. Immense quantities of smelts are caught during the winter months in nets, seines and by hook and line. They are usually shipped to market in the frozen condition, packed in snow or crushed ice. The fish which have not been frozen, however, are more highly prized than any others.

Family **COREGONIDÆ** (The White Fishes).

Genus **COREGONUS** (Artedi) Linnæus.

The white fishes of Pennsylvania belong to four species, representing the four divisions of the genus *Coregonus*. In two of the species the lower jaw is included within the upper; the mouth is small and the intermaxillary bone broad and more or less vertical in position. These two may be readily distinguished by the structure of the gill rakers and the size of the mouth. The remaining two white fishes have the lower jaw as long as, or longer than, the upper; the mouth large, and the intermaxillary narrow and not vertical in position. They are easily separated from each other by the shape of the body, and the size and contour of the scales. The relations of the species are shown in the following key:

1. Lower jaw shorter than upper.
   - 1 a. Mouth very small, upper jaw not reaching to eye; gill rakers short and stout, 13 to 16 below angle of first arch (*Prosopium*).
     QUADRILATERALIS.
   - 1 b. Mouth moderate, upper jaw reaching beyond front of eye; gill rakers long and slender, 20 or more below angle of first arch (*Coregonus*).
     CLUPEIFORMIS.
2. Lower jaw equal to or longer than upper.
   - 2 a. Body slender, elongate; scales small and convex on their free margin; lower jaw longer than upper (*Argyrosomus*).
     ARTEDI.
   - 2 b. Body deep, short; scales large, deep, the free margin scarcely convex; jaws equal (*Allosomus*).
     TULLIBEE.

84. Coregonus quadrilateralis RICHARDSON.

The Round Whitefish. (*Figure 47.*)

This is a small species and very readily distinguished from all other American species except Williamson's whitefish by its diminutive mouth. The body is slender, elongate and subterete, its greatest depth slightly exceeding one-fifth of total length to base of caudal. The head is long, its length one-fifth of total without caudal, and the snout is thin and obtuse at tip. The broad maxilla does not reach to below the front of the eye; its length less than one-fifth length of head. D. 11; A. 10; scales in lateral line, 80 to 90. Upper parts dark bluish; sides silvery.

Names.—This species is called frost fish in the Adirondacks; other names are Menomonee whitefish, round-fish, shad-waiter, pilot-fish and chivey. The last term is applied to the fish in Maine.

Distribution.—The round-fish is found in lakes of New England, sometimes running into streams, the Adirondack region of New York, the Great Lakes and northward into British America and Alaska. Its distribution has been extended by transplanting on account of its great value as food for the lake trout and other large fish of the salmon family.

Size.—It seldom exceeds a length of twelve inches and a weight of one pound.

Habits.—Like some other species of whitefish it spawns in shallow parts of lakes or ascends their small tributary streams for that purpose. The food consists of small shells and crustaceans. The species frequents deep waters, where it falls an easy prey to the voracious lake trout.

Uses and Capture.—The round-fish is excellent for the table, and as food for the larger trout and salmon it is unsurpassed. Its capture with hook and line is difficult, because of its very small mouth and its habit of retiring into deep water. In the Great Lakes it does not constitute an important element of the fishery, but in northern regions it is one of the most useful and highly prized of the food fishes.

85. Coregonus clupeiformis Mitchill.

The Whitefish. (*Figure 3.*)

The common whitefish of the Great Lakes is so well known that it scarcely needs an elaborate description. The body is stout and deep, its depth at the nape greatly increased in adults. The greatest depth is two-sevenths of the total length to caudal base. Caudal peduncle short, its depth one-half length of head, which is about one-fifth of total without caudal. The snout is sharp conic, two-sevenths as long as the head and about twice as long as the eye. The maxilla reaches to below front of eye. The dorsal origin is above the twenty-third scale of the lateral line and the ventral begins under the middle of the dorsal. The longest dorsal ray equals length of head without snout. Adipose fin stout and low. The dorsal and anal bases are equal to each other and two-thirds length of head.

D. 10 divided rays; A. 11 divided rays; V. 11; P. 15; scales in lateral line 74 to 80. The upper parts are grayish or light olive in color; the sides white and lustrous in life.

Names.—The name whitefish is thoroughly identified with this species and is seldom varied except by means of the prefix "common" or "lake." A well-marked variety in Otsego Lake, New York, has long been known as the Otsego bass.

Distribution.—The common whitefish occurs in the Great Lakes and northward into British America; its northern limit is not definitely known. In Alaska, where the species was formerly supposed to exist, it is replaced by a similar, but well-marked form, the *Coregonus richardsoni* of Günther. The variety known as Otsego bass is found in Otsego Lake, N. Y. If we may judge from the yield of the fisheries, Lake Michigan has more whitefish than any of the other lakes, Superior ranks second, Erie third, Huron fourth and Ontario is sadly in the rear.

Size.—The largest individual on record was taken at Whitefish Point, Lake Superior; it weighed twenty three pounds. A seventeen-pound specimen was caught at Vermillion, in Lake Erie, in 1876. The size varies greatly with locality, ranging all the way from one and three-fourths pounds, on the average, to fourteen pounds. In Lake Erie in 1885, the average weight was between two and three pounds. The length of adults will average twenty inches.

Habits.—There is a movement of the whitefish in many lakes from the deep water early in the summer into the shoal water near the shore. In midsummer, however, the usual retreat of this species is in the deep and cold portions of the lakes which it inhabits. Again, as the spawning season approaches in October, the whitefish come towards the shore to deposit their eggs. It is said that they do not spawn until the water has reached a temperature of about 40°. After spawning they again retire to deep water, where they remain during the winter. Mr. Milner observed that the shoreward migration varies with locality, and is influenced also by depth of water and temperature. In Lake Erie, for example, which has a high summer temperature, there is no shoreward migration in summer. It is to be noted, also, that the whitefish moves along the shore, and in some cases it ascends rivers for the purpose of spawning. It is believed also that when the feeding grounds of the whitefish are polluted by mud the fish temporarily seek other localities. There appears to be a spring and summer migration also from lake to lake. Spawning takes place during October, November and December, upon shoals or occasionally in rivers. The female is larger than the male. According to the observations of Mr. George Clark, the two sexes, in the act of spawning, frequently throw themselves together above the surface, emitting the spawn and milt with the vents close together. Spawning operations are most active in the evening, are continued at night, and the eggs are deposited in lots of several hundred at a time. The number of eggs in a fish of seven and one-half pounds was 66,606; the average number being nearly 10,000 for each pound of the female's weight. The period of incubation depends on the temperature. The usual time of distribution of the young is in March and April. The very young are described as swimming near the surface and not in schools. They are very active and soon seek deep water to escape from their enemies. Their food consists chiefly of small crustaceans. The adults subsist upon the same food with the addition of small mollusks.

Growth.—The only means of determining the rate of growth of the whitefish is by artificial rearing. Mr. Samuel Wilmot had young fish which were five inches long at the age of four months. The growth under natural conditions must be even greater than this. Mr. Wilmot himself has seen whitefish measuring seven inches in December in his ponds.

Enemies and Diseases.—The eggs of the whitefish are destroyed in immense numbers by the lake herring (*Coregonus artedi*). The water lizard (*Menobranchus*) also consumes vast numbers of the eggs. The young whitefish are eaten extensively by the pike perch, black bass, pike, pickerel, and fresh water ling. The lake trout also feeds upon the whitefish. A leach parasitic on the whitefish proves very troublesome to that species, and the scales are liable to a peculiar roughness which has been observed late in November or during the spawning season. There is also a lernæan which fastens itself to the gills and other portions of the white fish.

Uses and Capture.—The excellence of the flesh of the whitefish is so well known as scarcely to require mention. Its commercial value is great. In Lake Erie, in 1885, according to statistics collected by the United States Fish Commission, 3,500,000 pounds of whitefish were caught, over 2,000,000 of these by fishermen from Erie alone. In this year Erie county had 310 persons employed in the fisheries. The capital invested in the business was nearly $250,000. The wholesale value of the fish products was upwards of $400,000. The whitefish was the third species in relative importance; blue pike ranking first and the lake her-

Figure 3.

THE WHITEFISH.

Page 67.

ring second. In Erie county whitefish are caught chiefly in July, August and November, and the bulk of them are taken in gill-nets, of which Erie, in 1885, owned 10,700. Pound-nets are also employed in the capture of whitefish, and Erie had 19 in 1885.

Artificial Propagation.—Carl Müller, of New York, and Henry Brown, of New Haven, are credited with the first attempt to propagate the white fish artificially. Their experiments were made in Lake Saltonstall, near the city of New Haven. The result of the experiments, which were repeated in 1858, is not known. In 1868 Seth Green and Samuel Wilmot began a series of experiments in the same direction, and in 1869 Mr. N. W. Clark, of Clarkson, Michigan, took up the same work. In 1870 a half million eggs were placed in hatching boxes by Mr. Clark. In 1872, through the aid of the United States Fish Commission, Mr. Clark's hatching house was doubled in capacity and a million eggs were taken from Lake Michigan. Since that time both the national and state governments have made the whitefish the object of their most extensive operations, and at this time Pennsylvania alone distributes sixteen millions annually, while the United States has hatcheries for this species accommodating nearly one thousand millions. The success of artificial propagation has been so thoroughly demonstrated as not to require additional mention.

86. Coregonus artedi (Le Sueur).

The Lake Herring. *(Figure 78.)*

The body of the lake herring is moderately elongated, compressed, and the head pointed. The greatest height of the body at the origin of the dorsal is one-fourth of the total length without caudal. The caudal peduncle is short and stout. Its least depth is somewhat more than one-third of greatest depth of body. The eye is contained four to four and one-half times in length of head; the snout, three and one-half times. The maxillary reaches to nearly below the middle of the eye. The lower jaw projects strongly. The dorsal begins midway between tip of snout and base of tail. Its longest ray equals length of head without snout. The ventral begins under the middle of the dorsal; its longest ray, two-thirds length of head. The pectoral is slightly longer than the ventral. The anal base equals the length of its longest ray, which is nearly one-half length of head. The adipose dorsal is slender; its width one-half its height and about one-half length of eye; twenty-five to thirty gill rakers below the angle of the first arch. D. 11; A. 10 (counting only divided rays in dorsal and anal); V. 10; scales 9-80-8.

The upper parts are greenish or bluish black; the sides silvery and with narrow, pale streaks along the rows of scales, especially above the lateral line.

Names.—This species is known as the lake herring or cisco. The name cisco is applied more particularly in the small lakes of Wisconsin, Indiana and New York.

Distribution.—The lake herring is most abundant in the Great Lakes, extending northward into British America; eastward it has been obtained from Labrador. It becomes variable in certain portions of its habitat, notably in Labrador and in the lakes in which it is known as cisco. In the Great Lakes, in 1885, more individuals of this species were taken in Lake Erie than in all the other lakes put together, a total of over nineteen million pounds having been caught there out of a total of less than twenty-six million pounds.

Size.—The average length of this species is about one foot, and the weight nine to twelve ounces, but examples measuring nineteen inches in length and weighing two pounds have been recorded.

Habits.—The lake herring frequents moderately shoal waters and occurs in enormous schools, as we may judge from the quantity captured in Lake Erie. Its food consists of insects and crustaceans. During the spawning season of the whitefish, however, it feeds exclusively upon the eggs of this species and proves very destructive. The lake herring will take the hook, and has been caught with live minnows. Spawning takes place about the end of November, in shoal waters.

Uses and Capture.—As a food fish this species is inferior to the whitefish, but it is in great demand over an extensive area of the country, and is shipped in the fresh condition many hundreds of miles east and west. I have elsewhere referred to the enormous number taken in 1885 in Lake Erie. These are caught chiefly in pound and gill nets. The catch in 1885 amounted to more than one-third of the entire quantity of fishes taken in this lake. There is no apparent diminution in the number of these fishes, and their artificial propagation has not been practiced.

87. Coregonus tullibee Richardson.

The Tullibee. (*Figure 49.*)

The body of the tullibee is very short, deep and compressed; its greatest height about one-third of the length without caudal. The head is pointed, as in the "black fin;" the mouth large, with the lower jaw scarcely longer than the upper. The maxilla extends to below the middle of the eye. The eye equals the snout in length and is two-ninths length of the head. Scales much larger on front part of the body than on the caudal peduncle. The gill rakers are long, slender and numerous, about thirty below the angle on the first arch. D. 11; A. 11; scales in the lateral line seventy-four, eight rows above and seven below lateral line. The upper parts are bluish; sides white and minutely dotted.

Names.—This species is usually called the tullibee, but in Lakes Erie and Michigan it is sometimes styled the "mongrel whitefish" on the supposition that it is a cross between the common whitefish and the lake herring.

Distribution.—The tullibee has been taken recently in Lake Michigan, and Dr. E. Sterling had a specimen from Lake Erie. It is found occasionally in other of the Great Lakes and extends northward into British America, but is comparatively little known to the fishermen and is very rare in collections.

Size.—This fish grows to a length of eighteen inches, but the few examples seen by me were about one foot long. Its scarcity makes it unimportant as a food fish in our waters; but in some parts of Canada it is a valuable species. The first account of its habits was published by Mr. F. C. Gilchrist in *Forest and Stream*, April 7, 1892.

Genus **THYMALLUS** Cuvier.

88. Thymallus ontariensis Cuv. & Val.

The Grayling. (*Figure 50.*)

The grayling may be readily distinguished from its relatives among the salmon, whitefish and trout by its very long and high dorsal, which contains about twenty rays. The jaws contain well-developed teeth and the scales are smaller than in the whitefishes. The body is oblong, not very deep, somewhat compressed. The head is short, its length a little more than one-fifth of the total without caudal, and nearly equal to the depth. The caudal peduncle is slender, its depth about one-third the greatest depth of body. Mouth moderate, the upper extending to below the pupil. A few slender teeth on maxillary, intermaxillary and mandible; a small vomerine patch of teeth and palatine teeth present. Tongue toothless or with a few small teeth. Seven or eight branchiostegals; gill openings wide; about eleven short, slender gill-rakers below the angle of the first arch. Eye from one-third to one-quarter as long as head. Distance of dorsal from snout equals one-third of total length without caudal; the dorsal base two-sevenths of total. Dorsal rays shorter in front than behind, the longest ray near the end of the fin, equal to length of head. The ventral origin is slightly behind the middle of the dorsal; the length of the ventral equals that of the pectoral, or about four-fifths length of the head. The anal origin is distant from ventral origin a space nearly equal to base of dorsal. The longest anal ray equals half length of head. The adipose fin is above the last rays of the anal; this fin is narrow, its width being less than half the length, which is but two-sevenths of the length of head.

D. 24; A. 12; V. 9. Scales, 9, 90-94, 13.

The sides are purplish gray, silvery below. Dorsal with blackish lines alternating with rose-colored ones and with green and rose-colored spots. A few small, dusky spots on the middle of the sides in front. Ventrals crossed obliquely by rose-colored lines.

The graylings of North America are found in Alaska and the northwest territory; in Montana and probably other portions of the Rocky Mountain region and in both northern and southern Michigan. The Michigan species is not native in Pennsylvania, but was introduced about 1874 in this state as well as in New York. The Alaska grayling appears to me to be sufficiently distinct from the Michigan species to be designated under the name by which it was described by Richardson. *Thymallus signifer.*

Dr. Jordan distinguishes a variety of grayling in the Rocky Mountain region, *Thymallus ontariensis cis-montanus.* I have never been able to make out more than two species of grayling, the Michigan and Alaskan.

The Michigan grayling is best known in the Muskegon, Manistee and Au Sable rivers. The Rifle and the Jordan also have the species, and Portage lake in the extreme northern part of the state is said to contain it. This fish rarely exceeds sixteen inches in length and a weight of two pounds, while the average length is ten or eleven inches and the weight one-half pound.

The grayling resembles the brook trout in its feeding habits. Its food consists of insects and their larvæ. It spawns in April and yields between three and four thousand eggs. According to Norris, the eggs are deposited in the main current of the rivers, and generally in the wider reaches, on loose, coarse, white sand or small pebbles. It prefers streams which have little variation in their volume of water and with equable temperature, never freezing in winter and not becoming warmer than fifty-four degrees in summer. Seth Green obtained a few fertilized eggs from the Au Sable in 1874, and Mr. Mather from the same river the following year. For the experiment in Pennsylvania, streams flowing from large limestone springs, such as are found in the Cumberland Valley, were suggested by Mr. Norris. Mr. Green found that the grayling did not spawn for him in confinement, and the effort to introduce them into Pennsylvania and elsewhere has been unsuccessful. This is a beautiful fish, but opinions are divided as to its game qualities and its desirability for food.

FAMILY **SALMONIDÆ** (SALMON AND TROUT).

GENUS **ONCORHYNCHUS** SUCKLEY.

89. Oncorhynchus chouicha WALBAUM.

The California Salmon.

The California or quinnat salmon is stout bodied and comparatively short; its greatest depth is contained about three to three and two-thirds times in the length without the caudal. The caudal peduncle is rather slender, its depth less than one-third greatest depth of body. Before the spawning season the head is conical, its length about one-fourth of total to base of tail. The maxilla is more than one-half as long as the head and extends far beyond the eye. The eye is one-seventh as long as the head. All the fins except the caudal are short for so large a species. The dorsal begins midway between tip of snout and base of caudal; its longest ray equals the length of dorsal base and nearly one-half length of head. The ventral begins under the posterior part of the dorsal; its length one-half length of head. The anal base is as long as the postorbital part of head; its longest ray little more than two-thirds the length of the anal base. B. 17–19; D. 11; A. 16; gill rakers 23, of which 14 are below the angle. The pyloric cæca are very numerous (about 150). Scales in lateral line 130 to 150. The upper parts are grayish, sometimes bluish; the head darker and with few black spots; the sides and lower parts are silvery. Numerous small black spots on the back and the dorsal and caudal fins. Males in the breeding season become very dark and dull in color, the sides blotched with reddish; their jaws also are greatly lengthened and hooked and the teeth become canine-like. The distortion is so great at this time that the mouth cannot be closed.

Names.—This widely known fish has received many names, among which are California salmon, quinnat salmon, king salmon, Columbia salmon, Chinnook salmon, Sacramento salmon, spring salmon, Takou salmon and chouicha, the last a Russian name. In the publications of the various fish commissions it usually appears as the California or quinnat salmon

Distribution.—The quinnat salmon is found native in the North Pacific, ascending rivers from California to Alaska and Siberia. It is especially known in the Sacramento, Columbia, Nushagak, Yukon and some other great rivers. Through the efforts of the United States Fish Commission it has been widely distributed in the East and beyond seas; but with comparatively poor results, as the species does not appear suitable for acclimation, or the proper method of introduction has not yet been discovered. In Pennsylvania the fry have been somewhat extensively planted, but without success. In certain ponds they have been reared to maturity, but were dwarfed in size. Ten thousand fry were placed in James Duffy's pond at Marietta, in the autumn of 1878. On November 12, 1880, 5,500 of eight to ten inches long were left alive and planted in the Susquehanna.

Size.—This is the largest species of *Oncorhynchus*, occasionally reaching a weight of one hundred pounds. The average weight, however, on the Columbia river is about twenty-two and one-half pounds, and on the Sacramento sixteen. A greater proportion of large individuals is taken in Alaska than in any other region and particularly in the Yukon, Nushagak, and some rivers of Cook's inlet. It is believed that the species will attain a weight of twenty pounds when four years old. The very large salmon of this kind must have successfully passed more than one spawning season, or else we must admit a more rapid rate of growth than appears possible. The length of an individual weighing sixty pounds was nearly four feet; the average length of the adults is three feet.

Habits.—Like other species of salmon the quinnat attains its principal growth at sea and enters the rivers only for the purpose of spawning. The young leave the streams, it is believed, at the age of six or seven months when they have reached a length of four to six inches. What their history in the ocean is no one can tell as they are not seen until their return for the purpose of reproduction. When the sea-run fish approach the shores they come in immense schools which break up when they have reached within a mile and a half of the land. They play around in the bays near the mouths of rivers for a short time before beginning the ascent, and it is known that they feed upon herring, capelin, and sand launce at such times. In fresh water they take no food. The quinnat makes very long journeys towards the headwaters of streams, in some rivers traveling upward of one thousand miles from the sea. Spawning takes place in little tributaries of the rivers. It is now generally believed that salmon which travel so great a distance all die after spawning. The want of food, the rough usage undergone in the ascent of the obstructed waters, and the fatigue incident to the process of spawning, combine to emaciate the fish; the injuries received from sharp rocks cause fractures of the skin, and these are speedily attacked by the dreaded salmon fungus, *Saprolegnia*, so that the last days of the once beautiful salmon are pitiful to look upon. The quinnat build a nest in clear, shoal water on gravelly bottom, scooping out the gravel with their noses and leveling it with their tails, making a circular depression a few feet in diameter in which the eggs and milt are deposited, and then covered by the parent fish again with gravel. Spawning takes place in the late fall months, and the eggs are hatched very early in the spring. The artificial culture of this species has attained to very great importance. The eggs have been sent to nearly all parts of the world by tens of millions. Numerous attempts have been made to acclimate the species in eastern waters, but the experiment has been unsuccessful mainly because of a lack of conditions similar to those of their native habitat, and because of the almost total destruction of the tender fry by their enemies soon after their deposit.

Uses.—The quinnat is one of the most important salmon of the world commercially. It is the chief salmon of the Columbia and Sacramento as well as those Alaskan rivers in which it occurs. In the canned condition it is known all over the world. The flesh of this salmon is a beautiful red and of most excellent quality. The fish is sometimes taken by trolling in the bays shortly after its arrival from sea. Herring is the most successful bait. For commercial purposes, however, seines, gillnets and fish wheels are mainly relied upon for its capture.

Genus **SALMO** (Artedi) Linnæus.

Pennsylvania has one representative of the marine salmon and two species of the river salmon. The first of these belongs to the genus *Salmo*, which is distinguished from the next group (*Fario*) by its seagoing habit, the feeble development of the vomerine teeth, and the great distortion of the jaws of the male in the breeding season.

The group *Fario*, to which the river salmon are referred, is not seagoing to any great extent, although a few individuals of some of the species go into salt water occasionally. The teeth of the vomer are well developed in a long, zig-zag row, or two alternating rows, and the sexual differences are never strongly marked.

90. Salmo salar Linnæus.

The Atlantic Salmon. (*Figure 5.*)

The Atlantic salmon has a moderately thick and elongate body. The greatest height at the origin of the dorsal fin is two-ninths of the total length without caudal. The caudal peduncle is rather slender; its least depth about one third of the greatest depth of body. The head is comparatively small; its length in the female about one-fifth of total without caudal. The eye is placed at a distance from the top of the head equal to its own diameter. It is one-half as long as the snout and about one-seventh length of head. The maxillary reaches a little past the eye in adults. Its length equals the depth of caudal peduncle. The dorsal origin is midway between tip of snout and adipose fin. The adipose fin is long and narrow; its width one-half its length and equal to length of eye. The dorsal base is slightly longer than its longest ray and nearly one-eighth of total without caudal. The last dorsal ray is about one-third length of dorsal base. The ventral origin is nearly under the end of the dorsal base. The length of the fin equals one-half length of head. The appendage is two-fifths the length of the fin. The pectoral is as long as the dorsal base. The distance

Figure 4.

THE ATLANTIC SALMON.

page 74.

of the ventral origin from the anal origin is a little more than length of head. The longest anal ray equals length of ventral. The last ray is two-fifths length of longest. B. 11; D. 11 divided rays and 3 rudiments; A. 9 divided rays and 3 rudiments. Scales 23, 120, 21. Vertebræ 60. Pyloric cœca 60 to 70. In the adult the upper parts are brownish or grayish; the sides silvery. Numerous X-shaped or XX-shaped black spots on the upper half of the body, side of the head, and on the fins. Males in the breeding season have red blotches along the sides. In the young there are from ten to twelve dark cross bars mingled with red blotches and black spots.

The land-locked salmon, which has received the name of Sebago, does not differ from the seagoing form in any important character. It grows to a smaller size and is usually darker in color and lives permanently in lakes as well as in streams out of which it could run to the sea if so disposed.

Names.—The salmon in America has but a single common name. When the young have reached a length of a couple of inches and taken on the vermilion spots and dark cross bands they are called parr, and retain this name while they remain in fresh water. Before descending to the sea in the second or third spring, the parr assumes a bright silvery coat and is then known as a smolt. After a sojourn in salt water lasting from four months to about two years it may return to its native river either as a sexually immature salmon or as a grilse, the female not yet ready for reproducing its species, although the male is sexually mature.

The land-locked variety of the Atlantic salmon has been variously denominated fresh-water salmon, schoodic trout, Sebago trout, dwarf salmon and winninish, the last name in use in the Saginaw region. In some Nova Scotian rivers a misnomer, grayling, is applied to the land-locked salmon.

Distribution.—This species inhabits the north Atlantic, ascending rivers of Europe and America for the purpose of reproduction. In Europe it extends southward to France, and in the United States the most southern river in which specimens have been obtained is the Potomac. It occurs in small numbers in the Delaware and in large numbers in the Hudson, but in the last three river basins mentioned its presence is the result of artificial introduction. It is not found abundantly south of the Merrimac, and in rivers of New England and Canada in which it is native it is maintained almost exclusively by artificial culture. The first efforts to introduce the salmon into Pennsylvania waters were made at the expense of a number of gentlemen of Easton and Philadelphia. Beginning in 1871, they deposited a small number of fry in one of the tributaries of the Delaware and repeated the experiment in 1872. In March, 1873, 20,000 fry purchased from Mr. C. G. Atkins, of Bucksport, Maine, were added to the deposits in the Delaware. In 1873 the State of Pennsylvania hatched and planted 27,000 in the Delaware, and the New Jersey commissioners also deposited 18,000 In 1874, 137,000 fry were planted in Bushkill creek near Easton, Swatara creek, Chiquessalunga creek, Codorus and Donegal creeks. The young, varying from four to eight inches long, have been taken by the hook. On November 9, 1877, a salmon thirty-two inches long was captured in the Bushkill in Groetzinger's mill race. This was a female. Several other adults, six or eight in all, were taken in the fall of 1877. A few individuals have been caught in the Susquehanna; one weighing nineteen pounds was taken, May 11, 1879, near Havre de Grace. Of the land-locked variety a small number were placed in Harvey's lake, Luzerne county, and in Rutter's pond adjoining, as early as 1876. In 1891 young salmon were abundant in the upper Delaware.

Size.—The usual weight of the Atlantic salmon ranges from fifteen to forty pounds, but individuals weighing sixty pounds have been recorded.

Habits and Reproduction.—The growth of the salmon is accomplished chiefly in the ocean. As a rule the adults enter the rivers on a rising temperature when ready to deposit their eggs; the spawning season occurring on the falling temperature in water not warmer than fifty degrees. The time of entering the rivers is April in the Delaware and Hudson, a little later in the Connecticut, still later in the Merrimac, and in the Penobscot they come most abundantly in June and July; in the Miramichi from the middle of June to October. The salmon is not much affected by changes in temperature of the water, enduring a range of fully forty-five degrees. The eggs are deposited in shoal water on sandy or gravelly bottom, the parent fish making deep depressions by means of their noses or by flopping motions of the tail. The period of egg depositing lasts from five to twelve days. The spawning season begins about the middle of October and may run into December. In some European rivers the season continues until February. The eggs are about one-fourth of an inch in diameter, and the female is estimated to have about one thousand for each pound of her weight. In the Penobscot, according to the observations of Mr. Atkins, an eight-pound female yields from 5,000 to 6,000 eggs, and a female of forty pounds about 15,000 eggs. The hatching period ranges from one hundred and forty to two hundred days or more, depending on the temperature. A newly-hatched salmon is about three-fourths of an inch long, and the yolksack is not absorbed until from a month to six weeks. It then begins to feed upon small organisms in the water. At the age of two months it measures one and a-half inches and begins to show cross bars and red spots, gradually coming into the parr stage which may last until the second or third spring of its life, when it becomes bright silvery in color and is known as a smolt. The smolt then goes into the ocean, from which it returns at the end of from four to twenty-eight months as a grilse or a mature salmon. In the sea the salmon feeds upon herring, capelin, sand launce, smelt and other small fishes, besides crustaceans; but during its stay in fresh water it takes no food.

Enemies.—Among the worst enemies of salmon eggs are trout, eels, suckers and frogs. Numerous species of birds destroy the fry, among them shelldrakes, kingfishers, gulls and terns.

Uses and Capture.—The value of the salmon as a food and game fish is so well known as to require no description here. Those that find their way into market are usually caught in pound-nets, gill-nets or seines, and the bulk of them are taken at or near the mouths of the streams which they are about to enter for the purpose of spawning. Many are captured in the upper reaches of streams by the spear.

91. Salmo irideus (GIBBONS).

The Rainbow Trout. (*Figure 5.*)

The rainbow trout has a short and deep body, its greatest depth equaling two-sevenths of the total length without caudal. The least depth of caudal peduncle equals one-half length of head. The head is short and deep; its length contained about four and two-thirds times in the total length without caudal. The snout is short, not much exceeding the eye in length and about one-fourth length of head. The length of the eye is contained four and two-thirds times in that of the head. The maxilla does not quite reach to the end of the eye. The origin of the dorsal is a little nearer tip of snout than root of tail. The length of its base is contained seven and one-half times in total without caudal, and slightly exceeds its longest ray. The last ray is one-half length of longest. The ventral origin is under the middle of the dorsal base. The length of the fin equals longest dorsal ray. The ventral appendage is about as long as the eye. When the ventral is extended the distance of its tip from vent is one-third length of head. The distance of ventral origin from anal origin slightly exceeds length of head. The length of the anal base is a little more than half length of head. Its longest ray equals the longest dorsal ray. Its last ray is somewhat less than the length of the eye. B. 11; D. 11 divided rays and 4 rudiments. A. 10 divided rays and 3 rudiments. Scales 21–135–20. The adipose fin is short, its width nearly equal to its length and two-thirds length of eye.

The upper parts greenish blue, often purplish. The sides more or less silvery and profusely spotted with small black spots, these most numerous above lateral line. Head, dorsal, adipose, and caudal fins also black spotted. Sea-run specimens are uniform silvery without black spots. In the breeding season the broad crimson lateral band becomes brighter, and the sides of both sexes are iridescent purplish. The jaws of the male in the breeding season are not much distorted, but they are very much larger than in the female.

Names.—The rainbow trout is known also as California mountain trout, specked trout, golden trout, and brook trout.

Distribution.—This species ranges from California, near the Mexican boundary, to southern Alaska. A small specimen was taken at Sitka in 1880 by Captain L. A. Beardslee, U. S. N. The rainbow is found chiefly in mountain streams west of the Sierra Nevadas. It rarely descends into the lower stretches of the rivers; but occasionally does so and passes out to sea. In Pennsylvania the rainbow has been rather extensively introduced, but with such imperfect results in most cases that the Fish Commission has practically given up its distribution. The species reproduces naturally in Cumberland county and in Mill creek in Pike county, and doubtless in other streams. This trout has been very widely distributed artificially, and in numerous localities thrives greatly beyond all expectations. Favorite states for this species are Wisconsin, Michigan, Missouri and North Carolina. In Missouri the growth of the species is most remarkable, at the Neosho station of the United States Fish

Commission averaging about one inch per month up to the age of one year.

Size.—The average individuals of this species are less than one foot in length, but specimens measuring nearly two feet and weighing eight pounds have been recorded. The Neosho station has individuals nearly one foot long at the age of one year.

Habits and Reproduction.—The rainbow feeds on worms, insect larvæ and salmon eggs. In streams in which the California salmon and rainbow exist together, the rainbow is the one species most destructive to salmon eggs. Spawning takes place in winter and early spring, varying with temperature and locality. The bulk of the eggs are usually taken in January, February and March, and the average yield from each female is about 900 eggs.

Uses.—The rainbow is a good table fish although held in variable estimation in different localities. In most places, however, it is considered fully equal to the common brook trout. On the McCloud river, Cal., it is regarded as superior to salmon.

92. Salmo fario LINNÆUS.

The Brown Trout. (*Figure 6.*)

The brown trout of Europe was introduced into the United States from Germany in February, 1883, and in subsequent years. It has now become thoroughly acclimated in the fresh waters of many of the states.

The body of this trout is comparatively short and stout, its greatest depth being contained about four times in the length without the caudal. The caudal peduncle is short and deep, its depth equaling two-fifths the length of the head. The length of the head in adults is one-fourth of the total length without caudal, or slightly less. The diameter of the eye is about one-fifth of the length of the head and less than length of snout. The dorsal fin is placed nearer to the tip of the snout than to the root of the tail; the longest ray of this fin equals the distance from the eye to the end of the opercle. The ventral is under the posterior part of the dorsal; its length is about one-half that of the head. The adipose dorsal is placed over the end of the anal base; it is long and expanded at the end. The caudal is emarginate in young examples, but nearly truncate in specimens ten inches long. The pectoral is nearly one-sixth of the length without the caudal. In the male the jaws are produced and very old ones have a hook. The maxilla extends to the hind margin of the eye. The triangular head of the vomer has a transverse series of teeth, and the shaft of the bone bears two opposite or alternating series of strong, persistent teeth. D. 13-14; A. 10-11; P. 13; V. 9; scales 25-120-30; pyloric cœca 38-51; vertebræ 57-58.

On the head, body and dorsal fin usually numerous red and black spots, the latter circular or X-shaped and some of them with a pale border. A yellowish margin, usually present on the front of the dorsal and anal and the outer part of the ventral. The dark spots are few in number below the lateral line. The ground color of the body is brownish or brownish black, varying with food and locality.

Names.—In European countries in which this species is native it bears the name of trout or brook trout, or the equivalents of these terms. In Germany it is *Bachforelle*; in Italy, *Trota*; in France, *la Truite*. In the United States it is known as the brown trout and von Behr trout, the latter in honor of Herr von Behr, late president of the Deutscher

Figure 5. THE RAINBOW TROUT.

Page 77.

Fischerei Verein, who was very active in the acclimation of the fish in America.

Distribution.—The brown trout is widely distributed in Continental Europe and inhabits lakes as well as streams, especially in Norway and Sweden. Tributaries of the White Sea, the Baltic, the Black Sea and the Caspian, contain this species. In Great Britain it lives in lakes and streams and has reached a high state of perfection; in Germany and Austria, however, the trout is a characteristic fish and our supply has been drawn principally from the former country. Moreau found it at an elevation of 7,000 feet in the Pyrenees and a color variety is native to northern Algeria in about thirty-seven degrees north latitude. In the United States the brown trout has been successfully reared in Colorado at an elevation of nearly two miles above sea level. It is now well established in New York, Pennsylvania, Maryland, Missouri, Michigan, Wisconsin, Nebraska, Colorado and several other states. This trout has proved to be well adapted to the region east of the Rocky Mountains, which has no native black-spotted species, although the western streams and lakes contain many forms in a high state of development.

Size.—Under favorable conditions the brown trout has been credited with a weight of twenty-two pounds and a length of thirty-five inches. In New Zealand rivers, where it was introduced with unusual success, it now approximates equal size, but in most localities ten pounds is about the limit of weight, and five or six pounds is a good average, while in some regions the length seldom exceeds one foot and the weight ranges from one-half pound to one pound. In the United States a wild specimen, seven years old, weighed about eleven pounds. In a well in Scotland, an individual aged fifteen years, measured only about one foot in length. These illustrations will serve to show how much the growth of a brown trout is affected by its surroundings and food supply. The species has been known to become sexually mature when two years old and eight inches long.

Habits.—The brown trout thrives in clear, cold, rapid streams and at the mouths of streams tributary to lakes. In its movements it is swift and it leaps over obstructions like the salmon. It feeds usually in the morning and evening, is more active during evening and night, and often lies quietly in deep pools or in the shadow of overhanging bushes and trees for hours at a time. It feeds upon insects and their larvæ, worms, mollusks and small fishes, and, like its relative, the rainbow trout, it is fond of the eggs of fishes. In Europe it is described as rising eagerly to the surface in pursuit of gnats and is said to grow most rapidly when fed upon insects.

Reproduction.—Spawning begins in October and continues through December and sometimes into January. The eggs are from one-sixth to one-fifth of an inch in diameter and yellowish or reddish in color. They are deposited at intervals during a period of many days in crevices between stones, under projecting roots of trees and sometimes in nests excavated by the spawning fishes. The parents cover the eggs to some extent with gravel. The hatching period varies according to temperature, from forty to seventy days. Females aged three years, furnish on the average about three hundred and fifty eggs each, but individuals of this age have yielded as many as seven hundred, and even at the age of two years some females produce from four to five hundred. When four or five years old the number of eggs has reached fifteen hundred to two thousand. The young thrive in water with a temperature of about fifty degrees Fahrenheit. Sterility in the females is common and breeding females have been observed to cease reproduction when eight years old.

Qualities.—The brown trout is in its prime from May to the last of September. Its flesh is very digestible and nutritious, and deeper red than that of the salmon when suitable food is furnished; the flavor and color, however, vary with food and locality. Insect food produces the most rapid growth and best condition. This species has been so long known as one of the noblest of the game fishes and its adaptability for capture with artificial flies, because of its feeding habits, is so well understood that I need not dwell upon these familiar details.

Genus **SALVELINUS** (Nilsson) Richardson.

In Pennsylvania waters this genus of salmonidæ includes the well-known brook and lake trouts. They are distinguished from the salmon and river trouts most readily by the dentition of the vomer. The teeth are present only in a small rounded cluster on the head of that bone in the brook trout, and in the lake trout they are planted upon a raised crest or chevron which is not consolidated with the shaft of the vomer. The lake trout indeed is worthy of the separate designation—Cristivomer—assigned to it by Gill and Jordan in 1878. There is no difficulty in distinguishing the brook trout from the lake trout, the former having the typical teeth on the head of the vomer and a square tail, while the lake trout has a peculiar dentition and a deeply-forked tail. The coloration, also, would readily serve to distinguish the two at all ages.

In the charrs the scales are very small; the sexes do not differ much in the prolongation of the jaws, although the male always has a much larger maxilla than the female. The typical charrs are usually small and the species are numerous, while the sub-genus Cristivomer is represented by a single large and in many respects peculiar species.

93. Salvelinus fontinalis (Mitch.)

The Brook Trout. (*Figure 7.*)

The brook trout varies greatly in the shape of the body, sometimes being short and deep and again elongate and moderately thin. The depth is usually about one-fourth or two-ninths total length without caudal, and is about equal to length of

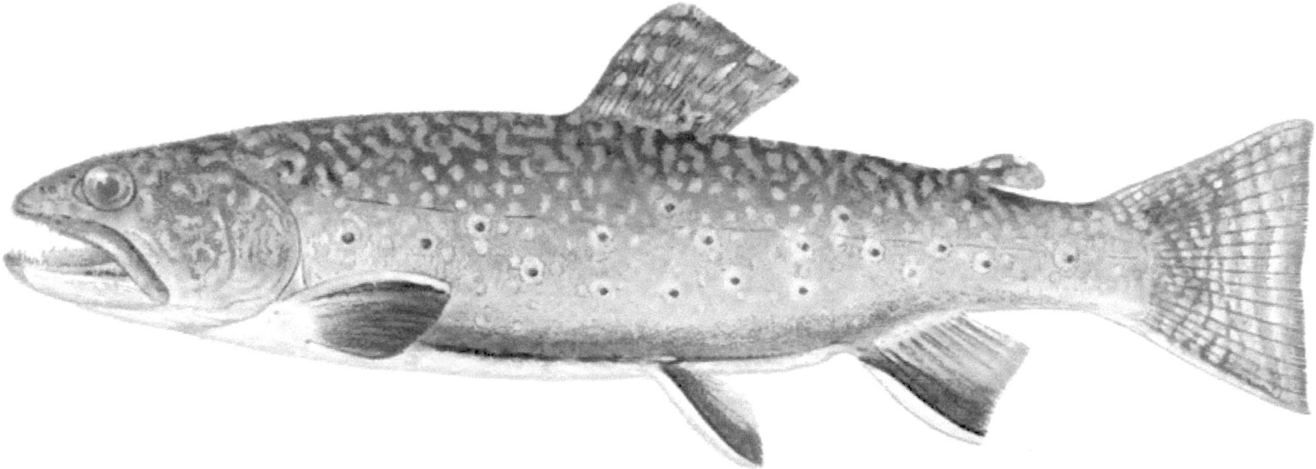

Figure 7.   THE BROOK TROUT.   Page 80.

head. The least depth of the caudal peduncle is a little more than one-third greatest depth of body. The head is large and the snout somewhat obtuse. The eye is in front of the middle of its length, a little more than one-half as long as the snout, and about one-sixth length of head. The dorsal fin is about midway between tip of snout and root of tail. The length of its base equals about half greatest depth of body. The longest ray equals length of ventral. The ventral origin is a little behind the middle of the dorsal. In the male when laid backward it reaches nearly to the vent. The length of the appendage equals that of the eye. The anal base is two-thirds as long as the ventral; its longest ray equal to ventral. The adipose fin is short and stout. Its width two-thirds of its length and about two-thirds length of eye. D. 10; A. 9. Scales in lateral line 225 to 235; 6 gill rakers above the angle of the first arch; 11 below.

The coloration is very variable with age and locality. The upper parts are usually grayish much mottled with dark olive or black. The dorsal fin and anterior portion of caudal base and top of head are also mottled. The caudal has narrow dark bars. The lower fins dusky with a creamy white anterior edge bounded behind by a narrow black streak. On the sides numerous pale brownish blotches encircling small vermilion spots.

Distribution.—The brook or speckled trout of the east is indigenous to the region east of the Allegheny mountains and the Great Lake region, extending from Georgia on the south to Labrador on the north. In Pennsylvania it is most abundant in the southeastern portion of the state and particularly in Pike and Monroe counties. The distribution of this trout has been wonderfully extended by artificial introduction, as it has always been a favorite with fish culturists. It is now to be found thriving in many of the western states and territories, and is particularly thrifty in Nebraska, Colorado, Nevada and California. It has also been sent to Mexico and to European countries. In Pennsylvania the Fish Commission distributes millions of this species annually.

Size.—The average brook trout seldom exceed seven or eight inches in length, and smaller individuals are much more abundant and require legal protection. In the northeastern part of its habitat the brook trout grows much larger, specimens weighing from three to six pounds being not uncommon, and in one of the Rangeley lakes an individual weighing eleven pounds is recorded; while Seth Green took a twelve-pound specimen in the Sault St. Marie, and Hallock mentions one which was said to weigh seventeen pounds.

Habits.—The book trout does not flourish in water warmer than 68°, and prefers a temperature of about 50°. It is an inhabitant of the cold clear mountain streams, and will leave a region which becomes polluted by mill refuse and other hurtful substances. In the Long Island region and around Cape Cod where the brook trout has free access to salt water, it has the habit of going to sea in the fall and remaining during the winter. It then grows rapidly and becomes a much more beautiful fish than many which live exclusively in fresh water. In hot weather when the temperature of the streams becomes too high and lakes are accessible, trout seek the deep parts of the lakes and the vicinity of cold springs. In streams they are to be found in deep pools or in chan-

6 FISHES.

nels. They feed in spring and early summer among the rapids upon insects and small crustaceans.

Reproduction.—The brook trout is a nest builder. Cavities are made in the gravel and the nest is shaped with the tail and the larger stones are carried in the mouths of the parents. After the eggs are deposited they are covered with gravel. The eggs are not all deposited at one time. Spawning usually begins in October, but brook trout are spawning at some locality in almost every month of the year except midsummer. The egg is about one-fifth of an inch in diameter, and varies in color from pale lemon to orange red. The average yield of the female is from 400 to 600. Mr. Livington Stone has taken 1,800 from a fish weighing one pound. The period of hatching will depend upon the temperature, ranging from 165 days in water of 37° to 32 days in water of 54°. The yolk sack is absorbed in from 30 to 80 days, and after its absorption the young fish begin to feed. The rate of growth will of course depend upon the amount of food consumed. In artificial culture, yearlings, according to Mr. Ainsworth's estimate, will average two ounces; two-year olds four ounces; three-year olds eight ounces, and four-year olds one pound.

The value of the brook trout as a food fish, and its game qualities are so well known that I need not refer to them here.

94. Salvelinus namaycush (Walb.)

The Lake Trout. (*Figure 8.*)

The lake trout or Namaycush has a stout and moderately elongate body. The caudal peduncle is slender, its height little more than one-third greatest height of body. The eye is large, placed near the top of the head, two-thirds as long as the snout, and contained four and a-half to five and a-half times in length of head. The maxilla reaches far behind the eye; its length is nearly one-half that of head. The origin of the dorsal is midway between the tip of snout and root of tail. The length of the base equals length of maxilla. Its longest ray one-sixth of total without caudal. The ventral is under the hind part of dorsal; its length half length of head. The appendage is very short, about one-half length of eye. The fin when extended reaches nearly to the vent. The distance between ventral origin and anal origin is one-fifth total length without caudal. The anal base is about one-third length of head. The longest ray one-half length of head. The last ray equal to eye. The pectoral is nearly two-thirds as long as the head. B. 11 to 12; D. 9 to 10, besides several rudiments; A. 9 and several rudiments; V. 9. Scales of lateral line about 200.

The coloration is extremely variable, generally grayish, in the variety known as the Tuladi, nearly black. Alaskan specimens are usually very dark; occasionally the upper parts are pale. The sides are profusely covered with roundish pale spots, sometimes with a reddish tinge. On the back and top of head there are fine vermiculations resembling those of the brook trout. The caudal in addition to numerous pale spots has many small dark blotches.

Names.—The lake trout has received many names, among which are the following: Mackinaw or Namaycush, Togue, Tuladi and salmon trout. Additional names of the species are Lunge, red trout, gray trout and black salmon. Togue and Tuladi are names applied in Maine, New Brunswick and Canada. Mackinaw and salmon trout in the Great

Figure 8.

THE LAKE TROUT.

Page 82.

Lake region; the latter is used also in New York. Namaycush is of course an Indian name.

Distribution.—The lake trout is native in the Great Lake region, lakes of New York and New England, Idaho, and northward into Labrador, British America and Alaska. Extending over such a wide range of country, it varies greatly in size, form and color, which will in part account for the various names which it has received. It has been found above the Arctic circle in Alaska.

Size.—This is one of the largest species of the salmon family resident in fresh waters. It reaches a length of three feet and specimens weighing forty pounds are not uncommon. It is said that an example of ninety pounds and measuring six feet in length has been taken. The species is found in its best condition in Lakes Huron, Michigan and Superior. In Alaska it grows to a large size and is a very shapely and beautifully colored fish.

Habits.—The lake trout is one of the most rapacious fishes of its family. In Lake Michigan it feeds largely upon the cisco and other small white fishes. At Two Rivers, Wis., a lake trout measuring twenty-three inches was found to contain a burbot about seventeen inches long. The gluttony of this species is proverbial. It will devour table refuse, and materials of this kind have frequently been taken from its stomach. Even twigs, leaves and pieces of wood have been eaten by this trout. The species is much more sluggish in its habits than the brook trout and is taken on or near the bottom. The gill and pound nets in which this species is principally captured are set in deep water.

Reproduction.—The spawning of the lake trout usually begins in October and continues into November. For this purpose they come up on rocky shoals and reefs in depths of from seventy to ninety feet and spawn near the edges of rock caverns, into which the eggs settle. The young are hatched late in the winter or early in spring. In some localities the depth of the spawning areas ranges from fifteen fathoms to only seven feet. Mr. Milner found 14,943 eggs in a lake trout weighing twenty-four pounds. In the hatchery, with a water temperature of forty-seven degrees, the young hatch about the last week of January, but their hatching may be retarded several weeks by lower temperatures.

Capture.—The fishery for the lake trout is most active in September, October and November, and the fish are taken chiefly in pound and gill nets. In some regions many of them also are caught with hooks. In Lake Erie a few large trout of this species weighing from twenty-five to forty pounds are taken off the city of Erie. In 1885, according to the statistics of the United States Fish Commission, 100,000 pounds of lake trout were taken in Erie county.

Uses.—This species is very extensively used for food, although it is not considered a choice fish. Being very abundant in some of the great lakes and a fish of extremely large size, it is important commercially.

In Pennsylvania a fertile hybrid between the lake and brook trout is held in much higher esteem than the lake trout as a food fish.

FAMILY **PERCOPSIDÆ** (THE TROUT PERCHES).

GENUS **PERCOPSIS** AGASSIZ.

95. Percopsis guttatus AGASSIZ.

The Trout Perch.

Body rather long and moderately compressed, covered with thin ctenoid scales; head scaleless and without barbels. Gill openings wide. Opercles well developed. Gill rakers short, tubercular. Skull highly cavernous; mouth small; the margin of the upper jaw formed by the short non-protractile intermaxillaries. No supplemental maxillary bone. Small villiform teeth on the intermaxillaries and mandible. The tongue is short, not free at tip. Pseudobranchiæ developed. Six branchiostegals. The lateral line is continuous. The first dorsal over middle of body, with nine to eleven developed rays. Adipose fin small. The anal and ventral eight-rayed. Caudal long, forked. Pectorals narrow, placed high. The stomach is siphonal and with numerous pyloric cœca as in certain *Salmonidæ*. The eggs are moderately large and are excluded through an oviduct. Air bladder present.

The greatest height of the body is about two-ninths of the total without caudal, the head about three-elevenths. The maxilla does not reach to the eye. The lower jaw is slightly included.

Scales in lateral line 47 to 50.

Color pale olivaceous, the upper parts with rounded dark spots made up of minute dots. A silvery median stripe, becoming obsolete in front. Peritoneum silvery.

The trout perch is a common fish in the Great Lakes and their tributaries. It ranges north to Hudson's Bay having been obtained at Moose Factory by Walton Hayden, also from Nelson river, near Rock Factory, by Dr. Robert Bell. It has been collected in the Delaware river by Dr. C. C. Abbott, in the Potomac by Professor Baird, in the Ohio by Drs. Jordan, Henshall and Bean, and Dr. Gill has recorded the species from Kansas. The trout perch is too small to be valuable for food, but is doubtless an excellent bait. It is one of the most remarkable fishes of our fresh waters, combining as it does the characters of the salmon and some of the perches. Its name indicates this singular relationship. It is voracious, takes the hook freely and spawns in the spring.

ORDER HAPLOMI. THE PIKE-LIKE FISHES.

FAMILY **CYPRINODONTIDÆ** (THE KILLI-FISHES).

GENUS **FUNDULUS** LACÉPÈDE.

96. Fundulus majalis (WALBAUM.)

The Striped Killifish. *(Figure 51.)*

The body is stout, oblong, not very deep nor greatly compressed. The head is contained nearly two and one-half times in the total length without caudal, and the depth four times. The snout is moderately long, one and one-half times as long as the eye. The eye one-fifth as long as head. The scales are moderately large, those on the head about equal to the average of those on the body. Scales on the cheeks in about three longitudinal rows; about twelve rows between dorsal origin and nape. The pectoral in both sexes equals the distance from the middle of the eye to the end of the head. The ventral and anal are longer in the male than in the female. In the male the ventral is one-half as long as the head, in the female only about two-fifths of the head. The longest anal ray of the male equals four-fifths of the length of the head, while in the female it is scarcely more than one-half as long as the head. The dorsal of the male is differently shaped from that of the female, its last rays being nearly as long as the longest, while in the female the last ray is not much more than one-half length of longest ray. D. 13-14; A. 11. Scales 35, 15.

The sexes may be at once distinguished by their difference in color, the female having several narrow lateral stripes, while the male has distinct cross-bands, varying from twelve to twenty in number. In the male the sides and upper parts are dark olivaceous. The sides are silvery, lower parts a beautiful yellowish green; the sides are also marked by a varying number of dark bands, the width of which varies also; a large black spot on the operculum. The dorsal is olivaceous with a black blotch, sometimes circular in form, on the last three or four rays. The pectorals are yellowish; ventrals yellowish green; anal olivaceous; caudal orange. In the female the lower parts are white, upper parts olivaceous and along the sides is a median dark band and below this two short interrupted dark stripes. Two or more short transverse dark bars on the caudal peduncle.

The striped killifish, also known as the banded or striped mummichog, bass mummy, bass fry, Mayfish, yellowtail and New York gudgeon, is the largest member of its family known on our eastern coast. Its range extends from Cape Cod to Florida. In Pennsylvania, Professor Cope states that it probably ascends the Delaware as far as the boundary of the state, and we see no reason to doubt its occurrence even in fresh water.

The female is usually larger than the male and examples measuring eight inches in length have been recorded. It swarms in shallow bays and salt marshes, and although not used as food it is extremely important for the subsistence of economic species and is also extensively used for bait. The name bass mummy, applied to the species on Long Island, refers to its use in the capture of striped bass. The species breeds in summer and the young are abundant in shallow water among eel grass and other aquatic plants.

97. Fundulus diaphanus (Le Sueur.)

The Barred Killifish.

The body is moderately slender and elongate, its greatest depth equaling about two-ninths of the total length without tail, or somewhat less than the length of the head. The head is flat above, the width between the eyes equaling nearly half length of head. The mouth is very protractile, small, its width somewhat greater than the length of the lower jaw. The upper jaw is as long as the eye, a little more than one-fourth length of head, which equals about one-fourth of total length without caudal. The length of the dorsal base equals the depth of the body and much exceeds length of anal base. Length of longest dorsal ray less than one-half head; longest anal ray two-thirds length of head. The dorsal is midway between the tip of the snout and the root of the caudal. The anal is wholly under the dorsal. Length of pectoral six and one-half times in total. Caudal large, convex behind.

D. 14; A. 12. Scales 44-46, 13.

The females are olivaceous with silvery; sides traversed by fifteen to twenty-five narrow dark cross bands; fins pale. The males, at least in the breeding season, are pale olive with about twenty pearly white cross bands.

The barred killifish, also known as the spring mummichog and toothed minnow, inhabits the Great Lakes, and their tributaries, east to Massachusetts, south to Virginia and Indiana, west to Colorado, according to Cope, south to Texas. In Ohio, and west, is found a variety with very distinct and somewhat irregular bands and the back always spotted, which has been called variety *menona* by Jordan and Copeland. Eastern specimens have the back unspotted and the cross bands faint and regular, but extremely variable in number. The difference in coloration of the sexes is very striking, especially in the breeding season when the adult males have silvery cross bands. The barred killifish grows to a length of four inches. It runs down into brackish waters along the east coast and ascends far up the streams, delighting in cold water. This fish has no importance except as bait and food for larger species. In the brackish waters along the coast it is eaten in large numbers by the striped bass and the weakfish. The black bass and trout also feed upon it.

98. Fundulus heteroclitus (LINNÆUS.)

The Common Killifish (*Figure 52.*)

The body is short and stout in both sexes; its depth one-fourth of the length including the tail and slightly greater than the length of the head. The head is moderately short, with an obtuse snout and the space between the eyes very flat. The lower jaw projects slightly. The eye is about two-thirds as long as the snout and one-fifth the length of the head. The pectoral reaches to the ninth or tenth row of scales; its length is equal to the base of the dorsal. The dorsal is considerably nearer to the end of the tail than to the tip of the snout; its longest ray in the female one-half length of head. The anal is entirely under the dorsal; its longest ray equals the longest of the dorsal, its base about one-third length of head. The ventral origin is under about the twelfth scale of the median line, its length, two-thirds that of the pectoral, considerably less than half head; when extended it reaches nearly to vent. The least depth of the caudal peduncle is one-seventh of the length including caudal. All the fins have rounded outlines and the caudal is especially convex. Scales 14, 35. D. 11; A. 11.

The females are nearly uniform olivaceous, lighter below; caudal with a median narrow band of a paler color; most of the scales have a narrow dusky submarginal streak; the scales of the head are very irregularly arranged and unequal in size. The males are dark greenish with many narrow irregular silvery bars on the sides and with the belly yellowish or orange. The sides are also more or less spotted with white or yellow. The dorsal, anal and caudal are dark with many small pale spots. On the last rays of the dorsal there is frequently a dark blotch, which sometimes is surrounded by paler giving it an ocellated appearance. In the young this blotch is often subdivided into two parts. Narrow dark bands are sometimes present in the young male.

The killifish is not a common fish in Pennsylvania, being for the most part a marine species, but has been found in the Delaware by Prof. Cope. It is frequently called mummichog or saltwater minnow, and the name mud-fish has also been applied to it. In the vicinity of Boston it is known to boys under the name of cobbler and on Long Island it is called mummy or chog-mummy. If we follow Dr. Jordan in considering *Fundulus grandis* of Baird and Girard as merely a variety of *heteroclitus* the range of the species will be extended from Maine to Mexico, usually in shallow salt or brackish water but sometimes ascending streams beyond tidewater. The killifish grows to a length of five or six inches; it has no importance as a food fish, but is eaten in large numbers by many of the valuable economic fishes, particularly the striped bass and the weakfish. Dr. Storer says it is an excellent bait for smelts. Piscivorous birds consume it in large quantities and domestic ducks have been known to swallow it with apparent great relish. Eggs have been found in this species as late as August. It spawns in the spring and early summer and the young are found in great schools in summer in the eel grass and on sandy beaches in company with other species of killifish, the common silverside and various other fishes. The sexes are so different in coloration that they have been described under distinct names by several of the older ichthyological writers.

GENUS **ZYGONECTES** AGASSIZ.

99. Zygonectes notatus (RAFINESQUE).

The Black-sided Top Minnow.

The body is slender; head long, low and flat with sharp snout and the jaws nearly equal. The width of the space between the eyes equals half the length of the head and one and one-half times the length of the eye. The depth of the body is less than the length of the head, which is one-fourth of the total length without caudal. The dorsal and anal in the male are higher than in the female. Teeth villiform, in a broad band with the outer series enlarged and canine-like.

The color is pale olive, with scattered specks on the back; a wide, purplish-black band extends from the snout through the eye to the base of the tail; its margin in the young somewhat uneven. The dorsal, caudal and anal fins with black dots. A translucent spot on the top of the head in life. Scales with strong, concentric striae. D. 9; A. 11; scales 34-11.

The black-sided top minnow or killifish is an inhabitant of the Mississippi valley and of streams flowing into the Great Lakes from the south. In the Mississippi valley it extends south to Texas. In Pennsylvania it is to be looked for in tributaries of the Ohio.

This species grows to a length of three and one-half inches. It is very abundant in still waters and frequents sloughs and ponds caused by the overflow of streams. In the rivers it seeks the shelter of aquatic plants. It is a surface swimmer and this fact gives rise to its common name. The species is useful for bait and is well adapted for the aquarium. It is a beautiful little fish and extremely hardy.

100. Zygonectes dispar AGASSIZ.

The Striped Top Minnow.

The head is short and broad; interorbital space flat, its width about twice the length of the eye; a very obtuse snout; fins rather small, the anal much larger than the dorsal. The depth of the body slightly exceeds the length of the head and equals two-sevenths of the total without caudal. The eye is about one-third as long as the head.

Color bluish-olive; sides with about ten longitudinal stripes formed by brownish lines following the edges of the rows of scales. The males have the stripes interrupted and they are further distinguished by about nine dusky bands. In adults there is a dark spot below the eye.

D. 7; A. 9. Scales 35–10.

The striped top minnow is found in lakes and sluggish streams in the Ohio valley and part of the Mississippi valley. Its known western limit is Iowa. It grows to a length of two and one-half inches and has no importance except as food for larger fishes. It frequents large bodies of water and swims at or near the surface and is very sluggish in its movements.

FAMILY **UMBRIDÆ** (THE MUD MINNOWS).

GENUS **UMBRA** (KRAMER) MÜLLER.

101. Umbra limi (KIRTLAND).

The Mud Minnow.

The mud-minnow has a comparatively short and stout body, its depth not equal to the length of the head and about one-fourth of total without caudal. The length of the head equals two-sevenths of the total. The head is flattened above and rather large.

D. 14; A. 9; ventral 6. Scales in lateral line 35; in transverse series 15.

The color is dark olive or greenish and the sides have irregular, narrow pale bars, which are sometimes obscure or absent. A black bar at the base of the tail.

The mud-minnow, mud-dace or dog-fish is found in the Great Lake region from Lake Champlain to Minnesota, being most abundant in Wisconsin. It is occasionally taken in the Ohio valley. It grows to a length of four inches and has no value whatever except as food for other species. Like the related mud-minnow next mentioned it is hardy and interesting in the aquarium. The name mud-minnow relates to a singular habit of the fish of burrowing into the mud when the water evaporates out of a pond. It has been stated that this fish has been plowed up in ponds and swamps which have become dried out. Professor Baird has recorded the following fact about this species: "A locality which with the water perfectly clear will appear destitute of fish will perhaps yield a number of mud-fish on stirring up the mud on the bottom and drawing a seine through it. Ditches on the plains of Wisconsin, or mere bog-holes affording lodgement to nothing beyond tadpoles may thus be found full of *melanurus*."

102. Umbra pygmæa (DEKAY).

The Striped Mud Minnow.

The body of this mud-minnow is oblong, robust; its greatest depth is contained slightly more than four times in the total length without the caudal and is not equal to length of head. The snout is short; eye moderate, about equal to snout, four and one-half in head. Cardiform teeth on premaxillaries, lower jaw, vomer and palatine bones. The gill-openings are very wide, the rakers short and rather numerous. Jaws short, gape of mouth rather wide. The body is covered with rather large cycloid scales and the head is almost entirely scaled.

D. 14; A. 8. Scales 8 or 9 in a traverse series; 35 from head to tail.

Color dark green, more or less mottled (in spirits brownish); sides with a dozen pale, longitudinal streaks, regularly arranged; a darker stripe through eye. A black bar at base of tail, which is present in very young examples as well as in the adult.

The eastern mud-minnow is found from New York to South Carolina in Atlantic streams. According to Professor Cope, it is very common near Philadelphia. It grows to a length of about five inches and is well adapted for aquarium life, but has no other value except as food for larger fishes. Its habits are similar to those of the species last described.

The body is stouter than in *Umbra limi*; the head is broader, less flattened on top, with a larger eye, shorter snout and the profile more convex.

Family **ESOCIDÆ** (The Pikes).

Genus **ESOX** (Artedi) Linnæus.

Subgenus **PICORELLUS**.

The genus *Esox* is readily sub-divided into three groups distinguished by their size, scaling and coloration. In the first group are three species of true pickerels, in which the cheeks and opercles are entirely scaly, the color greenish, usually with dark reticulations and the largest species reaches a length of about two feet. To this group the subgeneric name *Picorellus* was formerly applied; it includes the banded pickerel, the little pickerel and the chain pickerel, all of which occur in Pennsylvania.

103. Esox americanus Gmelin.

The Banded Pickerel. (*Figure 53.*)

The banded pickerel has an elongate body; its depth contained about five times in the total length without caudal; the length of the head three and one-fourth times in the standard length. The snout is contained two and two-thirds times in the length of the head and the eye five and one-half times in the same length. The maxillary extends to vertical through middle of eye; the lower jaw projects considerably beyond the upper. Teeth in the jaws strong, directed backward. The ventral is placed in middle of body, the dorsal and anal fins far back, opposite each other; their longest rays of about the same length, much longer than the bases of the fins. Caudal deeply emarginate.

B. 11-13; D. 11-14; A. 11-12; scales in lateral line 105. The body is usually dark green, sometimes brownish black, above; the sides greenish yellow with about twenty dark curved bars, which are generally very distinct. Dorsal and caudal fins dark brown; the other fins lighter, sometimes reddish. A dark bar from the eye to angle of jaw; another from the snout through the eye to the upper edge of opercle.

The banded pickerel is probably identical with the "mackerel pike" of Mitchill. It is a small fish, seldom exceeding twelve inches in length and will not average more than one-half pound in weight. It occurs only east of the Alleghenies from Massachusetts to Florida in coastwise streams. In Pennsylvania it is limited to waters in the eastern part of the state.

This pickerel is too small to have much importance as a food fish. It resembles in general appearance and habits the little pickerel of the West. It frequents clear, cold and rapid brooks and is said to associate with the brook trout without injury to the latter.

104. Esox vermiculatus Le Sueur.

The Little Pickerel. (Figure 54.)

The little pickerel has a short, stout body and a long head. The greatest depth is nearly one-fifth of the length without caudal and two-thirds length of head. Length of head two-sevenths of total without caudal. Eye two-fifths length of snout, one-sixth length of head. The maxilla reaches to below middle of eye. Cheeks and opercles fully scaled. Dorsal origin twice as far from eye as from end of scales; its base two-fifths head; its longest ray nearly one-half head. Anal under dorsal and with slightly longer rays. Ventral nearly midway between tip of snout and end of scales; its length equal to snout and to pectoral. B. 11-13; D. 12; A. 11 or 12; scales in lateral line 105.

Body green or grayish, usually with many irregular streaks or reticulations, which are sometimes entirely lacking. Sides of the head generally variegated. A dark bar extends downward from the eye and another one forward. Fins plain, but the caudal is sometimes mottled at its base.

This pickerel inhabits the valleys of the Ohio and Mississippi rivers and streams flowing into the Great Lakes from the southward. In ponds formed in the spring by the overflow of river banks it is one of the characteristic fishes and is often destroyed in great numbers by the drying up of such bodies of water. In Pennsylvania the little pickerel, or trout pickerel, is common in the Ohio and its tributaries. Prof. Cope mentions it also as an inhabitant of the Susquehanna river, wherein it is probably not a native.

This fish grows to the length of one foot and is, therefore, too small to have much importance for food.

105. Esox reticulatus Le Sueur.

The Chain Pickerel. (Figure 55.)

The chain pickerel has a long and slender body, its depth near the middle equaling about two-thirds the length of the head and contained five to six times in the total without caudal. The caudal peduncle is slender, its depth little more than one-third greatest depth of body. The snout is long and pointed, as long as the post-orbital part of the head and about three times the length of the eye, which is one-seventh to one-eighth length of head. The dorsal base equals two-fifths length of head; its longest ray equal to snout. The anal begins under the third or fourth ray of the dorsal; its longest ray nearly one-half as long as the head. Caudal deeply forked. Ventral halfway from tip of snout to end of scales; its length equal to snout and slightly greater than length of pectoral. B. 15; D. 15; A. 14; scales in the lateral line about 125. The cheeks and opercles are completely scaled.

The color is usually greenish sometimes brown or almost black. On the sides are many narrow dark lines connected by cross streaks forming a network which suggested the name *reticulatus*. Occasionally the body is uniform greenish as in a specimen taken in the Potomac river a few years ago. In the young the reticulations are very obscure and a pale stripe is found along the middle line on the second half of the body. In adults the sides are often golden or olive yellow and have dark reticulations. A distinct dark band under the eye.

The chain pickerel is known under other names; it is the jack of the South, the federation pike of Oneida Lake, New York, the green pike of the Great Lakes and the eastern pickerel of many writers. It does not occur west of the Alleghenies, but is found from Maine to Florida and Alabama east of this range of mountains. It lives in ponds, lakes and streams.

This pickerel is the largest of its group, reaching a length of two feet and a weight, occasionally, of eight pounds, although this is much above the average.

Like the pike, this is one of the tyrants among fishes, a fierce and hungry marauder, and yet it has been introduced by fishermen into many waters in which it is not native and has greatly multiplied. In the Potomac, the Connecticut, the Delaware and other large rivers the pickerel abounds; it is to be found in large numbers lying in wait among the river grasses or in ponds under the shelter of leafy water plants for the minnows which it consumes in enormous numbers, or some unlucky insect, frog or snake which attracts its voracious appetite.

Spawning takes place in winter and early in the spring and the young soon become solitary and woltish like their elders.

As a food fish not much can be said in praise of the chain pickerel although it is eaten and doubtless liked by a good many people. The flesh is often coarse and watery and is always full of small bones. This fish, however, furnishes considerable sport to the angler since it is a very free biter and fights with great boldness and stubbornness when hooked. It is caught by trolling with the spoon or still-fishing with live shiners, pickerels, frogs and many other baits. A minnow gang is often very effective in pickerel fishing. The hooks must be tied on gimp as a protection for the line from the sharp teeth of the fish.

Subgenus ESOX.

The longest known and most widely distributed species of *Esox* is the common pike—the typical species of the genus. In the sub-division into groups this would be the sole representative of the *Esox* group, which has the cheeks fully scaled and the lower half of opercles naked.

The sides are pale spotted, on a darker ground and the size is very much larger than in the pickerels. Fossil remains of the pike have been found in quaternary deposits in Europe.

106. Esox lucius LINNÆUS.

The Pike. (*Figure 55.*)

The pike has a stout, elongate body and a long head, with broad and produced snout. The greatest depth is about one-fifth of the length without caudal. The caudal peduncle is nearly equal to one-half depth of body. The eye is nearly median and about one-sixth length of head, which is three-elevenths of total without caudal. The mouth is very large and strongly toothed. The tongue, roof of mouth, pharynx and gill arches bristle with teeth in card-like bands, giving the fish extraordinary power in seizing and holding its prey. The dorsal and anal fins are near the caudal. The dorsal base is a little longer than its longest ray and equals depth of body at its origin. Ventral fin midway between tip of snout and end of tail fin. B. 14 to 16 ; D. 17 to 20 ; A. 16 or 17 ; scales in lateral line 120 to 125.

The ground color of the body is grayish, varying to bluish or greenish gray. The sides are thickly covered with pale blotches, none of them as large as the eye, arranged nearly in rows. The dorsal, anal and caudal fins have many rounded, dark spots. Adults without dark bar below eye. Naked part of opercle bounded by a whitish streak. In the young the sides are covered with oblique yellowish bars, which afterward break up into the pale spots of the adult.

Names.—Pike is the best known name for this species, although the misnomer "pickerel" is rather extensively used. The origin of pike is involved in uncertainty ; some trace it to the resemblance in shape of the snout to the pike or spear, while others believe it to refer to the the darting motion of the fish when speeding through the water. The name pickerel is used in Vermont and around Lake George, New York. "Frank Forrester" (Herbert) styles it the great northern pickerel. The name jack is applied in Great Britain to the young pike. *Brochet* is the French name, *hecht* the German and *luccio* the Italian designation of the species. In Prof. Cope's paper in earlier reports of the Pennsylvania Fish Commission the names lake pike and grass pike are used for the fish.

Distribution.—In the North Temperate and Arctic regions of North America, Europe and Asia the pike is equally common. In North America it extends from Pennsylvania to high northern latitudes. In Alaska Townsend and others found it above the Arctic Circle, and Dall and Nelson took it in abundance in the Yukon. From Greenland and the islands of the Arctic Ocean the pike appears to be absent. The identity of our American pike with the common one of Europe was recognized by Cuvier and Richardson more than half a century ago ; the former compared specimens from Lake Huron with European examples and Richardson with the English pike and both were unable to find specific differences between the two.

Size.—On the continent of Europe the largest recorded specimen was taken at Bregenty in 1862 ; this was said to weigh one hundred and forty-five pounds. In Scotland a pike measuring over seven feet and weighing seventy-two pounds has been reported. We do not find monsters like these in America. "Frank Forrester" mentions individuals of sixteen to seventeen pounds. Lake George, New York, is famous for its large pike. Dr. Frank Presbrey, of Washington, D. C., caught one there in 1889 weighing a little more than sixteen pounds and over thirty examples, averaging above ten pounds each, were taken that season by another Washington party in the same waters ; some of the largest pike were upward of four feet long. The average length of adults is about two feet.

Season.—The fishing season generally begins June 1 and ends December 1 ; but many of the states have no close season. In Pennsylvania the close time lasts from December 1 to June 1.

Habits.—The pike is a voracious fish and destroys everything within its reach in the form of animal life—other fish, water birds and mammals are consumed in enormous numbers. From its concealment, like a beast of prey, it darts out suddenly upon its victims and seldom misses its mark. The pike is even more destructive than the pickerel and two of the latter, measuring five inches in length, have been reported to eat more than one hundred minnows in a day. Spawning takes place in winter and early spring on shallows and frequently upon overflowed meadows. The eggs are about one-eighth inch in diameter and a female weighing thirty-two pounds was estimated by Buckland to contain 595,000. The young pike has a very large yolk sac. The period of hatching varies with the temperature of the water, from fourteen to thirty days. The female is said to be larger than the male; the fish breeds at the age of three years. At the age of one year the fish may reach a length of twelve inches and, if well supplied with food, it will increase in weight from two to three pounds yearly.

Uses and Capture.—The pike is a fairly good food fish and forms an important element of the Lake Erie fisheries. As a game fish the species is widely known. It can be readily caught by trolling or spinning or on lines set under the ice. Live minnows and frogs are favorite baits and Dr. Henshall says it will rise to a large gaudy fly. In Lake George the white chub is one of the best known baits.

Subgenus MASCALONGUS.

The largest member of the pike family is the single representative of the section *Mascalongus*, in which the lower half of the cheeks, as well as of the opercles, is scaleless. The scales are smaller than in the other groups. The sides and vertical fins are profusely covered with roundish black spots on a pale ground. The branchiostegals number 17 to 19. A color variety is occasionally met with having the body uniformly dark gray, unspotted.

107. Esox nobilior Thompson.

The Mascalonge. (*Figure 52.*)

The mascalonge has a stout and moderately elongate body, its greatest depth midway between the pectoral and ventral fins, one-fifth to one-sixth of the total length to the end of the scales. The caudal peduncle is short and slender, its depth one-third of greatest depth. The length of the head is two-sevenths of the total without the caudal, and the small eye equals less than one-fourth length of snout. The eye is nearly in the middle of the length of the head. The mouth is very large; the maxilla extends to below the hind margin of the eye; the teeth are as in the pike, but even more formidable; dorsal and anal far back, the origin of the former a little in advance of the anal origin; the length of dorsal base about two-fifths head; longest dorsal ray one-third head; caudal deeply forked; ventral midway between end of head and end of anal, its length equal to one-half depth of body; pectoral nearly equals post orbital part of head. B. 17 to 19; D. 17; A. 16; V. 12; scales in lateral line, 150.

The color is usually dark gray, sometimes immaculate as in the color variety *immaculatus*, but generally with numerous distinct, roundish, black spots about as large as buckshot. The dark spots are present only on the basal parts of the dorsal, anal and caudal fins. The lower parts are pale, the belly white.

Names.—The name of this giant pike is apparently derived from the Ojibwa or the Cree Indians; it is variously spelled and its meaning is uncertain, although the roots, according to Mr. H. W. Henshaw, are probably *más̄k* (ugly) and *kinongé* (fish). In the books it appears as muscalonge, muskellunge, muskallunge, mascalonge and maskinonge—all variations of the same term. Some writers style it the great pike, and by others it is confused with the common pike (*E. lucius*). Professor Cope mentions also the name blue pike.

Distribution.—The mascalonge is recorded by Professor Cope from Conneaut Lake, Crawford county, Pa., the specimen measuring seventeen inches in circumference behind the eyes. It is found occasionally in the Ohio Valley. The species, however, is most abundant in the Great Lake region. In Lake Erie favorite localities are Dunkirk and Barcelona, N. Y., Erie, Pa., and Mills Grove, Ohio. The northern limit of the fish is not definitely fixed.

Size.—It is recorded that in 1865 Mr. Schultz caught a mascalonge at Milwaukee weighing one hundred pounds. In 1864 Mr. Fred Alvord claimed to have taken an eighty-five-pound specimen in Maumee Bay. The average length of the species is about three feet, and there is reason to believe that a length of eight feet is sometimes reached. Individuals weighing fifty pounds are moderately common. With the exception of the lake trout and some of the salmon this is undoubtedly the largest game fish in the United States.

Habits.—The fish seem not to be gregarious, but occur usually in pairs. Their food consists mainly of smaller fishes and their voracity is notorious. In the spawning season in small rivers falling into Lake Simcoe, Richardson states that they feed upon small fishes and upon gelatinous green balls which grow on the sides of banks under the water.

Spawning takes place in the spring. In Chantauqua Lake, New York, Mr. Monroe Green and Mr. Jonathan Mason obtained the eggs in April and May, 1890, and these were artificially hatched. A large female yielded sixty thousand eggs. With the water at the temperature of 40° to 46° very few of the eggs were developed, but when it neared 60° in May better results were secured. On May 27 seventy-five thousand young fish were planted in the lake. The eggs were hatched in a box suspended about four feet from the bottom in eighteen feet of water.

Uses and Capture.—This is an excellent food fish, but not common enough to have much commercial importance. As a game fish it has few superiors. The spoon bait is very effective in the capture of mascalonge, and live fishes are extensively used. A correspondent of *Land and Water* describes a singular and successful lure made from a young brown calf's tail, through the center of which the shank of the hook was passed and fastened to a swivel.

ORDER APODES (THE EELS.)

FAMILY ANGUILLIDÆ.

GENUS ANGUILLA THUNBERG.

108. Anguilla rostrata LE SUEUR.

The Eel. (*Figure 58.*)

In the eel the body is elongate, roundish throughout most of its extent, compressed behind. The scales are deeply imbedded and very irregularly placed, some of them at right angles to others. The head is conical, elongate, with pointed snout and small eye, except in the male. The lower jaw is longer than the upper; the jaws with small teeth in bands; a long patch of teeth on the vomer. The gill openings are partly below the pectoral fins, small and slit-like. The beginning of the dorsal is at a distance of nearly twice the length of the head behind the gill opening. The anal begins still farther back and the vent is close to its origin. The dorsal and anal fins are continuous around the tail; height of body nearly two-thirds length of head, which is contained about eight and one-fourth times in the total. The distance from the gill opening to the vent equals two and one-half times the length of the head; the color varies greatly, but is usually dark brown, more or less tinged with yellow, lower parts paler. In the male referred to the upper parts were silvery gray, sharply separated from the satiny white of the abdomen. In the eel the lateral line is very distinct.

The eel appears to have only one common name. It is one of the best known and most singular of our fishes, yet its breeding habits are even now enveloped in doubt. The species ascends the rivers of eastern North America from the Gulf of St. Lawrence to Mexico, the former being the northern limit of the species on our coast. In the Ohio and Mississippi Valleys it is extremely common, and its range has been much extended by the opening of canals and by artificial introduction. It has been transferred to the Pacific coast. A similar and perhaps identical species is found in northern Europe and Asia.

The eel has been known to exceed a length of four feet. Dr. Mitchill records a Long Island specimen which weighed sixteen and one-half pounds. The average length of individuals, however, is about two feet. The female is larger than the male, paler in color, and is different in certain other particulars, which will be mentioned in the description of the specimens referred to below.

In Pennsylvania the eel is a very important food fish. It is caught chiefly when descending the rivers in the fall. In 1869 about a ton of eels were caught in a single fish basket above Harrisburg. At the present time this method of capture is illegal. Both adults and young eels ascend the streams in spring, the young coming in millions, but in the fall run small eels are seldom seen. Until a comparatively recent date it was not certainly known that the eels have eggs which are developed outside of the body. Even now the breeding habits are unknown, but it is supposed that spawning takes place late in the fall, or during the winter near the mouths of rivers on muddy bottoms. Dr. Jordan has expressed the belief that the eel sometimes breeds in fresh water, since he has found young eels less than an inch long in the headwaters of the Alabama river about five hundred miles from the sea. It is estimated that a large eel contains about nine million eggs. The eggs are very small, measuring about eighty to the inch, and can scarcely be seen by the naked eye. The ovary of an eel containing this number of eggs was nearly a foot in length and about one-half an inch in greatest diameter. When the eels meet obstructions in streams they will leave the water and travel through wet grass or over moist rocks. They have not been able to surmount the falls of Niagara. At the foot of this barrier hundreds of wagon loads of young eels have been seen crawling over the rocks in their efforts to reach the upper waters. For the sake of completing the record of the habits of the eel I quote from W. H. Ballou's description: "They are among the most voracious of carnivorous fishes. They eat most inland fishes except the gar and the chub. * * * They are particularly fond of game fishes, and show the delicate taste of a connoisseur in their selections from choice trout, bass, pickerel and shad. * * * On their hunting excursions they overturn huge and small stones alike, working for hours if necessary, beneath which they find species of shrimp and cray fish, of which they are exceedingly fond. * * * They are among the most powerful and rapid of swimmers. * * * They attack the spawn of other fishes open mouthed, and are even said to suck the eggs from an impaled female. They are owl-like in their habits, committing their depredations at night."

The difference of size in the sexes has already been referred to. According to one writer the males are much smaller than the females, rarely exceeding fifteen or sixteen inches in length. The question whether eels will breed in fresh water has an important bearing upon their introduction into places from which they cannot reach the sea. The generally accepted belief is that while the eels will grow large and fat they will not reproduce under such circumstances. The male eel has only rarely been recognized on the American coast. I had the good fortune to collect five examples on Long Island in the fall of 1884, and several specimens have been taken at Woods Holl, Mass. One of these latter specimens and several of those collected by myself were studied by Prof. John A. Ryder, of the University of Pennsylvania, and found to contain the male organs so well developed as to leave no doubt concerning the sex of the individuals. These eels, which were known to the fishermen as silver eels, have remarkably large eyes, short snout, and long pectoral fins when compared with the common form.

ORDER SYNENTOGNATHI.

Family **BELONIDÆ** (The Silver Gars).

Genus **TYLOSURUS** Cocco.

109. Tylosurus marinus (Bloch and Schneider).

The Silver Gar.

Body long, slender and somewhat compressed. The depth of the body is less than one fifth length of head; the eye is rather large, two-fifths of the length of the postorbital part of the head. The pectoral is as long as the postorbital part of the head and twice as long as the ventral. The distance of the dorsal from the root of the caudal is one-fourth its distance from the tip of the lower jaw. The anal ends under the end of the dorsal and begins in advance of the dorsal origin. The ventral is almost equi-distant from the root of the caudal and the hind margin of the eye.

D. 15 to 16; A. 15 to 17; V. 6.

The body is green with a broad silvery band along the sides and a dark bar on the operculum. The scales and bones are green.

The silver gar, soft gar, bill fish or needle fish is found along our coast from Maine to Texas, and although a marine species it ascends rivers far above the limits of tide. It has been found in the Susquehanna at Bainbridge, Pa., and it also runs up the Delaware. This species reaches a length of four feet. It is very destructive to small fishes, which are readily seized in its long and strongly-toothed jaws. The species has no value as a food fish. In the Gulf of Mexico the habits of the silver gar have been observed by Mr. Silas Stearns, whose notes are to be found in the *Fishery Industries of the United States*. It is found at Pensacola, Florida, in the summer, but retreats farther south in the winter.

The silver gar swims at the surface and feeds upon schools of small fish. Its movements are swift and its aim certain. It has been known to seize mullets and other fish one-third as large as itself and is sometimes killed by attempting to swallow spiny fish too large to pass through its throat. It spawns in the bays in May and June. Mr. Stearns found it to be an excellent food fish although it is seldom eaten on the Florida coast.

7 Fish.

ORDER HEMIBRANCHII (THE HALF-GILLED FISHES).

FAMILY **GASTEROSTEIDÆ** (THE STICKLEBACKS.)

GENUS **EUCALIA** JORDAN.

110. Eucalia inconstans (KIRTLAND).

The Brook Stickleback.

The body is more elongate than in the other sticklebacks described, and stouter; the caudal peduncle has no keel and the skin is entirely smooth. The ventral spines and pubic bones are very small, the latter concealed under the skin. The thoracic processes are covered by the skin, slender and widely separated. The dorsal spines are short, nearly equal in length, placed in a straight line; the anterior spines shortest. The ventral spines are small and serrated. The depth equals one-fourth and the depth two-sevenths of the total length without caudal.

D. III-IV, I, 10; A. I, 10.

Males in the breeding season are jet black, tinged entirely with coppery red. The females and young are greenish, variegated with darker.

The brook stickleback occurs in the freshwaters from New York westward to Dakota and is said to extend north to Greenland. A variety from Cayuga Lake has been described by Dr. Jordan. It has the ventral spines longer than the pubic bones.

In Pennsylvania the brook stickleback inhabits the Ohio valley. It grows to a length of two and one-half inches and has no value as food, but is an interesting aquarium fish. It is, however, extremely pugnacious and when kept in confinement great mortality is caused by its quarrels. The species is abundant in small streams, where it secretes itself among aquatic plants and is always on the alert for an attack upon small fishes and insects. Specimens have recently been obtained from an artesian well in South Dakota, the well having a depth of seven hundred feet. From this great depth the fish were brought up in full strength and vigor and were kept in an aquarium several months afterwards. A similar occurrence has been recorded by Mrs. Eigenmann in the Proceedings of the National Museum for 1883, p. 217, of Williamson' stickleback at San Bernardina, Cal. The well in this case was only one hundred and ninety-one feet deep. There is no doubt that the fish reach the wells through streams which become subterranean in a certain part of their course.

This species is a nest builder and is vigorous in the defense of its eggs and young.

GENUS **GASTEROSTEUS** (ARTEDI) LINNÆUS.

111. Gasterosteus aculeatus LINNÆUS.

The Two-spined Stickleback.

The body is fusiform, moderately elongate and compressed; the caudal peduncle is short and slender and distinctly keeled. The height of the body is less than the length of the head and about one-fourth of the total without caudal. The eye is one-fourth as long as the head. The sides are covered by about thirty-three bony plates. The processes from the shoulder girdle cover the breast except a small naked area between them. At the base of each dorsal spine is a large rough bony plate to which the spine is hinged in such a way that it may be fixed and immovable at the will of the fish. The pelvic bone is lanceolate. A cusp at the base of the ventral spine. The spines are all closely serrated; those in front of the anal and soft dorsal smallest.

D. II, I, 11-13; A. I, 9.

The living fish is greenish olive, lighter on the sides, the lower parts silvery. The gill covers are silvery with dusky spots; the iris silvery; pupil black; fins pale; the ventral membrane sometimes red.

The two-spined stickleback or burn stickle is found on both sides of the Atlantic, its range on our coast extending southward at least to New Jersey and northward to Greenland. This is the largest of the sticklebacks and is said to grow to a length of four inches. In the North Pacific and Bering Sea there is a related species, *G. cataphractus* Pallas, which has been styled the salmon killer. In Pennsylvania Mr. Seal has found this fish abundant in pools and ditches along the Delaware.

GENUS **APELTES** DeKay.

112. Apeltes quadracus (MITCHILL).

The Four-spined Stickleback.

The body is fusiform in shape, the snout pointed and the caudal peduncle slender. The sides are somewhat compressed. The depth of the body equals the length of the head and is one-fourth of the total without caudal.

D. III-IV, I, 11; A. I, 8.

The skin is scaleless. The first dorsal spine is the highest, its length about half that of head.

The living fish has the upper parts greenish brown. Below the lateral line the color is darker and is mottled by the extension upward of the white color of the abdomen. Young specimens have the brown color aggregated into several cross bands, which become indistinct in the adult. The ventral membrane is broad, scarlet in color, giving rise to one of the popular names.

The four-spined stickleback is known in Great South Bay as the "thorn back." In Massachusetts it is sometimes called the bloody stickleback.

This species reaches a length of two inches. It swarms in the shallow waters, especially in the northern portion of its habitat and is particularly plentiful in brackish streams where there are numerous aquatic plants. In salt marshes it is one of the commonest of the little fishes and it is not uncommon in the mouths of rivers. In Pennsylvania Prof. Cope records it as abundant in the tidewater streams and ditches of the Delaware. It is a beautiful fish for the aquarium. Its spinning habits have been described by Prof. John A. Ryder in the Bulletin of the United States Fish Commission for 1881. As a nest builder this is a most interesting species.

ORDER PERCESOCES.

Family ATHERINIDÆ (The Silversides).

Genus MENIDIA Bonaparte.

113. Menidia beryllina Cope.

The River Silverside.

The body is shorter than usual among the silversides. The spinous dorsal is well separated from the soft dorsal and its posterior margin extends almost to the vertical from the first anal ray. The ventral reaches to below the first ray of the dorsal. The length of the head is contained four and one-fourth times in the total length without caudal. The eye large, orbit one-third as long as the head. Mouth small. The mandible slightly longer than the maxilla and slightly curved. Greatest depth of body one-sixth of total length without caudal. Scales in lateral line thirty-six, transverse series ten. The lateral line is represented by a pore on the anterior part of the exposed portion of each scale, except on the caudal peduncle where it runs through a groove.

D. VI, 11; A. I, 18; V. I, 5; P. 15.

The caudal is deeply forked. Pale olivaceous in color with a silvery lateral band, on two and one-half rows of scales, with a lead colored margin. The anal base is lead colored; sides of the head silvery.

This species corresponds in many particulars with *Menidia peninsulæ*, of Goode and Bean, but in that species the silvery streak covers only one and one-half rows of scales. The soft dorsal in *M. peninsulæ* appears to show considerable variation in the number of rays.

The river silverside has been found only in the Potomac river so far as present information goes. It is believed to occur in the Susquehanna and probably will be found in that river. It is distinguished among the *Menidias* by its long soft dorsal fin, which contains eleven rays besides a rudiment. The silvery band along the sides also is very wide, covering two and one-half rows of scales. The species has no importance except as food for larger fishes.

Genus LABIDESTHES Cope.

114. Labidesthes sicculus Cope.

The Brook Silverside.

The body is slender and elongate, its depth one-sixth or one-seventh of the total without caudal. Length of head about two-ninths of total. Eye two-sevenths length of head, two-thirds length of snout.

D. IV, I, 11; A. I, 23; scales 14, 75. Caudal deeply forked.

Color olivaceous, the fish in life translucent. The upper parts with small black dots. The silvery lateral band edged above with lead color and covering one row and two half rows of scales. Cheeks silvery.

The genus *Labidesthes* has a very oblique mouth, with the upper jaw flat above and concave beneath, the intermaxillaries forming a roof-like beak. The mandible is convex.

The brook silverside or skip jack is found in streams and ponds in the Ohio and Mississippi valleys. It has also been discovered recently in some of the southern states from South Carolina to Florida.

This fish grows to a length of four inches and is important only as food for larger species. It has been kept in the aquarium but does not endure captivity. The brook silverside is a surface swimmer, and the name skip jack is derived from its habit of skipping out of and along the surface of the water. It abounds in "clear pools left in summer by the fall of the waters in the stream, which has filled them."

ORDER ACANTHOPTERI (THE SPINY-FINNED FISHES).

FAMILY **APHREDODERIDÆ** (PIRATE PERCHES).

GENUS **APHREDODERUS** LE SUEUR.

115. Aphredoderus sayanus (GILLIAMS).

The Pirate Perch.

The body is moderately stout, oblong, somewhat compressed posteriorly. Scales ctenoid. The dorsal fin is continuous, with three or four spines and eleven soft rays; the anterior spines much the shortest. The anal has two spines and six rays. The mouth is rather large for the size of the fish; the lower jaw somewhat longer than the upper; the maxilla reaches to front of eye. Jaws, vomer and palatine bones with villiform bands of teeth. Lateral line wanting. The depth of the body is two-sevenths and length of the head one-third of the total without caudal. The eye is two-ninths as long as the head. The origin of dorsal is much in advance of the middle of the total length. The pectorals do not reach as far back as the ventrals; ventrals more than one-half length of head. The long anal spine three-sevenths length of head; the caudal is rounded. Scales in 48 to 55 series. The color is variable, sometimes olivaceous at other times dark brown with numerous dark punctulations; a dark bar at the base of the caudal followed by a light one.

The pirate perch ranges from New York westward to Minnesota and in the Mississippi valley it extends to Louisiana. In Pennsylvania the species occurs in Lake Erie, probably in tributaries of the Ohio and in the lower Delaware. It grows to a length of four inches. Nothing is recorded about its habits except that it is very voracious and feeds at night. It is common in sluggish streams and ponds in the shelter of aquatic plants. In a pond near Patchogue, Long Island, we found the pirate perch to be quite common and the owners of the pond mistook it for the young of German carp which they had introduced.

This is one of the most interesting little fishes of the fresh waters, particularly because the position of the vent varies with age. In the young it is behind the ventrals while in the adult it is in the throat.

Family CENTRARCHIDÆ (The Sun Fishes).

Genus POMOXYS Rafinesque.

116. Pomoxys sparoides Lacepede.

The Calico Bass. (*Figure 9.*)

In the genus *Pomoxys* the body is deep, compressed, with long dorsal and anal fins, having the soft portion as long as or longer than the spinous portion. The dorsal fin is continuous, its spines from five to eight in number, and rapidly increasing in size backward. The dorsal and anal are about equal in length and with nearly the same number of spines. The operculum is emarginate, the caudal deeply notched, and the gill rakers numerous, long, thread-like, finely toothed. The mouth is large, with the lower jaw strongly projecting. The calico bass has the depth about one-half the length not including the tail, the head about one-third. The mouth is very oblique and smaller than in the crappie. The eye is as long as the snout and one-fourth as long as the head. The maxilla reaches to slightly behind the middle of the eye. The dorsal and anal fins are very high; the longest rays are half as long as the head. The pectoral is as long as the ventral, slightly shorter than the longest ray of the dorsal. The ventral reaches to third anal spine. D. VII, 15; A. VI, 17-18. Scales 7, 42, 15.

The sides are olivaceous with silvery reflections and mottled with pale green. The dorsal, anal and caudal show pale spots surrounded by green reticulations.

The calico bass, on account of its wide distribution and variability, has received a profusion of names. Many of these are variations of the term bass. It is known, for example, as strawberry bass; grass bass, lake bass, Lake Erie bass, bank lick bass, silver bass and big-fin bass. Other names for the species are strawberry perch, chinquapin perch, goggle-eyed perch, silver perch and sand perch. Still other names of local application are bar fish, bitter head, tin mouth, sac-a-lait, lamplighter, razor-back, goggle-eye, black croppie and lake croppie. The species is mentioned in the fish laws of Pennsylvania under the name of Lake Erie bass or grass bass.

The distribution of the calico bass is naturally extensive, and it has been still further increased by artificial introduction. The fish has been carried to France, and examples measuring about eight inches in length were recorded there several years ago. There is, however, some confusion in that country between the calico bass and the common sunfish, and there is no doubt that some of the latter species have been introduced into Germany under the mistaken belief that they were calico bass.

This bass is indigenous east of the Alleghenies from New Jersey southward to Georgia. It abounds in the Great Lake region, Mississippi valley south to Louisiana, most common northward, and it occurs in the Missouri. In the Ohio valley it was rather uncommon until its introduction in large numbers. It was introduced into the Susquehanna

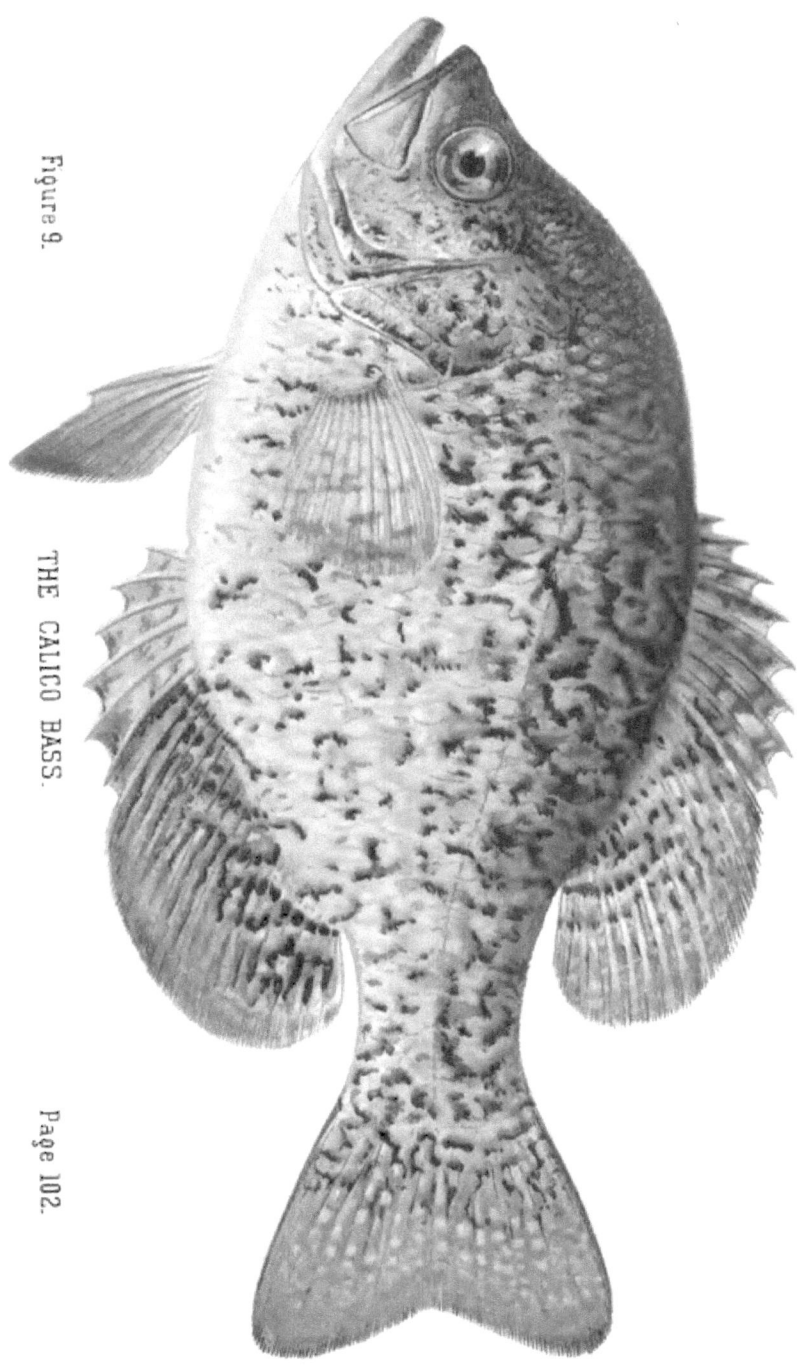

Figure 9. THE CALICO BASS. Page 102.

by the Pennsylvania Fish Commission and has become acclimatized there. Two very fine examples were obtained at Port Deposit in 1890. In October, 1877, one hundred and thirty of these fish, weighing from three-fourths to one pound, were obtained at Licking reservoir, about ten miles from Newark, Ohio, and carried in cans and planted in the Susquehanna at Harrisburg. In 1878 one thousand seven hundred and twelve calico bass were brought from Ohio and deposited at Hollidaysburg, in the Monongahela at Pittsburgh, the Lehigh and the Susquehanna at Harrisburg. The report for 1878 contains mention of the capture of this species thirty miles above Harrisburg at the Clark's Ferry dam.

This bass grows to a length of about one foot and a maximum weight of nearly three pounds, but the average weight is about one pound. It spawns in the spring and the close season in some states extends to June 1. Gravid females were caught near Havre de Grace, Md., in May. These were taken in the Susquehanna and Tidewater canal where the species is becoming rather abundant. The food of the calico bass consists of worms, small crustaceans and fishes. Although a native of deep sluggish waters of western rivers and lakes, it readily adapts itself to cold and rapid streams, and thrives even in small brooks. The species is suitable also for pond life, and may be kept in small areas of water provided they have sufficient depth. It does not prey upon other fishes, and its numerous stiff spines protect it from larger predaceous species. It swims in large schools and is often found in comparatively shoal water. The nest building habits have been described by Duclos from observations made at Versailles, France. This writer, unfortunately, had under observation both the calico bass and the common sunfish and his statements need confirmation. The game qualities of this bass are noteworthy. It is a vigorous and free biter, and its endurance is rather remarkable considering its size. As a food fish this species is highly prized, and its increase in rivers of Pennsylvania is greatly to be desired.

117. Pomoxys annularis RAFINESQUE.

The Crappie. (*Figure 59.*)

In the crappie the depth of the body is two-fifths of the total length not including the tail. The length of the head is one-third of the total; the mouth is oblique and larger than in the calico bass. The eye is about equal to the snout and nearly one-fourth the length of the head. The upper jaw nearly one-half length of head; the maxilla reaches slightly beyond the middle of the eye. The longest rays of the dorsal and anal are about one-half as long as head. The pectoral is longer than the ventral and reaches to above the origin of the anal. The ventral when laid back reaches to the vent.

D. VI, 16; A. VI, 17. Scales 7, 45, 13.

There is considerable variation in the the number of spines and rays in the dorsal and anal fins.

Color clear silvery olive, the sides mottled with dark greenish blotches. On the upper part of the body are traces of narrow vertical bars. The dorsal and caudal are mottled, but the anal is usually uniform pale.

Among the many names which have been applied to the crappie are: bachelor, newlight, Campbellite, sac-a-lait, bridge perch, strawberry perch, chinquapin perch, speckled perch, tin perch, goggle-eye, John demon, shad, white croppie and timber croppie.

In the lower Mississippi valley the crappie is one of the commonest fishes. It is abundant also in the Ohio valley and occurs rarely in Lake Erie. The Ohio, Illinois and Mississippi rivers are particularly noted for an abundance of crappies, and it is very plentiful in Lake Pontchartrain, Louisiana where it is one of the most highly prized of the smaller game fishes.

The crappie is a very general favorite for pond culture, can be readily transported and under favorable conditions multiplies prodigiously. Its range has been very much extended by artificial means. The best distinguishing marks between the crappie and the calico bass are the more elongated form of the crappie, the presence of six spines in the dorsal and the nearly uniform whitish color of the anal. In the crappie the greatest depth of the body is usually contained two and one-half times in the total length without the tail, while in the calico bass the depth equals one-half the length. These two species are so closely similar in size and habits that they are rarely distinguished except by ichthyologists.

The crappie grows to the length of about one foot and usually weighs one pound or less, but in a lake near St. Louis an individual weighing three pounds has been recorded.

Crappie fishing usually begins in June and lasts until the coming of cold weather. Large numbers of this fish are collected near Quincy, Illinois, for distribution to other waters. At Peoria, Illinois, Professor Forbes has taken them in March and April; he has found them also in Pistakee Lake and at Ottawa. Cedar Lake, Indiana, and King's Lake, Missouri, are celebrated crappie waters. Near Covington, Kentucky, in private ponds belonging to Joseph Schlosser there are myriads of crappie as well as other game fishes.

Prof. S. A. Forbes has studied the feeding habits of the crappie and finds that the young live chiefly upon *entomostraca* and small insect larvæ. The adults subsist upon the same food when obtainable, but in times of scarcity they feed to some extent upon other fishes. Small minnows and darters have been found in their stomachs. In the autumn Prof. Forbes has found a larger percentage of small fishes, sometimes constituting nearly two-fifths of their food. The helgramite is eaten by the crappie. In cold weather it does not consume one-fourth the amount of food which it takes in the early spring. The crappie prefers still waters, thriving even in warm and muddy water, and has been taken in large numbers in mid-summer at depths of only a few feet; in cold weather it retires to deeper water, becomes rather sluggish and takes little food. Dr. Henshall states that the crappie is found about dams and in deep still portions of streams and ponds, especially about logs, brush and drift.

The crappie is a very free biter and can be caught readily with minnows or worms. Spoon bait has been successfully used in trolling for this species. It is recorded that two men have taken a thousand crappies in three days' fishing with hook and line. As the fish is gregarious, congregating in large schools, and fearless, it can be taken in the immense numbers cited. The best bait for crappie is a small shiner. It rises well also to the artificial fly. As a food fish this is one of the best in our inland waters and its adaptability for life in artificial ponds should make it a favorite with fish culturists.

Genus **AMBLOPLITES** Rafinesque.

118. Ambloplites rupestris (Rafinesque).

The Rock Bass. (*Figure 16.*)

The rock bass has a robust, oblong body; its depth is contained two and one-third times in the total length without caudal, the head two and four-fifths in this same length. The caudal peduncle is stout, almost as deep as long. The dorsal profile is rather steep, strongly concave over eye. The eye is large, about one-fourth length of head, equal to snout. The mouth is large, the maxillary reaching to vertical from posterior end of pupil. The heavy lower jaw projects slightly. The vomer, palatines, tongue and pterygoid bones all toothed; those on the tongue in a single patch. The pharyngeal teeth are sharp. The opercle ends in two flat points; preopercle serrated at its angle. Gill-rakers long and strong, less than ten in number. Six branchiostegals. Scales large; those on the cheeks in about eight rows. Caudal rather deeply emarginate. The dorsal base is about one and one-half times as long as that of the anal. The spines of both fins are stout and rather short. The first spine of the dorsal is over the seventh scale of the lateral line, and the last spine is over the twenty-fifth scale. The first soft ray is over the twenty-sixth scale and the last ray over the thirty-fifth. The anal origin is under the middle of the spinous dorsal and the last anal ray is opposite the last dorsal ray. First dorsal spine shortest, one-half length of longest spine which is about three fifths as long as the longest ray. The spines and rays of the anal are in about the same proportion to each other as are those of the dorsal, the first spine being the shortest and the longest about three-fifths as long as the longest anal ray. The soft portions of the dorsal and anal are high and rounded. The pectoral is rather short and broad. The ventral long and slender, directly under base of pectoral. The lateral line is complete, placed high on body and follows the contour of the back. D. XI, 11; A. VI, 11. Scales 5-46-14.

The specimen described, No. 9101, United States National Museum, nine inches long, was collected at Ecorse, Michigan.

The rock bass is known under a variety of names. Among them are the following: red-eye or red-eyed perch, goggle-eye and lake bass. It is found in lower Canada, Vermont and throughout the Great Lake region, west to Manitoba, and it is native in Minnesota and Dakota; southward it ranges through the Mississippi valley to Texas. In the Ohio valley it is very common, while in the Middle Atlantic states, east of the Alleghenies, it has probably been introduced. Its existence in the Susquehanna has been known for about twenty years.

Whether it is indigenous in Pennsylvania waters is uncertain. It has been introduced into some parts of Virginia, while in other portions of that state it is native. It is indigenous in North Carolina. Its distribution in Pennsylvania has of late years been greatly extended through the efforts of the Fish Commission and it is now well established in the Delaware, especially in its upper waters.

Under favorable circumstances as to water and food supply the rock bass grows to a length of fourteen inches and a weight of two pounds. It increases in depth and thickness with age. The largest example we have examined is one of two pounds weight, length fourteen inches, from the James river, Va., taken near Richmond. Dr. Wm. Overton reports that rock bass weighing three and three-fourths pounds have been taken in his vicinity at Stony Creek, Va.

In February and March this fish frequents the mouths of small streams and in summer it seeks shady places under high banks or projecting rocks. The species is gregarious, going in large schools. It thrives where there is not much current and is very well adapted for culture in artificial ponds. It is as common in lakes and ponds as in the streams. Sluggish, pure, dark water suits it best.

The fishing season begins in June and lasts until the approach of cold weather.

The rock bass feeds upon worms, crustaceans and larvæ of insects early in the season; later its food consists of minnows and crawfish. The young feed upon insects and their larvæ.

The spawning season is May and June and gravelly shoals are resorted to for depositing the eggs.

The rock bass bites very freely and is a fair game fish and excellent for the table. It fights vigorously, but its endurance is not great. Suitable baits are white grubs, crickets, grasshoppers, crawfish and small minnows. Common earthworms are also successfully used. Dr. Henshall recommends for fly fishing a light trout fly rod of five or six ounces, light click reel, enamelled line, size G, and a fine trout leader. The flies he recommends are Montreal, ibis, soldier, professor, aureole and polka, also the brown, red and ginger hackles. He would tie them on drawn gut snells on No. 5 to 7 Sproat hooks. For bait fishing the Doctor recommends a light cane rod, ten feet long, weighing four or five ounces, with a No. 9 twisted silk line as long as the rod, a three-foot leader of the finest gut, No. 4 or 5 Sproat hooks tied on drawn gut and a quill float. In bait casting from a reel instead of the twisted silk line he would substitute one of braided silk, size H.

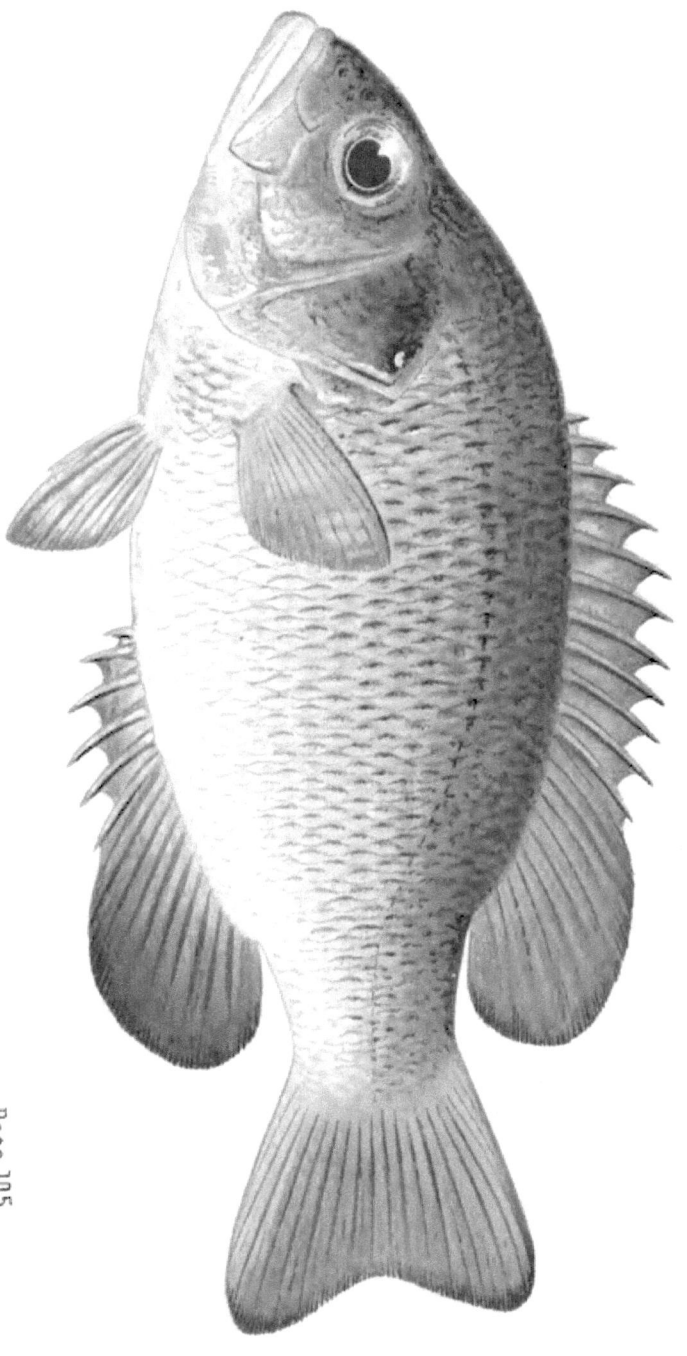

Figure 10.

THE ROCK BASS.

Page 105.

Genus **ACANTHARCHUS** Gill.

119. Acantharchus pomotis (Baird).

The Mud Sunfish.

The mud sunfish has an oblong and moderately elongate body, its greatest depth near the vent two-fifths of the total length without the caudal. The greatest thickness is a little less than one-half the depth. The caudal peduncle is short and deep, its least depth two-fifths of greatest depth of body. The head is moderately large, rather more than one-third of total length without the caudal, its width equal to the length of its postorbital part. The snout is very short and obtuse, its length about one-half that of the eye. The eye is placed high, its diameter contained three and two-thirds times in the length of the head. The interorbital space is slightly convex, its width three-fourths the length of the eye. The mouth is large, the maxilla broadly expanded behind and reaching nearly to below the hind margin of the eye. A well developed supplemental maxillary bone two-thirds as long as the eye; six rows of scales on the cheeks. The operculum ends in two thin, flat points, between which there is a black spot about two-fifths as long as the eye; gill-rakers short and few; five developed on the first arch, the longest two-fifths as long as the eye. The spinous dorsal begins over the fifth scale of the lateral line; its base is as long as the head without the snout; the first spine is very short, one-half as long as the eye; the spines increase very gradually in length to the last, which is as long as the eye and snout combined; the soft dorsal base is two-thirds as long as that of the spinous dorsal; its rays are longer than the spines, the longest (fourth to sixth) about one-half as long as the head ; the anal begins under eighteenth scale of the lateral line; the first spine one-half as long as the eye; the spines increase in length to the last, which is one-third as long as the head; the rays are long, the longest (fourth) equal to postorbital length of head; the ventral reaches to the vent; the pectoral reaches to below the fifteenth scale of the lateral line; the caudal is rounded, its middle rays five-sevenths as long as the head; the lateral line is complete and runs parallel to the dorsal outline. D. XII, 11; A. VII, 10; V. I, 5; P. 14. Scales 6-43-12. In spirits the color is dark brown; two or three dusky stripes on the sides below the lateral line; a dark shade around the nape extending backward behind the eye; two dark stripes across the cheeks and operculum; a dark opercular flap as described above; the fins unspotted. In life the fish is dark green. The example described, No. 17,844, United States National Museum, from New Jersey, is four and one-fifth inches long; it has more dorsal and anal spines than are usually present in this sunfish.

Prof. Baird, who first described the above species, called it the bass sunfish, because of its resemblance in shape to some of the basses. The mud sunfish ranges from New York to North Carolina in sluggish streams near the coast. Prof. Baird found it not rare in Cedar Swamp creek, near Beesley's Point, N. J., in 1854, and the writer obtained a single individual in Gravelly Run, not far from this locality, in 1887, associated with the pirate perch, striped mud minnow, barred killifish and young pickerel.

This fish reaches a length of six inches. It prefers muddy water and may even lie embedded in mud.

The colors of living specimens were described by Prof. Baird as follows: " Dark greenish olive, with three or four irregular longitudinal bands of dull greenish yellow, and occasionally cloudy spots of golden green. Sides of the head of this color, with three indistinct bands of dark olive. Iris purplish brown; cornea olive green. Fins quite uniform, very dark greenish olive, with darker margins, except the pectorals, which are light olivaceous, and the ventrals, the spinous rays of which are uncolored. Some specimens may be better described as dark golden green, with longitudinal bands of dark olive, broken up by cloudings of greenish."

Genus **ENNEACANTHUS** Gill.

120. Enneacanthus obesus (Baird).

The Banded Sunfish.

The body of the banded sunfish is elliptical in form, its depth more than one-half total length without caudal; its thickness equals two-fifths of its depth. The caudal peduncle is short and stout, its least depth one-third greatest depth of body; the head is short, two-fifths of total length without the caudal; the snout is very short and oblique, its length about two-thirds of the diameter of the eye, which is one-third as long as the head and exceeds the width of the interorbital space; the mouth is oblique, moderate in size, the maxilla broadly expanded posteriorly and reaching to below the middle of the eye; a supplemental maxillary bone; a black opercular flap two-thirds as long as the eye; scales on cheeks in four rows; gill-rakers short and spiny, thirteen developed on the first arch, the longest scarcely one-half as long as the eye. The first dorsal spine is over the pectoral base, minute, less than one-half as long as the second, which is two-thirds as long as the eye; the spines increase in size to the last, which is one-half as long as the head; the fourth and longest soft ray is two-thirds as long as the head; the ventral begins a little behind the pectoral base; the spine is two-fifths as long as the head; the fin reaches to the second anal ray, its longest ray produced into a filament; the anal begins under the thirteenth scale of the lateral line; the base is two-thirds as long as the head; the first spine is two-thirds as long as the second, which is as long as the eye; the last spine is as long as the eye and snout combined; the anal rays increase in length to the fifth, which is as long as the head without the snout; the pectoral is below the median line and reaches to above the third anal spine; the caudal is rounded, the middle rays as long as the head without the snout; the lateral line is imperfect after the seventeenth to the nineteenth scale. D. IX, 11; A. III, 10; V. I, 5; P. 12. Scales 5-32-10. The type of the species, No. 6538, United States National Museum, from Beesley's Point, N. J., is here described; it is three and three-fourths inches long.

The banded sunfish inhabits coastwise streams from Massachusetts to Florida. It occurs in southeastern Pennsylvania but is rare.

This species grows to a length of three inches. It is olive green in color, with five to eight dark cross bars intermingled with golden or purplish spots. There are lines and spots also on the cheeks. The flap on the opercle contains a velvety black spot with a purple border. Below the eye there is a dark bar. This is a beautiful little species but has no economic importance.

121. Enneacanthus simulans (Cope).

The Blue-spotted Sunfish.

The blue-spotted sunfish has an elliptical body, its greatest depth one-half of its total length without the caudal, and its thickness nearly two-fifths of its depth. The caudal peduncle is short, its least depth one-third of the greatest depth of body; the head is moderate in size, three-eighths of the total length without the caudal; the snout is very short and oblique, its length two-thirds that of the eye, which is nearly one-third as long as the head; the mouth is moderate in size, oblique, the broadly-expanded maxilla nearly reaching to below front of pupil; the lower jaw projects slightly; the operculum ends in two flat points, between which there is a dark spot two-thirds as long as the eye, and bordered below by a narrow pearly stripe; the gill-rakers are short and stout, eleven developed on the first arch, the longest one-third as long as the eye; four rows of scales on the cheeks; the spinous dorsal begins over the fourth scale of the lateral line; its base is two-thirds as long as the head; the first spine is nearly one-half as long as the eye; the spines gradually increase in length to the fourth, which is equal to those that follow it and to the length of the postorbital part of the head; the fifth and longest soft ray equals in length the head without the snout; the last soft ray equals the postorbital part of the head in length; the anal origin is under the fourteenth scale of the lateral line; the base of the fin is as long as the head without the snout; the first spine is one-fourth as long as the head; the third and longest equals length of postorbital part of head; the third and fourth soft rays are longest, equal to the head without the snout; the ventral reaches to the second anal ray, its spine equal in length to postorbital part of head; the pectoral is placed below the median line of the body; it reaches to below the fourteenth scale of the lateral line; the caudal is rounded, its middle rays three-fourths as long as the head; the lateral line is usually complete, sometimes imperfect on one side. D. IX. 11; A. III, 10; V. I, 5; P. 11. Scales 4-31-10. In spirits the color is brownish; about seven or eight rows of scales below the lateral line with pearly blotches forming interrupted stripes; a dark band under the eye; the dorsal, anal and caudal profusely spotted with roundish, pearly spots; young individuals are obscurely banded; in life the spots of the male are blue, and the fins are higher than in the female. The specimens described No. 20,356, United States National Museum, are from Trenton, N. J. The largest is three inches long.

The blue-spotted sunfish is found from New Jersey to South Carolina, and is very common in southeastern Pennsylvania according to Cope. It is a small species, not much exceeding the banded sunfish in length. In the male the head, body, dorsal, caudal and anal fins are profusely covered with bright, round, sky-blue spots; the opercle bears a pearly-blue spot. The female is not so brightly colored as the male, and the fins are not so high; the spots, also, are fainter. The young are faintly barred; the general color of adults is dark olive. It is a handsome species but not used for food.

Genus **MESOGONISTIUS** Gill.

122. Mesogonistius chætodon (Baird).

The Black-banded Sunfish. (*Figure 60.*)

The black-banded sunfish has an oblong body, its greatest depth one-half of the total length without caudal and its thickness one-third of the depth. The caudal peduncle is short and slender, its least depth equal to the thickness of the body. The head is moderate in size, its length one-third of the total without caudal. The snout is short and oblique, two-thirds as long as the eye, which is one-third as long as the head. The mouth is small, obliquely placed, the jaws about equal in front. The maxilla is not broadly expanded behind; it reaches to below the front of the eye. The operculum ends in two flat points and has a dark flap at its angle, which is one-half as long as the eye. Scales on the cheeks in three rows. The gill-rakers are comparatively long and slender; thirteen developed on the first arch, the longest one-third as long as the eye. The spinous dorsal begins over the third scale of the lateral line; the length of its base equals five-sixths that of the head. The first spine is minute, scarcely one-half as long as the eye, the second is nearly as long as the eye, the fourth (longest) about one-half length of head; from thence they decrease in length to the one before the last which is two-fifths as long as the head; the last is nearly one-half as long as the head. The base of the soft portion is as long as the head without the snout; the fourth and longest ray is as long as the base of the fin. The last ray is half length of longest. The anal origin is under the twelfth or thirteenth scale of the lateral line. The first spine is short, two-thirds as long as the second, and a little less than the eye in length; the third and longest is as long as the eye and snout combined. The longest soft rays (fourth to sixth) are as long as the head without the snout, and the last ray is about one-half as long as the longest. The ventral reaches to the first anal ray, its length about equal to the head without the snout. The pectoral reaches to the ventral and is slightly longer than that fin. The caudal is convex, its middle rays nearly as long at the head. The lateral line follows the outline of the back.

D. X, 12; A. III, 12; V. I, 5; P. 13. Scales 4–31–11.

The length of the specimen here described, No. 20,354, United States National Museum, from Trenton, N. J., is three inches.

This species was first described by Professor S. F. Baird, from specimens obtained by him in Cedar Swamp creek, Cape May county, New Jersey, in 1854. The Professor found it abundant in the muddy water of that creek. He described the colors as follows: "General color dirty white, with clouds of olivaceous; the tints clearer in smaller specimens; sides of abdomen silvery. Six well defined vertical bands of black on each side, covering each a breadth of two or three scales; the first passes through the pupil across the cheeks; the second is posterior to the edge of the preoperculum, but interrupted in the middle so as not to cross the operculum; the third is posterior to the first ray of the dorsal. * * * * Between the third and fourth bands are short bars, one proceeding from the dorsal, the other from the ventral outline in the same vertical line, and parallel to the others. This may in fact be described as an additional bar interrupted in the middle. Fins greenish yellow, with mottlings of dark. Ventrals black centrally, yellow posteriorly, and deep red on the two anterior rays and intermediate membrane. Dorsal with the three anterior rays and their membrane black; the membrane between the third and fourth rays red. Pectoral plain. In large specimens the tints are darker, and the ground color tinged with olivaceous. The red of the dorsal is not distinct. Length three inches."

Genus **LEPOMIS** Rafinesque.

123. Lepomis cyanellus Rafinesque.

The Green Sunfish. (*Figure 61.*)

The green sunfish has an oblong body, its greatest depth at the ventrals equaling three-sevenths of the total length without caudal, and its thickness three-eighths of its depth. The least depth of the caudal peduncle equals four-fifths of its length and about one-third of greatest body depth. The head is one-third of total length without the caudal; its width nearly one-half its length. The snout is moderately pointed and as long as the eye, which is two-ninths as long as the head. The interorbital space is nearly flat, its width a little greater than the length of the eye. The nape is moderately arched. The mouth is moderately large, the maxilla not widely expanded behind and reaching to below the front of the pupil. Supplemental maxillary bone well developed. Seven rows of scales on the cheeks. Gill rakers short and stiff, eleven developed on the first arch; the longest one-third as long as the eye. A short, broad opercular flap, its width and length about equal and two-thirds length of eye. The spinous dorsal begins over the sixth scale of the lateral line; its base nearly equal in length to the head; the first spine is two-thirds as long as the eye; the spines increase gradually in length to the seventh, which is two-fifths as long as the spinous dorsal base and one-half length of head without the snout. The tenth spine is nearly as long as the seventh. The seventh and longest soft ray is one-half as long as the head; the last ray is one-third as long as the head. The base of the soft dorsal is about two-thirds as long as the spinous dorsal base. The anal begins under the twenty-fourth scale of the lateral line; the first spine is three-fourths as long as the eye; the second is nearly twice and the third two and one-half times as long as the first. The length of the anal base equals one-fifth of the total without the caudal. The fourth and longest anal ray is as long as the postorbital part of the head; the last ray is a little more than one-half as long as the fourth. The caudal fin is emarginate, the middle rays three-fourths as long as the external. The ventral reaches to the vent; its spine one-half as long as the head without the snout; its length one-fifth of the total without the caudal. The pectoral reaches to below the seventeenth scale of the lateral line. The lateral line follows the outline of the back. D. X, 11; A. III, 10; V. I, 5; P. 13. Scales 7-47-14. In spirits the color is pale brown, the fins paler. The opercular flap has a dark spot as described above. In life there is generally a black blotch on the hinder part of the dorsal and anal; the ground color is greenish with a brassy tinge on the sides; the lower parts yellowish; blue spots and gilt borders usually ornament the scales and faint dark bands are often present. The dorsal, anal and caudal have blue or green markings, and the anal is margined in front with orange. The iris is red and the cheeks are striped with blue. The specimen described, No. 36,313, United States National Museum, from the Sac River, Mo., is seven inches long.

The blue-spotted sunfish, also known as the green sunfish and redeye, occurs from the Great Lake region throughout the Ohio and Mississippi valleys south to Mexico. It does not occur in the Middle Atlantic states east of the Alleghenies. The species reaches a length of seven inches and is an extremely variable one. Professor Cope refers to it as a good pan fish and states that it is abundant in the Ohio basin. In the Ohio valley it is one of the characteristic fishes, inhabiting ponds and ascending small streams. It frequents deep holes and the shelter of overhanging roots.

124. Lepomis macrochirus Rafinesque.

The body is oblong, its greatest depth contained two and two-fifths times in the total length without caudal. The head is one-third of total without caudal. The mouth is large and the snout is pointed. Mucous pores on the head well developed. Five to seven rows of scales on the cheeks. Opercular flap small. Eleven slender gill rakers. The dorsal spines are high. Pectorals long, reaching to the anal. D. X, 10; A. III, 10; scales, 6-42-15. The colors are described below.

The chain-sided sunfish, called by Prof. Cope the chain side, is one of the small and very handsome species of the sunfish family. It does not exceed five inches in length, and is known only in the Ohio valley, where it is rare.

This species is easily distinguished by its mottled coloration, the chain like bars making it conspicuous. It is not a food fish but is very hardy and active and consequently desirable for the aquarium. Its voracity is said to be remarkable.

The sides are steel blue overlaid with bronze orange spots arranged so as to form chain-like bars. The fins are mottled with bronze, and generally with a pale orange border. The sides of the head have a purplish tint.

125. Lepomis pallidus (MITCHILL).

The Blue Sunfish. (*Figure 62.*)

The blue sunfish has a deep, elliptical body, its greatest depth at the ventrals one-half of the total length without the caudal; the thickness equals about one-third of the depth. The caudal peduncle is short and deep, its least height nearly one-half length of head. The head is one-third of the total length without the caudal; its width equals one-half of its length. The snout is short, obtuse and oblique, less than the eye in length. The interorbital space is slightly convex, its width one-third of the length of the head. The mouth is small, oblique, the maxilla not greatly expanded behind, reaching to below the front of the eye. The width of the preorbital equals one-half the diameter of the eye. Scales on the cheeks in five rows. The gill-rakers are short and stout, about fifteen developed on the first arch, the longest little more than one-fourth as long as the eye. No supplemental maxillary bone. No palatine teeth. The lower pharyngeal bone narrow, with teeth in only about four series, chiefly acute. The spinous dorsal begins over the fourth scale of the lateral line; the spines are stout, the first as long as the snout and one-half as long as the fifth and longest; the spines following the fifth are not much shorter. The first seven soft rays are about equal in length and one-half as long as the head; the last ray is one-third as long as the head. The base of the spinous dorsal is nearly as long as the head; the soft dorsal is two-thirds as long as the spinous. The anal begins under the twentieth scale of the lateral line; its base is as long as the head without the snout; the spines are short and heavy, the first five-sixths as long as the eye, the second a little longer than the eye, and the third one-half as long as the head without the snout; the longest rays are the fourth to the seventh, which are one-half as long as the head. The caudal is notched, its middle rays three-fourths as long as the outer. The ventral reaches almost to the anal, its spine being one-half as long as the head without the snout. The pectoral is broad and reaches to below the eighteenth scale of the lateral line. The lateral line follows the curve of the back.

D. X, 11; A. III, 10; V. I, 5; P. 13; scales 7-41-15.

In spirits the color is pale brown, the scales with a pale margin. A large dark blotch on the hind part of the soft dorsal. A black opercular flap, its width and length about equal, shorter than the eye. The living fish varies with age from light green to dark green. The young have the sides silvery, tinged with purple and with many vertical greenish bands, which are sometimes chain-like. The dark blotch of the soft dorsal is often indistinct in the young. In very old individuals the belly is often coppery red. The specimen described, No. 27,845, United States National Museum, from Peoria, Ill., is seven and one-half inches long.

The propriety of using Mitchill's name *pallidus* for the blue sunfish is extremely doubtful. His description can be much more readily referred to a species of *Enneacanthus* and the locality "near New York" probably does not possess this sunfish among its native species.

The blue sunfish, blue bream, copper-nosed bream or dollardee, is a very widely diffused species and varies greatly in size, color and length of the ear flap. It is found in the Great Lakes and throughout the Mississippi valley to Mexico. East of the Alleghenies it ranges from New Jersey to Florida. In Pennsylvania it is abundant only in the western part of the state including Lake Erie. Dr. Abbott has recorded it from the Delaware river.

The blue sunfish grows to a length of nearly one foot and individuals weighing nearly two pounds are on record. Adults, however, average eight inches in length with a weight of less than one pound. The size of the individuals depends on the habitat. In large lakes and streams it grows to a greater size than in small bodies of water. In southern waters it attains to a larger size than in northern waters. It lives in ponds as well as in streams and thrives in warm waters. It is considered equal to the rock bass as a pan fish and can very readily be taken by hook fishing.

126. Lepomis auritus LINNÉ.

The Long-eared Sunfish. (*Figure 63.*)

The long-eared sunfish has an oblong, moderately elongate body, its depth nearly one-half of the length without the caudal and its thickness a little more than one-third of its depth. The caudal peduncle is moderately short, its least depth three-fourths of its length and one-third of greatest depth of body. The head is rather large, its length without the flap one-third of the total without caudal; its width one-half of its length. The space between the eyes is convex, its width a little more than the length of the snout, which is two-ninths as long as the head including the flap. The upper edge of the snout is oblique. The eye is one-fourth as long as the head without the flap. The mouth is moderate in size, the maxilla not very broadly expanded behind and extending to below the front of the pupil. The scales on the cheeks are very small, in about eight rows. The opercular flap is long, narrow and pointed, its length equal to that of the snout and about twice its width. The gill-rakers are short and stout, about eleven developed on the first arch, the longest one-third as long as the eye. The spinous dorsal begins over the sixth scale of the lateral line; its base is two-sevenths of total length without caudal. The first spine is two-thirds as long as the second, which is as long as the eye; the fourth (longest) is one and one-half times as long as the eye; after the fourth the spines slightly decrease in length, the last being little longer than the eye. The fifth (longest) soft ray is as long as the base of the soft dorsal and equal to the snout and eye combined. The last soft ray is a little more than one-half as long as the longest. The anal begins under the twenty-first scale of the lateral line; the length of its base equals that of the soft dorsal; the spines are short and stout. The first two-thirds as long as the second and one-half as long as the third, which is one and one-half times as long as the eye; the fourth (longest) soft ray is as long as the base of the fin; the last ray is two-thirds of this length. The caudal is emarginate, the middle rays two-thirds as long as the outer. The ventral reaches beyond the vent, sometimes to the origin of the anal. The ventral spine is one-half as long as the fin. The pectoral has a broad base and extends to below the nineteenth scale of the lateral line.

D. X, 10; A. III, 9; V. I, 5; P. 14. Scales 7-45-13. The lateral line follows the curve of the back.

In spirits the color is pale brown; the fins somewhat paler; the ear flap black; a brownish streak in front of the eye and another horizontal one beneath it.

In life the color is olivaceous; the belly, especially in breeding males, orange. The scales on the sides have reddish spots on a bluish ground. Dorsal, anal and caudal usually yellowish. The stripes on the head are bluish.

The specimen described, No. 33,152, United States National Museum, from Bainbridge, Pa., is five and one-half inches long.

The long-eared sunfish has a very extensive range and is known under many common names, among which are the following: Bream, red-tailed bream, red-head bream, red-bellied bream, perch, sun perch, red-bellied perch and red breast.

8 FISH.

The species is common in streams east of the Alleghenies from Maine to Florida, and in tributaries of the Gulf of Mexico to Louisiana. In the southern states the typical long-eared sunfish is replaced by a variety with larger scales on the cheeks and belly and a dusky blotch on the posterior part of the soft dorsal fin.

In size the long-eared sunfish averages about eight inches when adult and weighs about one pound. In the South the size and number of individuals is greatly increased. This fish feeds upon worms, insect larvae, crustaceans, mollusks and small fishes. In the Susquehanna this is one of the commonest of the sunfishes, in the Delaware, also, it is abundant and reaches a large size. Although not important commercially, it is taken in large numbers on the hook and is an excellent food fish. It takes any kind of live bait very readily and furnishes good sport also with the artificial fly.

127. Lepomis megalotis (Rafinesque).

The Red-bellied Bream. (Figure 64.)

The red-bellied bream has a deep, oblong and thin body; its greatest depth at the ventrals one-half of the total length without caudal; its thickness less than one-third of its depth. The caudal peduncle is rather short and deep, its least depth two-thirds of its length and nearly one-third of the greatest depth of body. The head is moderately large, its length without flap about one-third of the total length without caudal. The back is strongly arched in front. The space between the eyes is very slightly convex, its width greater than the diameter of the eye. The snout is moderately short and obtuse, as long as the eye, which is one-fourth as long as the head without the flap, or one-fifth as long including the flap. The mouth is rather small and oblique, the lower jaw very slightly projecting. The maxilla is not very broadly expanded behind; it reaches a little past front of eye. Scales on the cheeks in five rows. The gill rakers are short and stout, eleven or twelve developed on the first arch the longest scarcely one-third the diameter of the eye. The dark opercular spot is one and one-third times as long as the eye; its width nearly equals the diameter of the eye. The spinous dorsal begins over the fourth scale of the lateral line, its base about one-third of the total without caudal; the first spine is two-thirds as long as the second, and nearly one-half as long as the fourth (longest), which is as long as the lower jaw; the fifth and sixth are about equal to the fourth, the seventh, eighth and ninth are shorter, and the tenth is a little longer than the ninth; the sixth and longest soft ray is one-half as long as the head, including the flap, and the last ray is one-half as long as the sixth. The base of the soft dorsal is as long as the eye and snout combined. The anal begins under the nineteenth scale of the lateral line; the spines are short and stout, the first two-thirds as long as the second and one-half as long as the third, which is one-third as long as the head, including the flap. The fourth and fifth soft rays are longest, one-half as long as the head; the base of the anal equals one-half of the depth of the body. The ventral reaches to the second anal spine; its spine is one-third as long as the head and about one-half as long as the fin. The pectoral reaches to above the first anal ray and below the twenty-third scale of the lateral line. The caudal is emarginate, its middle rays three-fourths as long as the outer. The lateral line follows the outline of the back.

D. X, 11; A. III, 10; V. I, 5; P. 13. Scales 6-42-13.

In spirits the body is pale brown; the fins dusky and a large black blotch on the hind part of the soft dorsal as large as the eye; the opercular flap is black. There is also a faint trace of a dark blotch on the hind part of the anal. In life the adult has a red or pale blue margin on the opercular flap; the upper parts are mainly blue, the belly orange, the sides spotted with orange and having undulating vertical blue streaks. The lips are blue, the cheeks orange, striped with blue. Iris red. Snout with blue streaks. The dorsal, anal and caudal membranes are blue on the rays and orange between them.

The specimen described, No. 36,394, United States National Museum, from the Poteau river, Indian Territory, is seven inches long.

The red-bellied bream or long-eared sunfish is very abundant in the Ohio valley and also in tributaries of Lake Erie and Lake Michigan. It extends west to Dakota, south to South Carolina and Mexico, but is absent from Atlantic waters of the northern and middle states. It is especially abundant in small brooks. The species grows to a length of eight inches and is one of the handsomest of the sunfishes. The specific name is derived from the large opercular flap, generally spoken of as the ear-flap.

The sides are blue and orange, the blue occurring in undulating streaks, and the orange in spots. There are distinct blue stripes on the head. The thin membranes are generally orange and the rays blue. This fish is extremely variable and has been described under about twenty different names. According to Dr. Jordan it avoids muddy water and frequents deep still places in rivers and clear ponds. It runs into very small streams. The red-bellied bream is used for food and takes the hook very freely.

128. Lepomis gibbosus LINNÉ.

The Common Sunfish. (Figure 65.)

The body of the common sunfish is nearly ovate, its depth one-half of the total length without caudal, its thickness one-third of the depth. The caudal peduncle is short and compressed, its least depth less than the thickness of the body. The head is moderately large, one-third of the total length without caudal. Its width one-half of its length. The snout is short and depressed, its length four-fifths the diameter of the eye, which is one-fourth as long as the head. The interorbital space is nearly flat, its width one and one-half times the diameter of the eye. The mouth is small and oblique; the maxilla not much expanded behind and reaching to below the front of the eye. Scales on the cheeks in four rows. The opercular spot is short, less than two-thirds the diameter of the eye, and has a whitish margin behind. The gill-rakers are very short, moderately stout, ten or eleven developed on the first arch; the longest less than one-fourth the diameter of the eye. The spinous dorsal begins over the third scale of the lateral line; its base is as long as the head without the opercular flap; the first spine is two-thirds as long as the eye; the spines increase in size; the fourth, fifth and sixth being nearly equal in length and about as long as the eye and snout combined. The sixth and longest soft ray is as long as the postorbital part of the head, while the last ray is less than one-third as long as the head. The base of the soft dorsal is as long as that of the spinous dorsal. The anal origin is under the twenty-third scale of the lateral line. The anal base is two-thirds as long as the head; the first spine is about one-half as long as the third (longest), which is two-fifths as long as the head. The first and second rays are the longest, nearly as long as the base of the fin. The last ray is two-thirds as long as the first. The ventral reaches beyond the vent; its spine is one-half as long as the head without the snout. The pectoral reaches to above the anal origin. The caudal is emarginate, its middle rays four-fifths as long as the outer. The lateral line follows the curve of the back.

D. X, 12; A. III, 10; V. I, 5; P. 14. Scales 6-42-13.

In spirits the color is pale brownish, the opercular flap black with a narrow whitish margin behind and beneath, and the dorsal fin with faint dusky blotches. In life this is one of the most brilliant of sunfishes, the upper part being greenish olive with a bluish tinge; the sides profusely spotted with orange, the belly and lower fins orange and the dorsal and caudal fins bluish with orange spots. The cheeks are orange, with undulating blue stripes; the opercular flap is black, margined behind and underneath with bright scarlet.

The specimen described, No. 20,304, United States National Museum, from the Susquehanna at Havre de Grace, is nearly six inches long.

The common sunfish or sunny, pumpkin seed, bream, tobacco box, and pond sunfish, is one of the best known of the fishes of Pennsylvania. It is found from Maine westward through the Great Lake region to Minnesota and in the eastern states south to South Carolina. In western rivers, however, it is seldom found south of the latitude of Chicago. In Pennsylvania it is everywhere common, reaching its greatest size in tidewater where it forms a valuable article of food. It grows to a length of eight inches and a weight of about one-half pound. Its food is similar to that of the long-eared sunfish and it is one of the readiest biters known to the angler. The habits of this fish have been described by Dr. Theodore Gill and Mr. W. P. Seal. The latter states that the male, in the breeding season, is readily identified by his brighter coloration, conspicuous ear flaps and a luminous border around the fins while in the water. The nest is a depression in the mud, sand or gravel, hollowed out by means of the fins. In the Potomac he found a number of nests which were located from a few inches to several feet apart. The male watches the nest and drives away all intruders. The eggs are only about one-thirty-second of an inch in diameter and not very numerous. They are attached to stones and aquatic plants. Mr. Seal has reason to believe that the male alone is concerned in building the nest and in the care of the eggs and young.

Genus **MICROPTERUS** Lacépède.

129. Micropterus dolomieu Lacépède.

The Small-mouthed Black Bass. (*Figure 11.*)

The small-mouthed bass differs most markedly from the large-mouthed in the size of its jaws, the shallower notch in the dorsal fin and the smaller scales. There are about eleven rows of scales above the lateral line and seven below it—72 to 74 scales in the lateral line. The ninth spine of the dorsal is longer than the eye and fully two-thirds as long as the fifth and longest spine; the upper jaw extends backward to below the hind margin of the eye; the body is ovate-oblong in shape, its greatest depth about equal to length of the head and one-third of the total without caudal, becoming deeper with age; the eye is less than two-thirds as long as the snout and about one-sixth length of head; the pectoral is not much longer than the ventral and slightly more than one-half length of head; the soft dorsal and anal are more scaly at the base than in the large-mouthed species; the scales on the cheeks and breast are very much smaller than those on the middle of the sides. D. X, 13-15; A. III, 10.

The young are dull, yellowish-green, the sides mottled with darker spots which sometimes form short vertical bars; three dark stripes on the head; caudal yellowish

Figure 11. THE SMALL-MOUTHED BLACK BASS. Page 116.

at the base; a broad black band near middle of tail and a broad whitish margin behind. The dark lateral band characteristic of the large-mouthed species is not found in the small-mouth. In the adult the prevailing color is olive-green, the stripes on the head remaining more or less distinct.

One of the early names for the small-mouthed black bass is that of growler, which appears in the writings of Cuvier, who was under the impression that the name was applied because of a noise sometimes produced by this bass. At the time of his writing the name growler was pretty generally identified with the black bass. Among the names applied to this fish by Rafinesque are lake bass, big bass, spotted bass and achigan. He also mentions it under the names painted tail, bridge perch, yellow bass, gold bass, brown bass, dark bass, minny bass, little bass, hog bass, yellow perch, black perch, trout pearch, black pearch, streaked head, white trout and brown trout. In the southern states the small-mouthed form is known as the trout perch and jumper. In Alabama it is called mountain trout. Some persons style it the bronze backer. The most appropriate name and the one by which it is best known is that of black bass, or small-mouthed black bass.

This species is indigenous to the upper parts of the St. Lawrence basin, the Great Lake region and the basin of the Mississippi. East of the Alleghenies it is native to the headwaters of the Ocmulgee and Chattahoochee rivers, but north of these streams, although not originally an inhabitant of the waters, it has been widely distributed by artificial introduction. In Pennsylvania the introduction of black bass at State expense, according to the report of the commissioners, dates from October 26, 1870, as may be seen from the following extract:

"On October 26, 1870, the first black bass, about four hundred and fifty, from Harper's Ferry, were placed in the Delaware just below the Lehigh dam. The project was suggested and urged by the late Thaddeus Norris, and the funds for the purpose were raised by him and by Howard J. Reeder, Esq., and G. W. Stout, the latter raising in Easton three hundred and thirteen dollars and Mr. Norris about one thousand dollars in Philadelphia."

In the report for 1878 is to be found the following account of the success attending the efforts to acclimate this valuable fish:

"It is to be found in all the streams of any size and is making its way into the smaller streams. It occupies a river stretch of one thousand miles, and is estimated to be worth forty-five thousand dollars a year."

This bass does not grow so large as the large-mouthed, seldom exceeding eight pounds in weight, and averaging but two and one-half pounds. A fish of the latter weight will measure fifteen inches in length, while one of eight pounds would measure two feet.

The food of the black bass consists of crawfish, frogs, insects and their larvæ, minnows and other aquatic animals of suitable size. The young can be fed on small fresh water crustaceans, such as *Daphnia* and *Cyclops*.

Among the successful baits for this species are stone catfish, helgramites and crickets.

This bass prefers rapid water, is extremely active, and frequents clear, rapid-flowing streams where the water is pure, and thrives in greater elevations than those preferred by the large-mouthed. It hibernates in the winter and spawns in the shallow or gravelly bottoms in spring. It follows its prey into shallow water, and frequently leaps far out of the water in its efforts to escape from the hook or when frightened by the sudden approach of an enemy. It swims in schools, and is often found in the shelter of sunken logs and in the vicinity of large rocks.

The spawning season begins in March and ends in July. The period of incubation lasts from seven to fourteen days. The eggs are bound together in bands or ribbons by an adhesive substance. They adhere to stones on which they are deposited. The parent fish build nests and protect the eggs and young. In the Delaware the current is more rapid and the temperature lower than in the Susquehanna, hence the bass spawn earlier in the latter than in the Delaware. The spawning fish have nearly all left their spawning beds in the Susquehanna early in July, but at this time most of the nests in the Delaware are still full of eggs. By some writers it is believed that the female prepares the nest before the male joins her. The males fight for the possession of the female and are said to help the process of ejecting the eggs by biting or pressing the belly of the female. After the eggs are deposited the female guards the nest from the attacks of the crawfish and some other enemies. The young are consumed by many birds and by frogs and snakes, yet notwithstanding the numerous enemies of the black bass its multiplication has been rapid and enormous.

130. Micropterus salmoides (Lac.)
The Large-mouthed Black Bass. (*Figure 66.*)

The large-mouthed black bass takes its common name from the size of its jaws; the lower jaw projects very strongly and the maxilla in the adult extends beyond the hind margin of the eye. The depth of the body is about one-third of the total without caudal, and does not equal the length of the head. The eye is shorter than the snout, about one-sixth of the length of the head. The pectoral is half as long as the head, much longer than the ventral. The spinous dorsal is very low, its ninth and tenth spines not so long as the eye; its fourth spine longest, about one-fourth length of head. Seven to eight scales above the lateral line, below sixteen and in the lateral line about 68. The color is greenish, silvery below. The young have a broad dark lateral band.

D. X, 13; A. III, 10–11.

This species may best be distinguished from the small-mouthed black bass by the size of its mouth and the number of rows of scales above the lateral line. The young of the small-mouthed species, also, never have a dark lateral band.

Common names for this species are Oswego bass, river bass, green bass, moss bass, bayou bass, trout, jumper, chub and Welshman. Throughout the North it is generally known as bass, in Virginia and North Carolina as chub and in Florida and west to Texas as trout. The average weight of the large-mouthed bass in southern waters is less than five pounds, and still less in northern waters. In Florida it attains a large size, as much as three feet in length and a weight of twenty-five pounds. Its growth and size depend upon the waters where found, the natural food supply of small fish, crawfish, frogs, etc.

The large-mouthed bass has a wide distribution, being indigenous to the eastern United States, from Manitoba to Florida and Texas, except New England and the Middle Atlantic states east of the Alleghenies, where it has been extensively introduced. It inhabits the fresh water ponds, lakes and sluggish streams. It is found also at the mouths of rivers emptying into the Gulf of Mexico, where the water is brackish. It is a very active fish; its movements are affected by seasonal changes, search for food and places of spawning. In polluted streams the bass are often compelled by the impurities to seek new haunts in pure water.

The young bass feed upon animal food at an early age. The large-mouthed bass is said to be more cannibalistic than the small-mouthed. Small fishes (minnows) of all kinds, crawfish, frogs, insects and their larvæ, and aquatic animals of all kinds, suitable in size, make up the diet of this fish. It feeds both at the surface and on the bottom, pursuing its prey with great activity. When surrounded by seines or caught on hooks this species will often leap five or six feet out of the water, and its habit of jumping over the cork lines of seines has given it the name of "jumper."

In cold weather the bass seeks deep places, often hibernating under rocks, sunken logs and in the mud. Favorite localities are under overhanging and brush-covered banks, in the summer, and among aquatic plants where the fish lies in wait for its prey. The spawning season of the large-mouthed bass is about the same as that of the small-mouthed species, beginning in April and lasting until July. Its eggs are adhesive, sticking to stones during the incubation period, which lasts from one to two weeks according to the temperature of the water. The young bass remain in the nest a week or ten days, and at the age of two weeks will measure about three-fourths of an inch in length. In suitable waters it is estimated that the large-mouthed bass will weigh at the age of three years from two pounds to four pounds.

FAMILY **PERCIDÆ** (THE PERCHES).

GENUS **ETHEOSTOMA** RAFINESQUE.

131. Etheostoma pellucida BAIRD.

The Sand Darter.

The body is slender, cylindrical and translucent. Its depth about one-seventh of the total length without caudal. The length of head two-ninths of the total. The maxilla reaches about to the eye, which is large and placed high. Interorbital space narrow, grooved. The pectorals extend to tips of ventrals and half way to vent. Scales on the cheeks, gill-covers and temporal region. The sides of the body with nearly smooth scales, not closely placed and more or less concealed in the skin. Scales of the lateral line and caudal peduncle more developed than the others. Space in front of the dorsal thinly scaled.

D. X, 10; A. I, 8.

Lateral line 75-80; six scales above it. The scales are thin, translucent, finely punctulated with black. Bluish blotches along the back and the lateral line; the median series united by a gilt line. The fins are pale.

The sand darter inhabits the Ohio valley and a portion of the Mississippi valley. It runs into several varieties one of which is without scales on the nape and the anterior portion of the sides except on the lateral line. Another variety from southern Illinois, southward and westward, has the nape more or less closely scaled, the scales firmer and rougher than in the typical form and with a dark bar along the base of the soft dorsal.

The species was first described by Prof. Baird from the Ohio valley. It reaches a length of two or three inches and is abundant in clear sandy streams. Its habits have been fully described in the *American Naturalist*, February, 1887, p. 86. The sand darter feeds upon insect larvæ, small crustaceans and other animals of suitable size.

132. Etheostoma olmstedi Storer.

The Tessellated Darter. (*Figure 67.*)

The head is contained four and one-fourth times in total length; depth five and one-fourth times. The cheeks and opercles are scaly; nape and breast naked. The lateral line is complete with about fifty scales.

D. IX, 14; A. I, 9.

The color is olivaceous; fins with many narrow bars; the back tessellated; sides with blotches and zigzag markings. Head in spring males black, a dark streak forward from the eye and another one downward.

The common darter or tessellated darter is found from Massachusetts to Georgia. It is replaced in Cayuga Lake and some other regions to the southward by a black spotted variety, which differs from the common form still further in having the nape and breast closely scaled.

This species grows to a length of three and one-half inches and is a near relative of the Johnny darter (*Boleosoma nigrum*) of Rafinesque.

This darter secretes itself on the bottom in small clear brooks, swimming rapidly for a short distance when alarmed. The sexes are very different in appearance, the males having higher and more brightly colored fins than the females. The males are also larger than the females and in the spring are much spotted with black.

133. Etheostoma nigrum Rafinesque.

The Johnny Darter.

This is one of the small species, attaining a length of only two and one-half inches. It is found on the bottom in clear small brooks, where it lies partly concealed by sand, and changes its colors according to its surroundings. The body is slender, spindle-shaped. The conical head is contained slightly more than four times and the depth about five times, in the total length. The snout is somewhat decurved. Mouth small and the lower jaw included within the upper. The gill-covers are scaly, cheeks naked except in occasional individuals, and the nape is usually scaled. The fins are high, but lower and smaller than in other species of *Boleosoma*.

Color olivaceous; the back with brown tessellations; sides with many w-shaped blotches. The head is speckled above; in males generally black. In the breeding season the whole anterior portion of the male is often black. A dark line forward from the eye and sometimes another one downward.

The Johnny darter ranges from western Pennsylvania to Missouri and Dakota. In the Great Lake region it is abundant and is one of the commonest darters in the streams of Ohio. It does not occur in eastern Pennsylvania.

134. Etheostoma æsopus (Cope).

The Spotted Darter.

[*Boleosoma æsopus* Cope, Proc. Amer. Philos. Society, 1870, p. 270.]

"The dorsal line descends regularly from the base of the first dorsal fin to between the orbits, and then curves more abruptly to the mouth. Mouth terminal; eye four times in head, once in advance of its front rim. The dorsal line descends from the first dorsal fin, to a somewhat contracted caudal peduncle. Dorsal fins much elevated, VII-14. Pectorals a little elongate, not reaching vent, but little exceeding the very moderate ventrals. A. 10. Scales 5-47-8. Color light brown, with six small dark dorsal spots, and ten similar small spots on the lateral line. A black bar round muzzle, and one below eye.

"Total length, 26.6 lines; of tail, 4.3 lines; of pectoral fin, 5.2 lines; depth at first dorsal, 4.6 lines; at nape, 3.4 lines; of caudal peduncle, 2.3 lines."

The form of this fish is rather that of a *Pœcilichthys*, while the absence of spinous anal rays is peculiar to the present species. From the number of rays, ten, in the anal, it is probable that the missing spinous ray is represented by the first cartilaginous ray, and is not wanting. In general it is so near to the *B. olmstedi*, as not to be removed from the genus.

"Found in the Loyalsock creek, in the Allegheny region, in Lycoming county, Pennsylvania, by Aubrey H. Smith, of Philadelphia."

This is a little species and has received no common name. Dr. Jordan thinks it may be identical with *B. effulgens* of Girard, which grows to a length of two and one-half inches, and that this again may be only a variety of the Johnny darter (*B. nigrum*.)

The species was originally described by Prof. Cope from an example two and one-fourth inches long which was taken in Loyalsock creek, a tributary of the Allegheny river. No other specimens of the species have since been recorded.

135. Etheostoma blennioides Rafinesque.

The Green-sided Darter.

The body is stout and long; the head moderate in size, its length contained four and one-half times in the total and slightly exceeding the depth of the body. Mouth small; lower jaw included within the upper. The eyes are large, placed high and narrowly separated by a longitudinal furrow. The scales are rather small except some larger ones on the belly which are not shed. The cheeks are finely scaled and the gill-covers have large scales. The nape is scaly, but the breast is naked. The males have a large anal papilla. The anal spines are stout and the caudal fin is notched. Males have the lower pectoral rays and the ventral and anal rays enlarged and thickened.

Color olive-green; the upper parts tessellated; the sides have seven or eight double cross bars each forming a y-shaped figure; these bars are sometimes joined above so as to form an undulating lateral band and are clear deep green in life and the sides are speckled with orange. There is a dark bar from eye forward and another downward, besides some olive stripes on the head.

The spinous dorsal is blue above with a pale margin and dark orange brown at base. The soft dorsal and the anal are deep blue green tinged with red. The caudal is greenish with faint bars. Females and young are less conspicuously colored, but in the same general pattern.

D. XIII, 13; A. II, 8; scales 65-78; 42 vertebræ.

The green-sided darter extends from Pennsylvania westward to Kansas and south to Alabama. It grows to a length of five inches and is a very beautiful species. It is common in gravelly streams and occurs only in clear water. Its habits are similar to those of the Johnny darter, but it is less tenacious of life than that species.

136. Etheostoma caprodes RAFINESQUE.

The Log Perch. (*Figure 68.*)

Body long, moderately compressed; head long, with pointed snout; mouth small, the lower jaw not reaching near to tip of snout, and the maxilla not extending to the front of the eye. The head forms one-fourth of the total length without the caudal, and the depth about one-sixth. Scales on cheeks and gill-covers, also on the space before the first dorsal; breast scaleless. A row of enlarged plates on the belly, which are sometimes deciduous. Fins moderately low and rather long. D. XV, 15; A. II, 9. Lateral line with 92 scales.

Color greenish yellow; sides with about fifteen dark cross-bands, extending from back to belly; alternating with these above the lateral line are fainter bars. Fins barred. A black spot at the base of the caudal.

The log perch, hogfish, hogmolly, rockfish or crawl-a-bottom is found in the Great Lake region, Quebec and the eastern states south to Virginia, also in the Mississippi valley south to Alabama and Texas.

This is the largest of the darters, reaching a length of eight inches. It takes the hook very readily and in many respects resembles the perches.

The log perch is found in rapid streams with gravelly or rocky bottom and prefers clear waters.

137. Etheostoma macrocephalum (COPE).

The Long-headed Darter.

The big-headed darter has a long and slender body, its depth not much greater than its width and equal to one-seventh of the total length without the caudal. The caudal peduncle is short and slender, its least depth equaling one-half of greatest depth of body. The head is long, its width and height about equal. The snout is conical and longer than the eye, which is about one-fifth as long as the head and nearly twice the width of the interorbital space. The eye is placed very high and is obliquely set. The mouth is large, the maxilla reaching to below the front of the eye. The lower jaw is slightly the longer. The cheeks are scaleless and the opercle is described as without scales, but the example before me has several large scales on the upper edge of the subopercle. The opercular spine is stout and short; the exposed tip one-fourth as long as the eye. The origin of the spinous dorsal is over the eleventh scale of the lateral line; the base of the fin is nearly as long as the head; the spines are all slender, the first as long as the snout, the fourth and longest one-half length of head without the snout, the last two-thirds as long as the eye. The interspace between the spinous and soft dorsals is shorter than the eye. The base of the soft dorsal is nearly two-thirds as long as the head; the fin is highest in front, the third ray being as long as the eye and snout combined, while the last ray is as long as the snout. The ventral origin is under the seventh scale of the lateral line; the fin is as long as the soft dorsal base. The anal origin is under the forty-sixth scale of the lateral line; the anal base is one-half as long as the head; the two spines are about equal in length, the first as long as the snout; the second and longest ray is as long as the eye and snout combined; the last ray is as long as the snout. The caudal is truncate, the middle rays as long as the snout and eye. The pectoral reaches to the twenty-fifth scale of the lateral line. The breast and the edge of the abdomen are scaleless, the belly shields having dropped off. The lateral line is very slightly decurved. D. XV, 14; A. II, 11; V. I, 5; P. 13; scales 10–76–12. Gill-rakers very short, stout, about nine developed on the first arch. In spirits the back is brown, the lower parts pale. A series of large dusky blotches forming an interrupted median band on the sides. A dark brown streak extending downward and forward from the eye. All the fins more or less barred. In life the dark spots on the sides are more conspicuous and there is an undulating whitish band from the head to the caudal fin. The specimen described, No. 1164, United States National Museum, from French Creek, Pa., is four inches long.

The long-headed darter inhabits the headwaters of the Ohio river in Pennsylvania. It grows to a length of three inches.

This darter was originally described from the Ohio valley in western Pennsylvania.

138. Etheostoma peltatum STAUFFER.

The Shielded Darter.

Body moderately stout; head one-fourth of total length; depth of body about one-fifth; muzzle blunt; scales wanting on cheeks, nape and breast; upper part of the gill-covers scaly; lower part naked; seven rows of scales above lateral line, nine below and fifty-three in the lateral line.

D. XIII or XIV, 12–13; A. II, 8 or 9; color olive. There are short bars across the back and the sides have broad, brownish shades. On the neck and opercle there is a dark blotch; bars present on the snout and the space below the eye. The fins are barred and the spinous dorsal has a black band.

The shielded darter (from the enlarged shield-like scales on the belly) was originally found by Jacob Stauffer in Conestoga creek, Lancaster county. Its range is now known to extend to South Carolina, east of the Alleghenies.

The species grows to a length of four inches.

139. Etheostoma aspro COPE AND JORDAN.

The Black-sided Darter.

The head is long and pointed, one-fourth of total length; the depth about one-fifth; the maxilla extends to past front of eye; the lower jaw is included; the body is spindle-shaped, compressed behind, moderately elongate; eye 4 in head, about equal to snout. The breast is naked, the nape scaled or naked; gill-covers with larger scales; cheek with very small scales, sometimes hardly visible; scales on the body small and rough, 9 above the lateral line, 17 below, and 65 from head to caudal base; lateral line straight, extending forward to the eye.

The sides are straw-colored or greenish-yellow, with dark tessellations and marblings above, and with about seven large dark blotches which are partly confluent; the fins are barred, and there is a small spot at the base of the caudal; on the belly there is a series of plates along the median line which are shed at certain seasons.

The black-sided darter or blenny darter is found from western Pennsylvania to Dakota and Arkansas. In Pennsylvania it is found only in tributaries of the Ohio. It grows to a length of four inches, and is among the most beautiful of the darters. It prefers clear streams with gravelly bottoms, and is more active in its habits than most of the other species, not concealing itself so closely under stones. It is admirably adapted for life in the aquarium.

140. Etheostoma variatum KIRTLAND.

The Variegated Darter.

The body is stout, the head short and heavy; snout blunt; the eye large, nearly one-fourth length of the head, which is more than one-fourth of the length without caudal; the depth about one-fifth; the upper jaw reaches to the front of the eye; the top of the head is rough, the head nearly scaleless; scales on the throat and nape; scales of the body large, in 54 rows from head to tail, 8 above and 9 below the lateral line. D. XIII, 13; A. II, 9.

The male is greenish, finely speckled with dusky spots; five orange bands on the hinder portion of the body; lower parts orange; a dark blue band on the spinous dorsal; the soft dorsal, pectoral and anal bluish black, with orange reflections. The female is less brilliantly colored than the male.

The variegated darter is known only from the Ohio valley, and is not common. It grows to a length of four inches.

141. Etheostoma zonale COPE.

The Zoned Darter.

The body is slender and moderately compressed; the head rather small, its length slightly less than one-fourth of the total without caudal; the depth equals one-fifth of the total; the snout is blunt and rounded; scales on the cheeks and gill-covers, also on the chest except in variety *arcansanum*; the teeth are weak and the dorsal fins separated by an interspace; the spinous dorsal is longer and lower than the soft dorsal; the caudal is notched.

D. XI, 12; A. II, 7. From 43 to 50 scales in the lateral line, 6 rows above it and 12 below.

Color olivaceous, lower parts golden; on the back are six dark brown quadrate spots; a brown lateral band, from which spots extend upward, alternating with those on the back, and eight narrow bands of dark bluish pass downward almost meeting around the belly; a crimson band on the middle of the spinous dorsal and crimson spots in a series on the base of the soft dorsal; a black spot on the top of the head, one at base of pectorals and on the operculum; pectoral, anal and caudal golden with brown spots; a dark bar from eye downward and forward. The female is plainer with barred ventrals.

The zoned darter ranges from western Pennsylvania through the Ohio valley and a portion of the Mississippi valley. Its western limit, according to Dr. Jordan, is Kansas. It is found in clear streams, reaches a length of about two and one-half inches, and varies considerably with locality. One of its varieties, *arcansanum*, differs from the typical zoned darter in having the breast naked.

142. Etheostoma maculatum KIRTLAND.

The Trout Darter.

The body is somewhat elongate, deep and compressed; the long head equals one-fourth of the total length without caudal; the depth about one-fifth; the eye is large, mouth moderately large with equal jaws, the maxillary reaching to the front of the eye; the dorsal fin is high, its longest rays reaching to the base of the tail.

D. XII, 12-13; A. II, 8-9. Lateral line 58-60; 9 scales above and 10 below.

Color dark olive, with an undulating light brown band on the back; throat blue; large crimson spots on the back and sides; a black spot anteriorly on the base of the spinous dorsal; the soft dorsal red; two carmine spots at the base of the caudal. The female plain, with speckled fins but lacking red markings.

The trout darter was originally described from the Mahoning river, Ohio. Its range is now known to extend from western Pennsylvania to eastern Tennessee. It grows to a length of two and one-half inches and is a species of surpassing beauty.

143. Etheostoma flabellare RAFINESQUE.

The Fan-tail Darter.

Body slender, elongate; head long, lower jaw strongly projecting. The species is readily recognized by its low fins, especially the spinous dorsal, and its prominent lower jaw. It runs, however, into several varieties one of which, occurring in Indiana and northwestward, has black spots on the scales forming lateral stripes; another variety from the Cumberland river is distinguished by its thick jaw and nearly plain coloration. In the male the spinous dorsal is one-half as high as the soft dorsal. The female has higher spines than the male; the spines have fleshy tips. No scales on nape, head and breast. A large black humeral scale. The length of the head equals one-fourth of the total length without caudal and the depth one-fifth.

D. VIII, 12; A. II, 8. Scales 7-50-7. The lateral line ends at the middle of the length.

The general color is olivaceous, the upper parts dusky. The sides with dark streaks formed by the spots at the base of the scales. The males have dusky cross bars; the soft dorsal and caudal barred. The spinous dorsal of the male has an orange margin.

The fan-tail darter is found from western New York to North Carolina, and in the Ohio valley. It grows to a length of two and one-half inches and abounds in clear rocky streams. It is very active and tenacious of life and is an excellent species for the aquarium.

144. Etheostoma cœruleum STORER.

The Blue Darter.

Body short, comparatively stout. Head large; mouth moderately large, with the lower jaw included within the upper. The maxilla extends to the front of the eye. The head is contained three and three-fourths times in the total length without the tail, and the depth four and one-fourth times.

D. X, 12; A. II, 7. Five rows of scales above the lateral line, eight below, and forty-five between the head and tail. Nape and breast generally scaleless.

The body of the male is olivaceous with darker blotches on the back. Twelve bars of indigo blue running obliquely downward and backward across the sides. The spaces between the bars are orange as are the throat, breast and cheeks. The base of the spinous dorsal is crimson, surmounted by orange and margined with blue. The soft dorsal is orange, the base and margin blue. In the female the blue and orange colors are chiefly wanting and the dorsal, anal and caudal are checked or barred.

The blue darter, blue Johnny, rainbow darter and soldier fish, is found in the Ohio valley and in some parts of the Mississippi valley. In Pennsylvania it is limited to the western portion of the state, in the Ohio and its tributaries. It reaches a length of two to three inches and is one of the most brilliantly colored of all the darters. It frequents gravelly bottoms in deeper parts of streams and is not common in small brooks. The blue darter is not so active as some of the other members of its family, but in coloration it is the most beautiful of all the darters.

GENUS **PERCA** (ARTEDI) LINNÉ.

145. Perca flavescens (MITCHILL).

The Yellow Perch. (*Figure 12.*)

The yellow perch has a fusiform and moderately elongate body, its greatest height at the ventral origin two-sevenths of the total length without the caudal and nearly equal to the length of the head. The least depth of the caudal peduncle equals one-third length of head. The greatest width of the body equals one-half its greatest height. The head is moderately large, its length contained three and one-fourth times in the standard, with pointed snout, one and one-third times as long as the eye. The interorbital region is flat, its width one and one-half times the diameter of the eye. The mouth is rather large, the jaws equal, and the maxilla reaching to below middle of pupil. The preopercle is coarsely dentate on its hind margin, the teeth on the superior border directed partly upward and partly backward, those on the lower limb pointing downward and some of them forward. The scapula and humerus are finely serrate. Scales on the cheeks in about thirteen rows from before backward. A single row or two imperfect rows of scales on the subopercle. Four short rows of scales on the upper anterior part of the opercle. Gill-rakers six + fourteen, the longest one-half as long as the eye. The spinous dorsal begins over the base of the pectoral; the first spine is one-third as long as the head to the end of the opercular spine; the fourth and longest spine is as long as the eye and snout combined; the last spine is minute and concealed in the dorsal furrow. The soft dorsal in the specimen described is preceded by two spines, the first two-thirds as long as the eye and one-half as long as the second. The longest ray is as long as the longest spine, and twice as long as the last ray. The ventral origin is under the fourth spine of the dorsal; the fin equals one-fifth of the total length without the caudal. The anal origin is under the fourth or fifth soft dorsal ray. The first anal spine is one-third as long as the head and nearly as long as the second. The last anal ray is less than one-half as long as the longest, which is one-half as long as the head. The caudal is notched, the middle rays contained one and one-third times in the length of the outer rays. The pectoral is as long as the ventral. D. XV, 11, 13; A. II, 8; V. I, 5; P. 15; scales 7-57-13. The lateral line curves upward in a long curve following the dorsal outline until below the end of the soft dorsal where it becomes straight and median. Color olivaceous varying into greenish or bluish, the sides yellow with about six to eight dark bands, the widest wider than the eye is long. The upper fins are olivaceous, the lower orange and rosy. The specimen described, No. 22,862, United States National Museum, from Washington, D. C., is nine inches long.

The yellow perch, ringed perch or striped perch is found throughout the Great Lake region, rivers and ponds of New England and northwestward, and in streams east of the Alleghenies south to Georgia. It does not occur in the Ohio valley or southwest.

The species reaches a length of one foot and weight of two pounds. It is one of the best known of our food fishes and has excellent game qualities. Its flesh, however, is rather soft and coarse and is far inferior to that of the black bass and other members of the sunfish family. It is a voracious feeder, its food consisting of small fishes, crustaceans and other animal matter.

The yellow perch spawns early in the spring. The eggs are adhesive and enclosed in thin translucent strips of adhesive mucus. The spawning of this species was described by Mr. Wm. P. Seal, in *Forest and Stream* of April 17, 1890. The spawning season extends from December to April. Mr. Seal describes the egg mass as having the shape of a long tube, closed at the ends and arranged in folds like the bellows of an accordion. When folded the mass was about eight to twelve inches long, but was capable of being drawn out to a length of three or four feet. Spawning in the aquarium took place at night and was observed by Mr. Wm. Maynard, who describes it as follows: "The female remained quiet in one spot on the bottom of one of the hatching aquaria tanks, one or more of the males hovering over and about her with pectoral fins vibrating with intense activity. The males would at times lie close alongside of her and at other times endeavor to force themselves under her with the evident intention of assisting in the extrusion of the eggs." Mr. Seal remarks that "the roe when taken from the dead fish not yet ripe is in a single compact mass, covered by a thin membrane; but in spawning the mass separates, one side being spawned before the other." This was noticed in a specimen which had spawned one side and appeared to be unable to get rid of the other. It was stripped from her and artificially fertilized successfully. Mr. Seal believes that the yellow perch spawns at the age of one year.

Genus **STIZOSTEDION** Rafinesque.

146. Stizostedion vitreum (Mitchill).

The Pike Perch. (*Figure 12.*)

The pike-perch belongs to the subgenus *Stizostedion*, which has been distinguished from the saugers by the structure of its pyloric cæca, which are three in number, nearly equal in size, and about as long as the stomach, and also by the presence of twenty-one soft rays in the second dorsal, while the saugers have eighteen. It may be remarked that all of these characters are more or less variable. The *S. vitreum* has the body long and moderately deep, its depth varying with age and equaling from one-sixth to one-fourth of the total length without caudal; the length of the head is contained in the same standard four and two-thirds times; the eye is moderate, about two-thirds as long as the snout and a little more than one-sixth of the length of the head; the lower jaw projects slightly; the maxilla reaches to beyond the pupil; the cheeks and opercles are more scaly than in the saugers; the soft dorsal is nearly as long as the spinous; length of longest dorsal spine about half length of head. D. XIII, I, 21; A. II, 12 to 13; about 90 scales in lateral line, 10 above and 19 below; the pectoral reaches to below the tenth spine of the dorsal; it is as long as the ventral and one-half length of head; the vent is under the fifth ray of the second dorsal.

Color olivaceous, mingled with brassy; sides of the head vermiculated; the dorsals, caudal and pectoral with bands; those of the dorsals and caudal not continuous; sides with about seven oblique dark bands, differing in direction; a jet black blotch on the membrane behind the last spine of the dorsal.

The pike-perch has received a great many common names. One of the most unsuitable is that of "Susquehanna salmon," which is used in Pennsylvania. In the eastern states the species is styled the perch-pike or the pike-perch, glass-eye and wall-eyed pike. In the Great Lake region it is known as blue pike, yellow pike, green pike and grass pike. In the Ohio valley and western North Carolina it is the jack; in Lake Erie and Canada, the pickerel; in some parts of the Ohio valley it is the white salmon or jack salmon. The Cree Indians call it the okow and the French Canadians doré or picarel. Among the fur traders of British America it is called the horn-fish.

The pike-perch or wall-eyed pike inhabits the Great Lake region and extends northward into British America, where it has been recorded as far as fifty-eight degrees north by Dr. Richardson. It ranges south in the Mississippi valley to Arkansas, and in Atlantic streams to Georgia. This species is said to reach a weight of fifty pounds, but the average weight of the market specimens is less than five pounds. In the Susquehanna it occasionally reaches ten pounds or upward in weight. The pike-perch feeds on the bottom upon other fishes, and has been charged even with destroying its own young. It prefers clear and rapid waters, and lurks under submerged logs and rocks from which it can readily dart upon its prey. Spawning takes place in April and May, and in Pennsylvania continues until June. Favorite spawning localities are on sandy bars in shallow water. The period of hatching varies from about fourteen to thirty days, depending upon the temperature of the water. The eggs vary from about seventeen to twenty-five to the inch, and a single female has been estimated to contain from two hundred thousand to three hundred thousand. In a state of nature only a small percentage of the eggs are hatched out; the greater portion are driven upon the lake shores by storms and devoured by fishes upon the spawning beds. The number of pike-perch annually hatched by artificial methods is enormous. This advance is due to improvements in the treatment of adhesive eggs. Formerly these were hatched by placing them on glass plates, to which they readily adhere. Recently it has been found that the sticky substance can be washed off the eggs, after which they are placed in jars and hatched like eggs of the shad and white fish. Pennsylvania distributed twelve millions of the fry in its eastern waters in 1889, and has greatly increased the distribution since that time.

"Dexter," in *Forest and Stream*, August 14, 1890, makes the following statement about its habits in the lakes: "These fish run up the rivers before or as soon as the ice is out, and after spawning lie off the rivers' mouth feeding on and off the sand flats, as the spring rains bring down plenty of worms, and probably other matter which they feed on. As soon as the water gets warm they sag off and work along the shores in ten to thirty feet of water, preferring cobbly bottom; from here they go into very deep water, coming on the reefs to feed, and when the wind blows very hard, or for a day or so after a big blow, you will find them right on top of a reef. I think the wind changes the water over the reefs, making a new current and cooler water, so they come up to feed. They are a bottom fish, and to fish for them successfully one must go to the bottom for them. They are nearly as particular as salmon-trout about the water they inhabit and consequently rank very high as a food fish, being white, solid and extremely free from bones."

The origin of the pike-perch in Pennsylvania is unknown, but it was doubtless transplanted from the North. In 1833 this fish was abundant in the Susquehanna and the Juniata within twenty miles of the headwaters. In the fall of the year it was caught in such quantities by the people that it was packed in barrels, salted, and in the spring carried to market and exchanged for goods and groceries. In 1840 it was abundant even up to the headwaters of the Juniata, and was caught and speared in great numbers, to be salted and carried to market in the spring by raftsmen.

The colors of the pike-perch change remarkably with age. The young have oblique dark bands very much like those of the king-fish of our east coast, and bear little resemblance in the pattern of coloration to the parent. The eye of the living fish is like a glowing emerald. The rate of growth must be rapid. In July, 1888, we took examples from four to six inches long, some of which seemed to be the young of the year.

This is one of the finest food and game fishes of the United States. Its flesh is firm and white, flaky and well flavored. Commercially the species ranks high in the Great Lake region, being next in importance to the white fish. Its multiplication by the Pennsylvania commission is one of the numerous evidences of sound judgment displayed by the commissioners.

In angling for the pike-perch live minnows are used in preference to all other baits, particularly such as are more or less transparent and with silvery sides, as the fall-fish or dace, the corporal roach, the red fin and the gudgeon. On some parts of the Susquehanna, between Columbia and Harrisburg, the favorite mode of capture is by trolling with the spoon with the same kind of tackle as is used for the black bass. Among the favorite fishing grounds are Fite's Eddy, Washington borough, Columbia dam and Conewago Falls. The species is well distributed throughout the river and its larger tributaries, especially the Juniata and the North Branch.

147. Stizostedion vitreum salmoneum (RAFINESQUE).

The Blue Pike. (*Figure 69.*)

The blue pike of Lake Erie, or white salmon of the Ohio river, was formerly distinguished by name from the common pike perch, but is now considered unworthy of a separate name.

This is a very small variety seldom exceeding fifteen inches in length and a weight of two pounds. The dorsal has fourteen spines and twenty rays. The spines are rather lower than in the pike perch, the coloration similar, but the adult is bluish or greenish and has no brassy mottling. The fins are darker and there is a trace of a band along the dorsal, besides the black blotch on the hind portion.

148. Stizostedion canadense SMITH.

The Sauger. (*Figure 70.*)

Body slender, not much compressed, roundish; its depth contained four and one-half to five times in the total without caudal. The head is pointed, about two-sevenths of standard length and contains the eye five to five and one-half times. The mouth is smaller than in the pike perch; the maxilla reaches to the hind margin of the eye.

D. XII to XIII, I, 17 to 18; A. II, 12. Scales 92 to 98; 4 to 7 pyloric caeca, unequal in size and all of them shorter than the stomach.

Color olivaceous above; sides brassy or pale orange, mottled with black in the form of irregular dark blotches, which are best defined under the soft dorsal. The spinous dorsal has several rows of round black spots on the membrane between the spines; no black blotch on the hind part of the spinous dorsal. Pectorals with a large dark blotch at base. Soft dorsal with several rows of dark spots irregularly placed. Caudal yellowish with dark spots forming interrupted bars.

The sauger is known also as sand pike, gray pike and green pike, pickering, pickerel and horse fish. It is found in the St. Lawrence river and Great Lake region, the upper Mississippi and Missouri rivers and in the Ohio where it is said to have been introduced from the lakes through canals.

This is a small fish, seldom exceeding eighteen inches in length, and embraces several varieties only one of which is found in Pennsylvania, the one called gray pike. It is a very common fish in the Great Lakes and is abundant in the Ohio river. It is doubtful whether it is native to Ohio or introduced. It is very extensively used for food but is not equal to the pike perch.

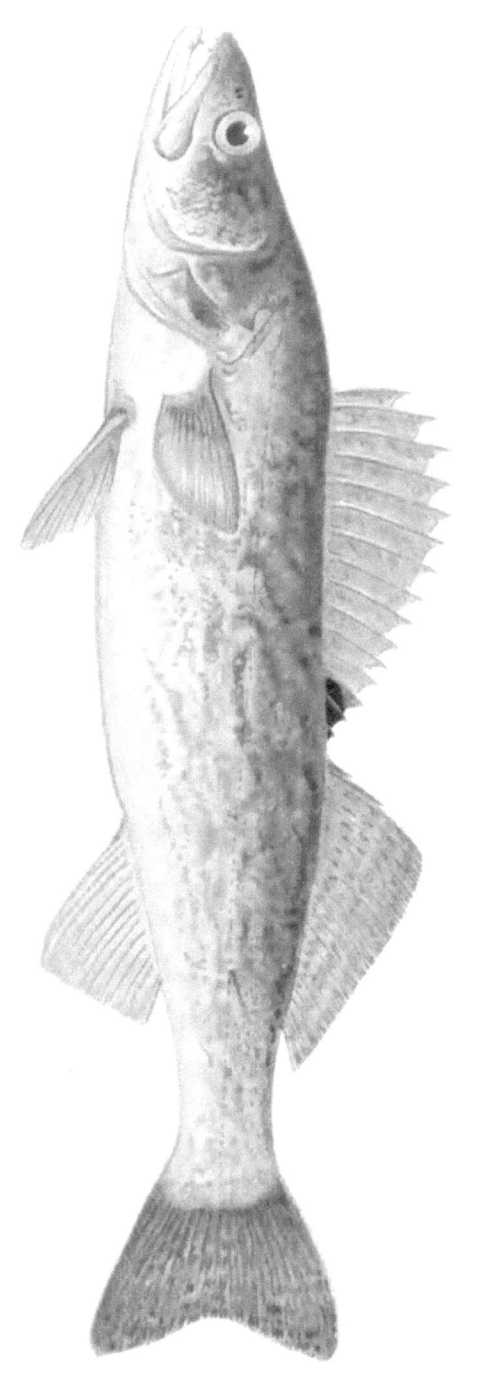

Family **SERRANIDÆ**.

Genus **ROCCUS** Mitchill.

149. Roccus lineatus Bloch.

The Striped Bass. (*Figure 14.*)

The genus *Roccus*, to which the striped bass belongs, has two patches of small teeth on the base of the tongue, the anal spines increasing regularly in size backward, the lower jaw much longer than the upper, the scales on the cheeks nearly smooth along their margin and the dorsal fins separated by a narrow interspace. The body is moderately elongate and rather stout; the caudal peduncle is slender. The greatest depth of the body is two-sevenths of the total length without caudal and equals length of head. Eye small, one-half as long as the snout and one-sixth to one-eighth the length of the head. The eyes are placed near the top of the head; the maxilla reaches to below the middle of the eye. The anal spines are slender, the third longest, about one-fifth length of head. The fourth and fifth dorsal spines are longest, about two-fifths length of head. Pectoral a little longer than ventral, one-half length of head.

D. IX, I, 11 to 12; A. III, 10 to 11. Scales 7, 65, 19.

Sides greenish above, silvery below, sometimes with a brassy lustre and marked by seven or eight longitudinal streaks none of which are half as wide as the eye, one of them passing along the lateral line; the lowermost stripe is somewhat below the middle of the depth.

In the southern United States from New Jersey to Florida the striped bass is known as the rock or rockfish. In the northern states the name striped bass is more generally used than the other, especially along the coast. In the Delaware, Susquehanna and Potomac rivers it is called rockfish. Green head and squid hound are names applied to large individuals found in the sea in New England waters. One of the old names of the fish is streaked bass.

The range of the striped bass or rockfish includes the entire Atlantic coast from the Gulf of St. Lawrence to the Gulf of Mexico, the fish entering rivers and ascending them long distances. In the Alabama river this fish is known to be taken every year and some large individuals have been obtained from that stream. It has been captured also in the lower Mississippi. It is very abundant in the great bays and sounds from North Carolina to Cape Cod. In Albemarle sound many large individuals are said to occur. In the St. John's river, Forida, according to Dr. Goode, the fish is rather rare. In the vicinity of Pensacola the late Silas Stearns occasionally obtained a specimen of the fish.

The striped bass has been introduced into California and has now become fairly acclimated there. In the Delaware and Susquehanna rivers this is one of the common fishes and it is one of the most highly esteemed.

This fish lives in the sea or in brackish or fresh water indifferently and it has been successfully kept in artificial ponds. In cold northern waters it becomes ice bound occasionally and is said to hibernate. It prefers cold water, is carnivorous and predaceous, feeding upon small fishes in the streams, consuming especially large quantities of the alewife or river herring and the young of the shad. In the shallow bays along the coasts its food consists of killifish, silversides, anchovies, lant and other small fishes, besides crabs, squid, clams, mussels and other marine invertebrates. Its movements while feeding depend greatly upon the tides. It is to be found frequently at the mouths of small creeks and in tideways, where it lies in wait for the large schools of small fishes, which constitute its food.

The largest striped bass recorded was said to weigh one hundred and twelve pounds. At Avoca, North Carolina, Dr. Capehart took a striped bass weighing ninety-five pounds. It reaches a length of four and one-half or five feet.

Spawning takes place from April to June, either in the rivers or in the brackish waters of bays and sounds. Eggs have been hatched artificially in May on Albemarle sound. Dr. Capehart took a fifty-eight-pound spawning fish April 22, 1891. The eggs are smaller than those of the shad and after fertilization they increase greatly in size and become light green in color. This fifty-eight-pound fish probably contained more than one-half million eggs. Dr. Abbott has found the young an inch long in the Delaware the second week in June and by the middle of October some of these had grown to a length of four and one-half inches. The striped bass has been kept in a small pool of fresh water and fed upon crabs and oysters increasing in about eleven months from six inches in length to twenty inches. In a Rhode Island pond it is stated that bass weighing one-half pound to one pound in June had reached a weight of six pounds in the following October.

In fresh water salted eel tail is a favorite bait for taking striped bass, and the spoon or spinner is also a good lure, but live minnows are preferred to all other baits. For surf fishing shedder crab well fastened to the hook is a very killing bait.

150. Roccus chrysops RAFINESQUE.

The White Bass. (*Figure 71.*)

The white bass has the body oblong, elevated and compressed; its depth contained two and one-half times in the total length without caudal, the length of the head about three and one-third times in this length; head sub-conical, depressed over eye; mouth moderate, the maxillary reaching to below middle of eye; length of eye almost equal to length of snout; villiform teeth in bands on jaws, palatines, vomer and tongue; the dorsal outline is much curved, the fins well separated.

D. IX, I, 14; A. III, 11 to 12. Scales 8-60-13. General color silvery, tinged with golden on sides; eight or more blackish longitudinal streaks on sides, those below more or less interrupted.

The white bass is sometimes called striped bass, and is probably the silver bass of Canada. Its center of abundance is the Great Lake region, but it is also widely distributed over the Ohio and Mississippi valleys. In Pennsylvania the species is found in Lake Erie and in the

Figure 14.

THE STRIPED BASS.

Page 130.

tributaries of the Ohio. The white bass weighs from one to three pounds, and its flesh is considered almost if not equally as good as that of the black bass. It prefers the deeper parts of rivers and thrives best in lakes and ponds. In April and May they leave the deeper waters and go in near shore or to the mouths of rivers where they spawn. The spawning period is in May and June.

The white bass feeds upon minnows, crawfish and other fresh water crustaceans, also minute mollusks or shell fish, and it is said to devour many young white fish upon the spawning grounds of that species.

It is a game fish and affords good sport to the angler.

GENUS **MORONE** MITCHILL.

151. Morone americana (GMELIN).

The White Perch. (*Figure 15.*)

The genus *Morone* of Gill differs from *Roccus* in having the dorsals joined, the spines strong, the anal with ten soft rays, its spines not graduated, the jaws subequal and base of the tongue toothless. It includes the common white perch and the yellow bass.

The white perch has an oblong body, with the back convex, mouth moderate, the maxillary reaching a little beyond the front of the eye; the eye is nearly as long as the snout, and is contained five and one-half times in the length of the head; the head is about one-third of total without caudal; the depth of body is contained two and two-thirds times in total without caudal; the fourth anal spine is the longest, two-fifths length of head; the second is stouter and slightly shorter than the third, its length one-third that of head.

D. IX, I, 12; A. III, 10. Scales 7-51-11. The dorsal fins are separated by a very deep notch, but connected by membrane; upper parts grayish or greenish; sides silvery; young individuals have pale, longitudinal streaks.

The white perch inhabits the sea coast from Nova Scotia to South Carolina, ascending streams and has been introduced into numerous fresh water lakes and ponds, where it thrives equally as well as in the sea. In Pennsylvania, according to Professor Cope, it is very common in the Delaware and Susquehanna rivers. In the latter its upward movement is prevented by obstructions so that it occurs only in that portion of the river below Columbia.

The average length of the white perch is about nine inches and its weight one-half pound or less, but numerous specimens measuring fourteen inches and weighing two pounds or more have been taken, especially in New England waters.

It is said that the white perch formerly extended south to Florida and the Gulf of Mexico, but this is discredited by competent observers. The perch of Lake Ponchartrain is very likely the species now known in many portions of the western states as the fresh water drum—*Aplodinotus grunniens*.

The white perch is a lover of brackish water, and may be found in tidal creeks in vast numbers associated with mummichogs, silversides and eels, feeding upon shrimp and minnows. Spawning takes place in

May and June. According to Professor John A. Ryder, of the University of Pennsylvania, the egg of the white perch is very adhesive, and on this account is troublesome to hatch artificially. In the experiments made by him the eggs were taken upon cotton yarn, which was drawn up through a funnel into which the eggs and milt had been squeezed from the spawning fish. The cord, covered with the adhering eggs, was then wrapped upon a wooden reel and sent under cover of damp cloths to the central station, where they arrived in fine condition, almost every egg being impregnated. This system was devised and carried out under the superintendence of Col. M. McDonald. After reaching the central station the cotton cord with the adhering eggs was cut into lengths of ten or twelve inches and suspended in the glass hatching jars. The development was soon interfered with by the growth of fungus. When the wooden reel with the adhering eggs was introduced into a wide aquarium fungus also attacked the eggs as before but the results were somewhat more favorable. With the water at fifty-eight to sixty degrees Fahrenheit the eggs hatched out in six days.

The white perch congregates in large schools and is one of the freest biters among fishes. The shrimp is one of the best baits, although worms, sturgeon eggs, minnows and strips of cut fish with silvery skin are equally effective. Dr. Abbott has known as many as twenty dozen to be taken with a line in a few hours, and Spangler mentions catches of six or seven hundred in a day by two rods, the fish ranging in weight from three-fourths to one and one-fourth pounds. He records good perch fishing from Fort Penn, at the head of Delaware bay, to considerably above Lambertville on the Delaware; also in all the tributaries of the Delaware river. One of the charges brought against the white perch is its destruction of the spawn of other fish, especially of the shad.

152. Morone interrupta GILL.

The Yellow Bass. (*Figure 72.*)

The yellow bass has an oblong body, its greatest depth equaling one-third of the total length without the caudal; the caudal peduncle is short and stout, its least depth three-eighths of the greatest depth of the body; the head is moderately large, nearly one-third of the total without the caudal; the snout is as long as the eye, which is one-fourth as long as the head; the mouth is rather large, the maxilla reaching to below the middle of the eye, moderately expanded behind and bearing a few small scales; the preopercle is strongly serrate on its hind margin; scales on the cheeks below the eye in seven rows; the gill-rakers are moderately long and slender, twenty developed on the first arch, the longest about one-half as long as the orbit; the spines are longer and more slender than in the white perch; the spinous dorsal begins over the sixth scale of the lateral line; its base is as long as the head without the snout; the first spine is shortest, two-thirds as long as the eye; the fourth and longest is four-fifths as long as the base of the fin; the last is two-fifths as long as the fourth; the spine in front of the second dorsal is one-half as long as the spinous dorsal base; the first and longest soft ray is as long as the base of the fin and nearly three times as long as the last; the anal fin begins under the twenty-seventh scale of the lateral line; the base of the fin is one-half as long as the head; the first spine is one-third as long as the second and two-fifths as long as the third; the second is a little longer

Figure 15.

THE WHITE PERCH.

Page 132.

than the anal base; the first and longest soft ray is as long as the anal base and more than twice as long as the last; the caudal is large and emarginate, the middle rays nearly two-thirds as long as the outer; the ventral reaches to below the twenty-first scale of the lateral line, its spine two-fifths as long as the head; the pectoral reaches to below the seventeenth scale of the lateral line; its base is broad, equaling two-thirds of the diameter of the eye; the lateral line is gently curved upward in the first half of its length.

D. IX-I, 11 or 12; A. III, 9 or 10; V. I, 5; P. 14. Scales 6-52-11.

In life the body is yellowish, the upper parts olivaceous and the sides with seven narrow dark stripes, the first one below the lateral line abruptly bent downward at its middle, the second interrupted and the third short; two short, oblique, dark streaks on the shoulders. The specimen described, number 3467, belonging to the United States National Museum, is seven and one-half inches long.

The yellow bass appears to have no other common name. It inhabits the lower Mississippi valley, extending northward to southern Indiana and Illinois. In Pennsylvania it has been introduced by the State Fish Commission into the Delaware, Perkiomen and Susquehanna rivers. The United States Fish Commission has recently sent examples east from Quincy, Illinois.

The species grows to the length of one foot. Nothing is recorded about its habits, which are supposed to resemble those of the white perch.

FAMILY **SCIÆNIDÆ** (THE DRUMS).

GENUS **APLODINOTUS** RAFINESQUE.

153. Aplodinotus grunniens RAFINESQUE.

The Fresh Water Drum. (Figure 75.)

The shape of the fresh water drum is similar to that of the saltwater species, the body being moderately elongate, its greatest height one-third of its length without the caudal; the sides are moderately compressed and the back very much so. The least depth of the tail is less than one-third of the depth of the body. The head is rather short, its length contained three and two-thirds times in the total without caudal. The eye is about four-fifths as long as the snout and one-sixth length of head. Snout obtuse. The maxilla reaches to below the middle of the eye; the lower jaw is shorter than the upper. The pectoral is nearly as long as the head and reaches to below the beginning of the soft dorsal. The ventral is about two-thirds length of head. The third dorsal spine is the longest, nearly one-half as long as the head. The second anal spine is much the longer and stouter, its length two-fifths that of head. The rays of the soft dorsal are longest near the end of the fin. The scales are very irregularly placed, about fifty-five in the lateral line.

D. IX, I, 30-31; A. II, 7.

The color is grayish, darker on the back; lower parts silvery. Young specimens have dark spots along the rows of scales, forming oblique lines.

The freshwater drum has received a great number of common names. In the Ohio valley and South it is known as the white perch; in the Great Lake region it called sheepshead or fresh-water drum on account of its resemblance to the salt-water drum. At Buffalo and Barcelona, New York, it is known as sheepshead. The name crocus, used on lakes of northern Indiana is a corruption of croaker, a name of a marine fish of the same family. In the southern states the name drum is generally applied to the species, and in addition the terms thunder pumper, gaspergou and jewel-head are used. Gaspergou is a term used in Arkansas, Louisiana and Texas. The names drum, croaker and thunder pumper have reference to certain sounds produced by the fish either by means of its air bladder or by grinding together the large molar-like teeth in the pharynx. The name jewel head probably refers to the otoliths or earbones, frequently called lucky stones, which are found in the skull of this species. In Texas, adjacent to Mexican territory, occurs the name gaspagie, a variation of the name gaspergou.

The fresh-water drum is widely distributed; it occurs in Lake Champlain and the entire Great Lake region, the Ohio and Mississippi valleys southward to Texas. It is found principally in large streams and lakes and rarely enters creeks and small rivers. In western Texas the species is rare. In the wilds of Texas, New Mexico and northern Mexico Mr. Turpe has found this fish in clear limestone streams emptying into the Rio Grande.

This species is usually found on the bottom, where it feeds chiefly on crustaceans and mollusks and sometimes small fishes. It is especially fond of crawfish and small shells such as *Cyclas* and *Paludina*. Mr. Turpe mentions water plants as forming part of its food and states that it will take a hook baited with worms or small minnows.

The fresh-water drum grows to a length of four feet and a weight of sixty pounds, but the average market specimens rarely exceed two feet in length and in many parts of the West much smaller ones are preferred. Nothing is recorded about the breeding habits of this species, and as to its edible qualities there is the greatest difference of opinion. Some writers claim that its flesh is tough and coarse with a disagreeable odor, especially in the Great Lakes. Individuals from the Ohio river and from more southern streams are fairly good food fish, while in Texas Mr. Turpe considers it one of the most excellent of the fresh-water fishes, comparing favorably with black bass. Mr. Robert Ridgway of the National Museum at Washington, pronounces the species from the Wabash river in Indiana, a fine table fish although, he says, other people there consider it inferior. Richardson described what is supposed to be a deformed specimen of this drum under the name of malashegany, which he had from Lake Huron. He described it as a firm, white, well-tasting fish, but never fat and requiring much boiling.

FAMILY **COTTIDÆ** (THE SCULPINS).

GENUS **URANIDEA** DEKAY.

154. Uranidea richardsoni GIRARD.

The Miller's Thumb. (*Figure 74.*)

The body is robust with a broad and rather short head; the preopercular spine short and sharp, nearly straight, turned upward and backward; two smaller spines below it. The depth of the body is variable, equaling from one-sixth to one-fourth of the total without caudal; the head equals three-tenths of the same length. The skin is usually smooth or with minute prickles behind the axil of the pectoral.

D. VI-VIII, 16; A. 12-13; V. I, 4.

The color is olivaceous, much speckled; sides usually with several distinct, rather broad cross bands.

Bull head, blob and muffle-jaws are names applied to the miller's thumb, which has been associated with Richardson's name.

The typical Richardson's miller's thumb is found in the upper Great Lakes, but in Pennsylvania there are two varieties of it. The one known as *Uranidea wilsoni*, inhabits the Ohio valley, and the other, *meridionalis*, frequents the Alleghenies. The typical form ranges from Canada and the Great Lakes to Georgia and Arkansas. It is most abundant in stony brooks, cold lakes, caves and springs. It is extremely variable in size, color and length of fins and number of rays.

This species grows to a length of seven inches under favorable circumstances and is one of the most destructive enemies of the eggs and young of brook trout and other members of the salmon family.

155. Uranidea viscosa HALDEMAN.

The Slippery Miller's Thumb.

Body stout; well supplied with mucus pores. Depth of body much less than length of head, which is two-sevenths of the total without caudal; the depth is scarcely more than one-fifth of this same length. A short sharp spine on the preopercle, turned obliquely upward. Fins low.

D. VI, 18; A. 14; V. I, 3.

The numerous mucus pores of the skin throw off a viscid secretion which has given rise to the specific name of this fish.

Color olivaceous, mottled with darker. The spinous dorsal has a red edge.

The slippery miller's thumb is a species of apparently limited distribution. It was originally found in Pennsylvania by Prof. Haldeman and is known from only two other states, Maryland and Virginia. This is a small species, reaching a length of but three inches, and belongs to the section without palatine teeth. Nothing is recorded of its habits except that it is frequently found in caves.

156. Uranidea gracilis HECKEL.

The Slender Miller's Thumb.

The body is moderately slender, spindle-shaped; mouth large, the upper jaw reaching nearly to the middle of the eye. The preopercular spine is moderately large, covered by skin. The pectorals reach to the origin of the anal, and the ventrals to the vent. The depth of the body is one-fifth, and the length of the head two-sevenths of the total without caudal. Teeth in villiform bands on the jaws and vomer, none on the palatine bones.

D. VIII, 16; A. 12.

The sides are olivaceous, mottled with darker. A red margin on spinous dorsal.

The miller's thumb or little star gazer is an inhabitant of New England and New York. In Pennsylvania it occurs in the headwaters of the

Susquehanna and Allegheny rivers. This species grows to a length of four inches and is represented by several varieties, one of which has the body robust instead of slender and another has the slender body as in *gracilis*, but with longer fins.

This fish is found under stones in clear, rocky and gravelly brooks. It has no importance either as food or bait and is very destructive to the eggs of other fishes.

FAMILY **GADIDÆ** (THE COD-FISHES).

GENUS **LOTA** COVIER.

157. Lota maculosa LE SUEUR.

The Burbot. (*Figure 75.*)

The body of the burbot is elongate, eel-shaped; its greatest height equaling the length of head without snout, and about one-sixth of total without caudal; it is roundish, somewhat compressed posteriorly. The eye is small, less than one-half length of snout and about one-eighth length of head. The upper jaw reaches slightly beyond the hind margin of the eye, its length three-sevenths length of head. The lower jaw is included within the upper, and has a stout barbel which is nearly one-fifth as long as the head; the ventral is longer than the pectoral, but does not reach half way to vent; the pectoral is half as long as the head; the distance of the first dorsal from the head equals the height of the body; the longest ray of the first dorsal equals half the length of its base; the dorsal fins are separated by a narrow interspace; the second dorsal is higher than the first, and the length of its base is nearly one-half total without caudal; the anal begins under the ninth ray of the second dorsal and extends as far back as that fin; caudal rounded; the scales are deeply imbedded in the skin, not imbricated. D. 13, 68 to 76; A. 67; V. 7; vertebræ, 22 to 23 + 38 to 39; pyloric cœca, 30 to 138.

The color is dark olivaceous, reticulated with blackish; the lower parts yellowish or dusky; the dorsal, anal and caudal fins with a narrow dark edge.

The American burbot was first described by Le Sueur from Lake Erie in 1817, and, also from Northampton, Connecticut, under a different name. This common fish has received a great many names, including the following: Marthy, methy, losh, eelpout, dogfish, club-eel, ling, lawyer, lake-cusk, fresh-water cod, aleby trout and mother-of-eels.

The southern limit of this fish appears to be Kansas City, Missouri; according to Prof. Cope, it has been once taken in the Susquehanna near Muncy, Lycoming county; it is extremely common in the Great Lakes; westward it ranges to Montana and northward throughout British Columbia and Alaska to the Arctic Ocean; it is most abundant in the Great Lakes and lakes of New York, New England and New Brunswick; it abounds also in rivers and lakes of Alaska.

The average length of this species in the Great Lake region is about two feet; in Alaska, according to Dr. Dall, it reaches a length of five feet and occasionally weighs sixty pounds; the size of the fish depends chiefly on the amount of food accessible to it.

It is stated that the burbot is usually found in deep water on mud bottom, except during the spawning season in March, when it frequents hard or rocky bottoms; the eggs are small and numerous, and are believed to be deposited in deep water; Dr. Dall estimates that some individuals contain several millions of eggs; in Alaska the eggs are of a creamy yellow color, and the fish are found full of spawn from November to January. From the observations mentioned, it will be seen that the spawning period extends at least from November to March; according to Dr. Dall the males are usually much smaller than the females and have a smaller liver; in some males he found two or three gall bladders opening into a common duct, but he never observed this phenomenon in the female; the eggs are laid separate or loose upon the bottom of the river. According to Baron Cederström, a medium-sized female of the European burbot, which is a near relative of the American species, contained about 160,000 eggs; in the European burbot, some eggs are clear, some yellowish and others almost colorless; the period of incubation occupies from three to four weeks; the eyes appear in fifteen or sixteen days; the embryos swim by quick movements of the pectorals, usually toward the surface of the water, whence they fall passively to the bottom.

The burbot is extremely voracious, and feeds upon bottom fishes and crustaceans. It destroys the pike and such spiny fishes as the yellow perch and sunfish. In Alaskan rivers it feeds upon whitefish, lampreys and other species; large stones have sometimes been found in its stomach; Mr. Graham took a stone weighing a pound from the stomach of a burbot.

In the Great Lake region the burbot is considered worthless for food, occasionally the livers are eaten; in Lake Winnepiscogee, when caught through the ice in winter the fish is highly esteemed; in the fur countries the roe is an article of food. On the Yukon river the liver is eaten and the flesh is liked by some persons; in Montana the burbot is in great demand for food; the quality of the flesh appears to depend chiefly on the nature of the habitat of the fish.

This is the only member of the cod family permanently resident in the fresh waters of America.

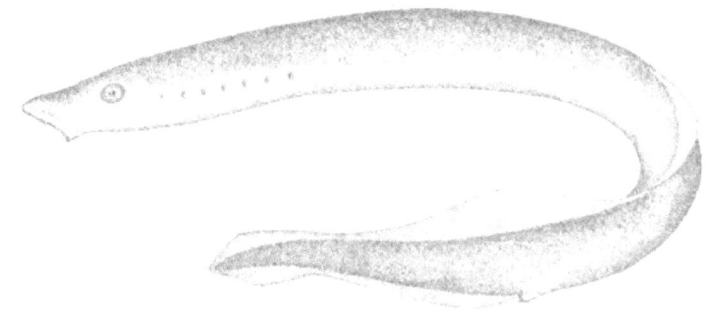

Figure 16.   THE BROOK LAMPREY.   Page 1.

Figure 17.   THE SEA LAMPREY.   Page 2.

FISHES OF PENNSYLVANIA – BEAN PLATE 17.

Figure 19.   THE COMMON STURGEON.   Page 6.

Figure 20.   THE LAKE STURGEON.   Page 8.

Figure 21.   THE SPOTTED CAT-FISH.   Page 12.

Figure 22.　　THE GREAT CAT-FISH.　　Page 13.

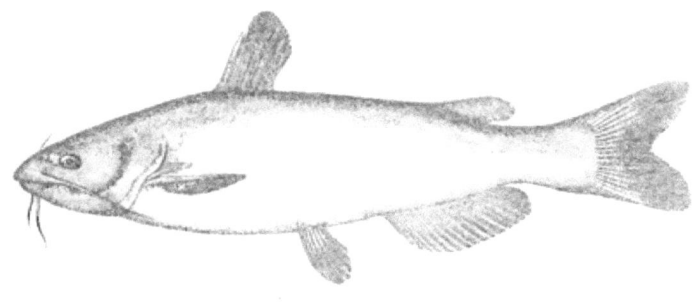

Figure 23.　　THE CHANNEL CAT-FISH.　　Page 14.

Figure 24.　　THE LONG-JAWED CAT-FISH.　　Page 15.

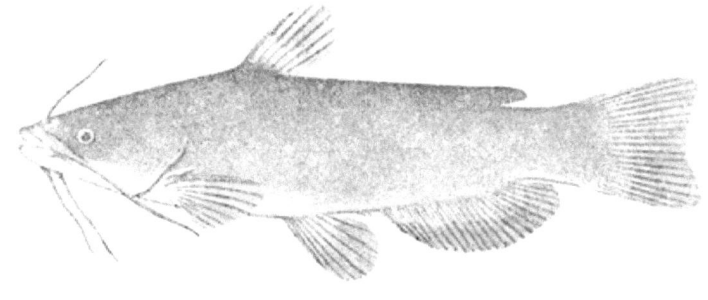

Figure 25. THE COMMON CATFISH. Page 16.

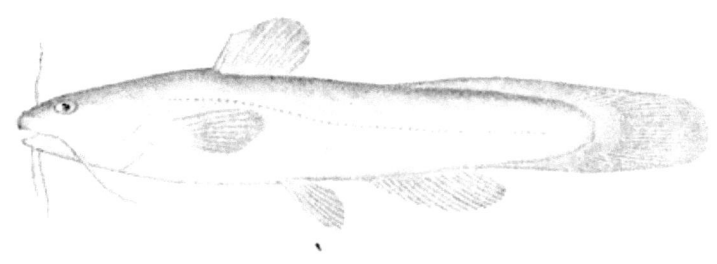

Figure 26. THE MARGINED STONE CATFISH. Page 19.

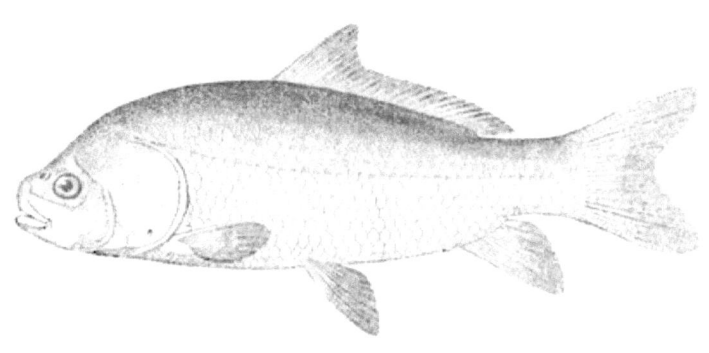

Figure 27. THE BIG-MOUTHED BUFFALO FISH. Page 21.

FISHES OF PENNSYLVANIA - BEAN   PLATE 20.

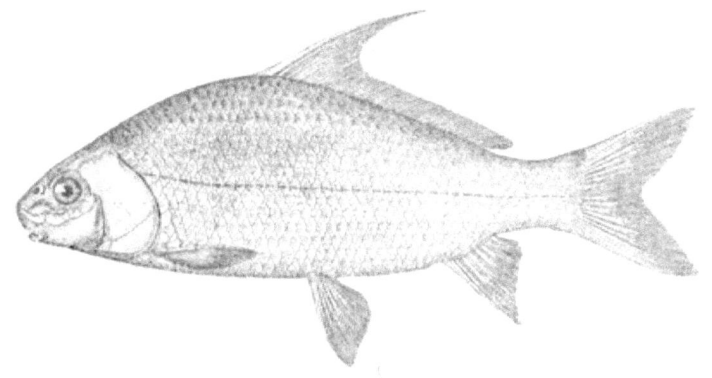

Figure 28.   THE CARP SUCKER.   Page 22.

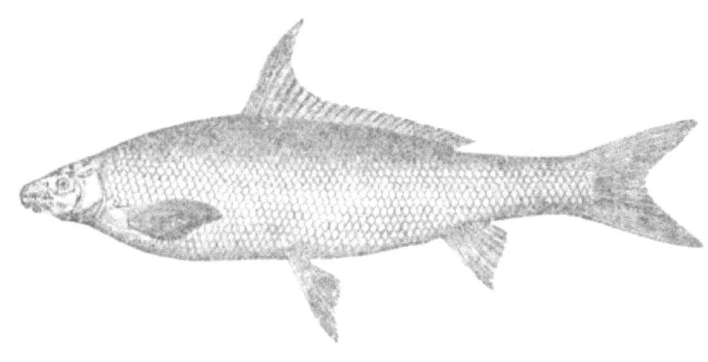

Figure 29.   THE BLACK HORSE.   Page 24.

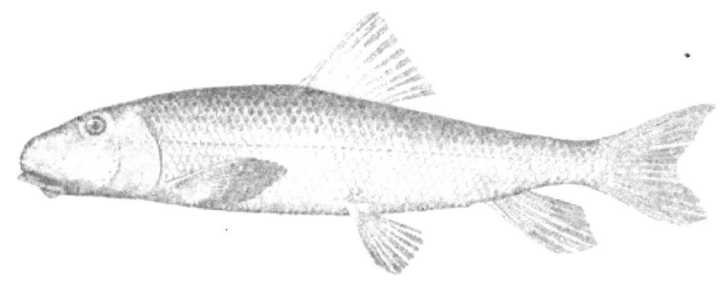

Figure 31.   THE STONE TOTER.   Page 26.

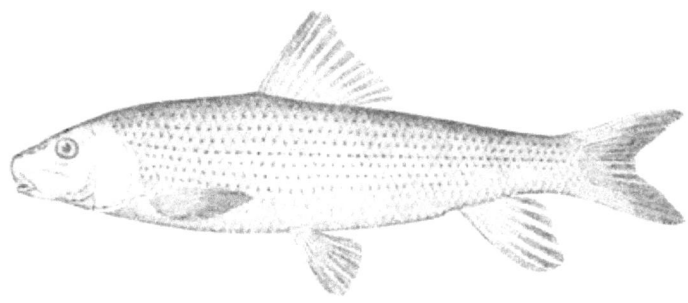

Figure 32.   THE STRIPED SUCKER.   Page 28.

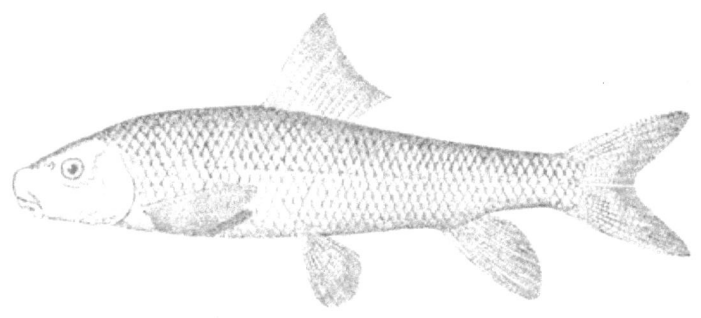

Figure 33.   THE RED HORSE.   Page 29.

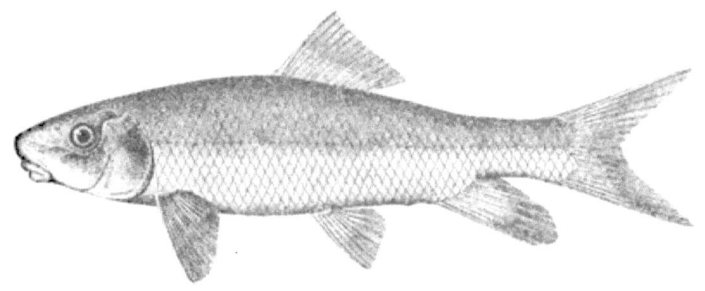

Figure 34. THE BIG-JAWED SUCKER. Page 31.

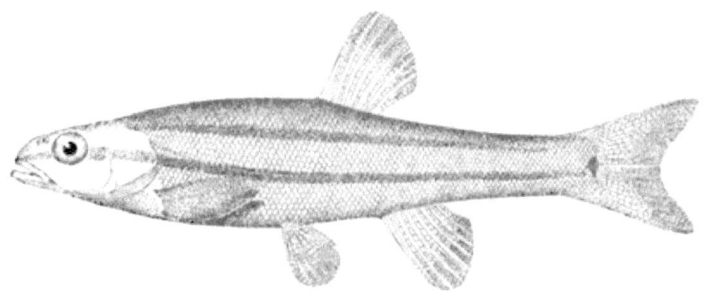

Figure 35. THE RED-BELLIED DACE. Page 32.

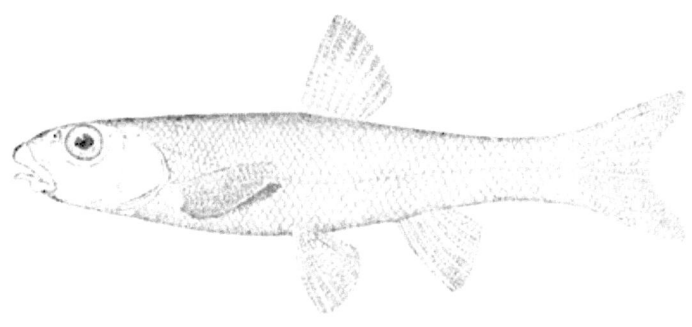

Figure 36. THE CUT-LIPS OR CHUB. Page 36.

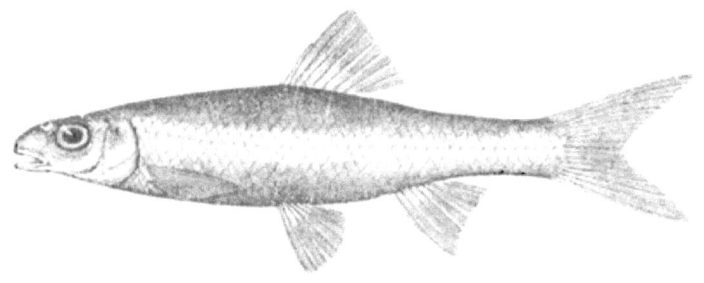

Figure 37.   THE GUDGEON OR SMELT.   Page 39.

Figure 38.   THE RED-FIN.   Page 42.

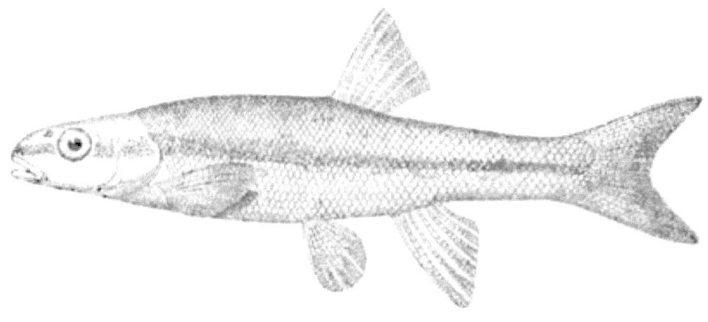

Figure 39.   THE BLACK-NOSED DACE.   Page 47.

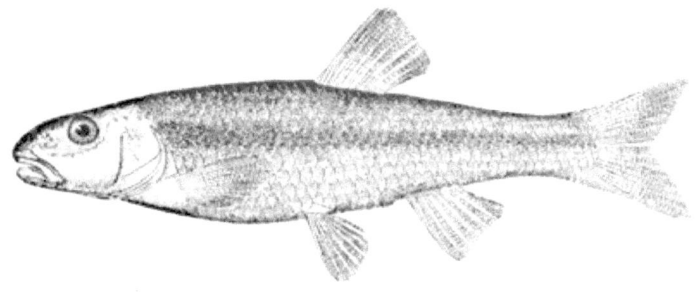

Figure 40. THE HORNED CHUB. Page 49.

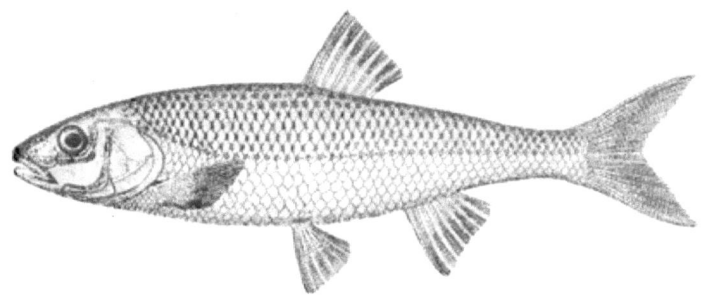

Figure 41. THE FALL FISH. Page 50.

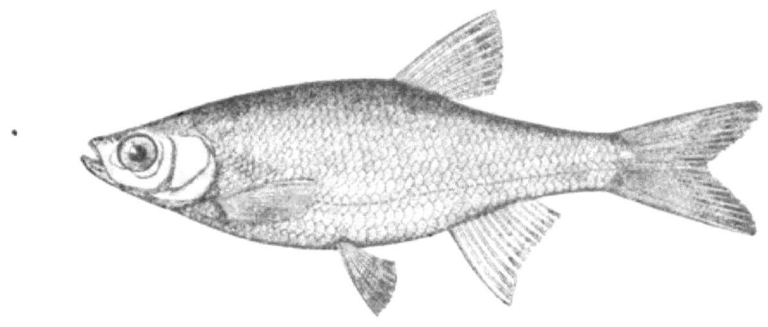

Figure 42. THE ROACH. Page 53.

FISHES OF PENNSYLVANIA. BEAN. PLATE 25.

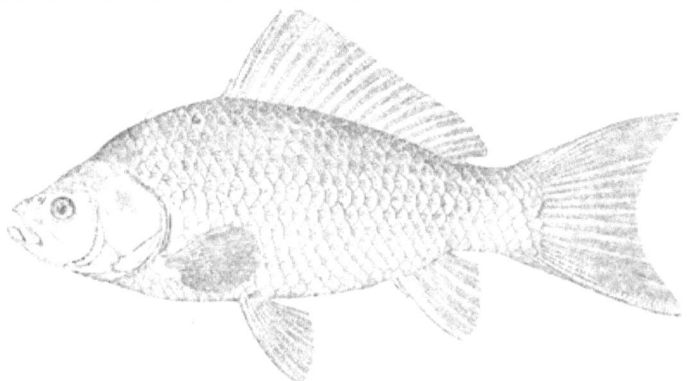

Figure 43.   THE GOLD FISH.   Page 54.

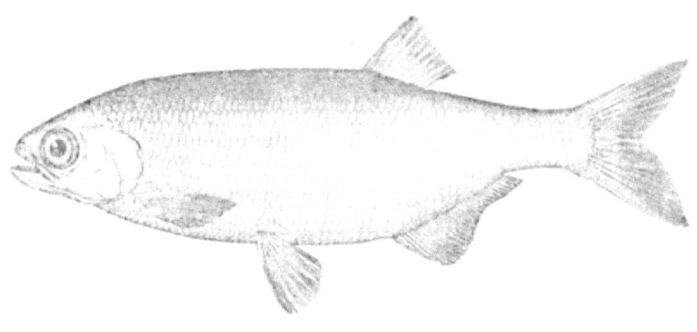

Figure 44.   THE NORTHERN MOON-EYE.   Page 57.

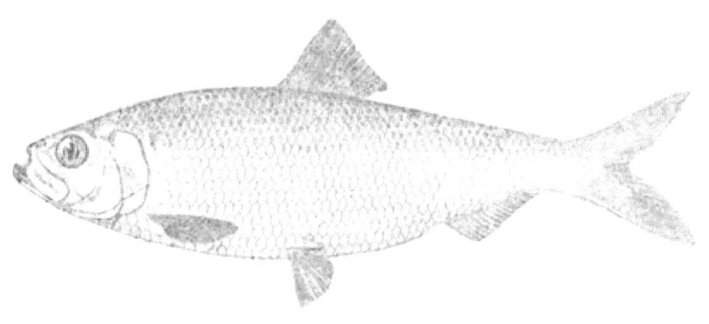

Figure 45.   THE BRANCH HERRING.   Page 58.

FISHES OF PENNSYLVANIA - BEAN. PLATE 26.

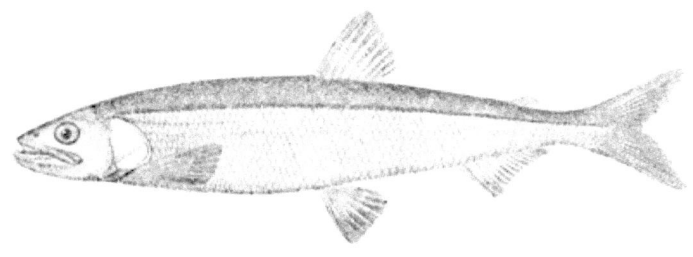

Figure 46.   THE SMELT.   Page 64.

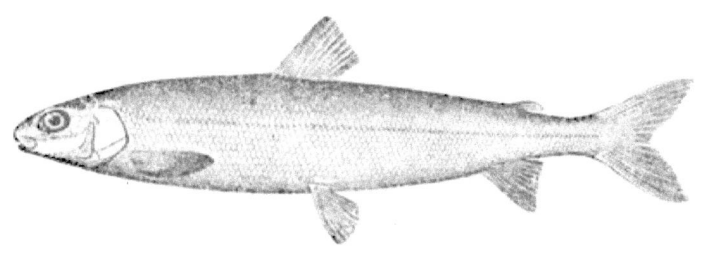

Figure 47.   THE ROUND WHITEFISH.   Page 66.

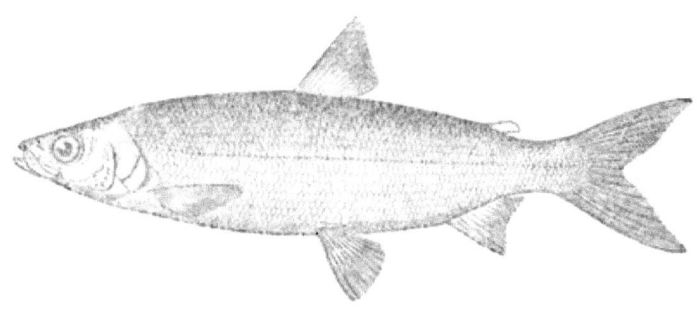

Figure 48.   THE LAKE HERRING.   Page 69.

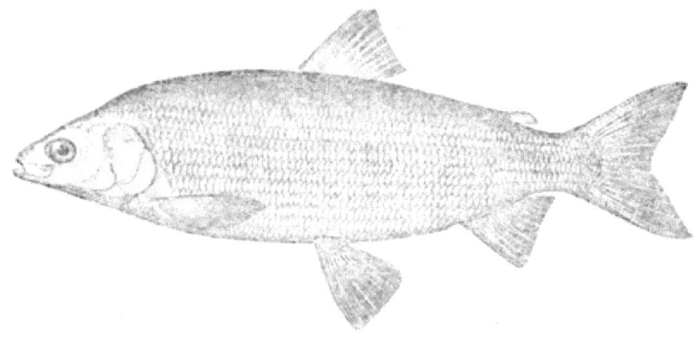

Figure 49. THE TULLIBEE. Page 70.

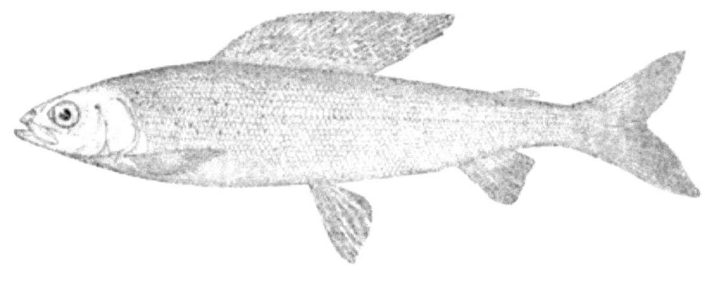

Figure 50. THE GRAYLING. Page 71.

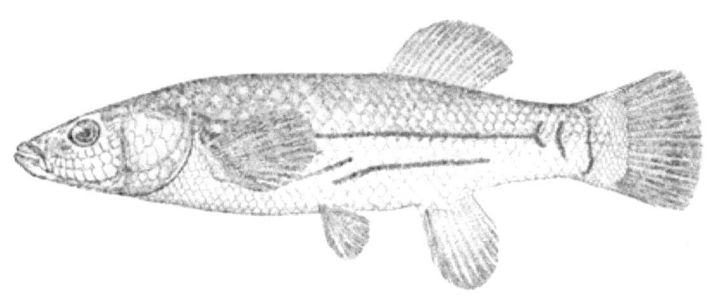

Figure 51. THE STRIPED KILLIFISH. Page 84.

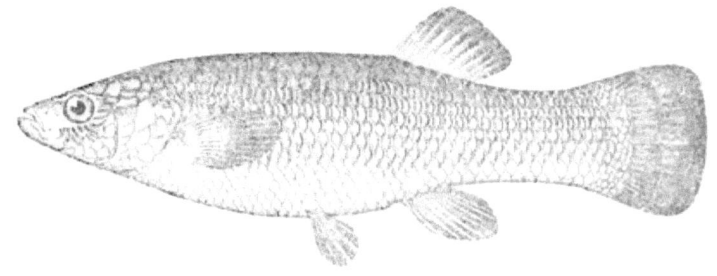

Figure 52. THE COMMON KILLIFISH. Page 86.

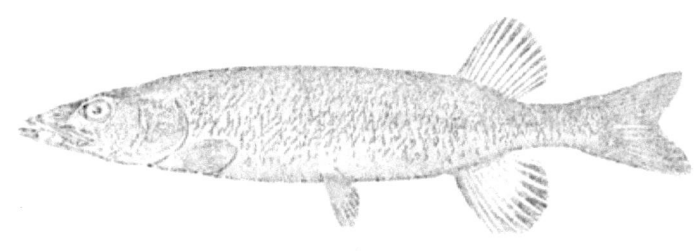

Figure 53. THE BANDED PICKEREL. Page 89.

Figure 54. THE LITTLE PICKEREL. Page 90.

Figure 55. THE CHAIN PICKEREL. Page 90.

Figure 56. THE PIKE. Page 91.

Figure 57. THE MASCALONGE. Page 93.

Figure 58.   THE EEL.   Page 95.

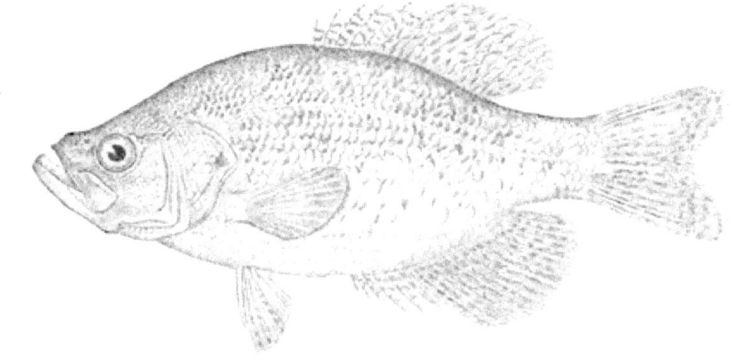

Figure 59.   THE CRAPPIE.   Page 103.

Figure 60.   THE BLACK-BANDED SUNFISH.   Page 109.

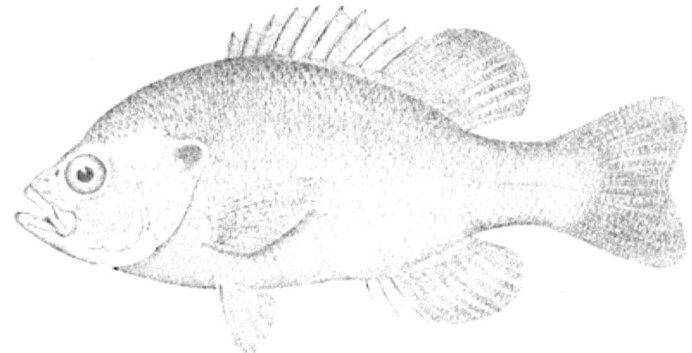

Figure 61. THE GREEN SUNFISH. Page 110.

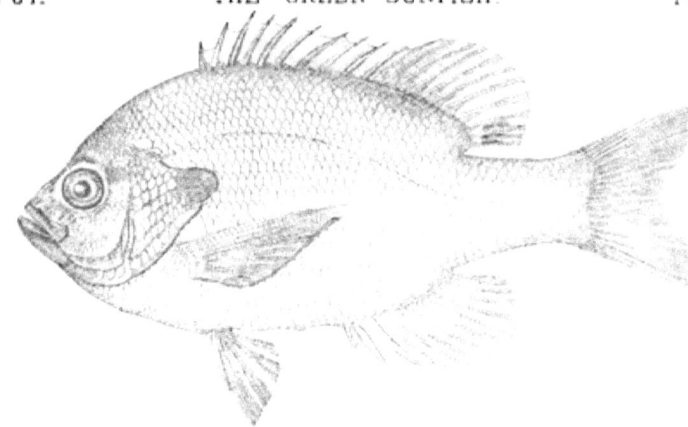

Figure 62. THE BLUE SUNFISH. Page 112.

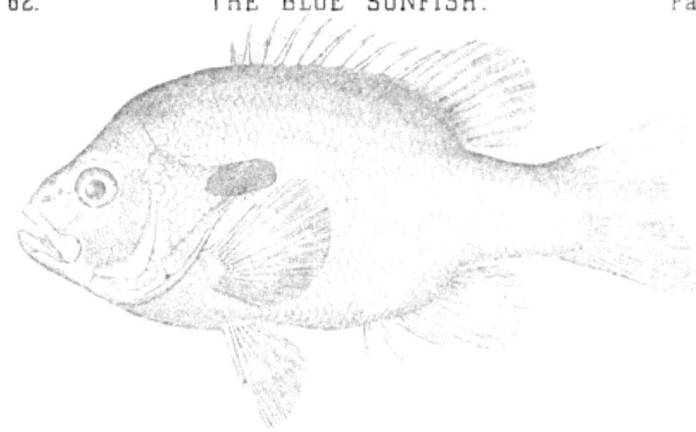

Figure 63. THE LONG-EARED SUNFISH. Page 113.

Figure 64.   THE RED-BELLIED BREAM.   Page 114.

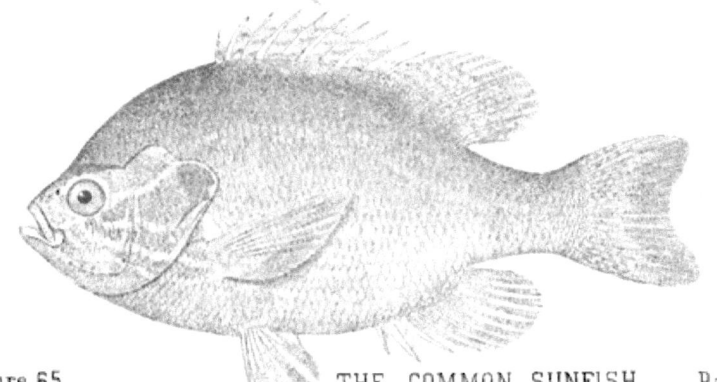

Figure 65.   THE COMMON SUNFISH.   Page 115.

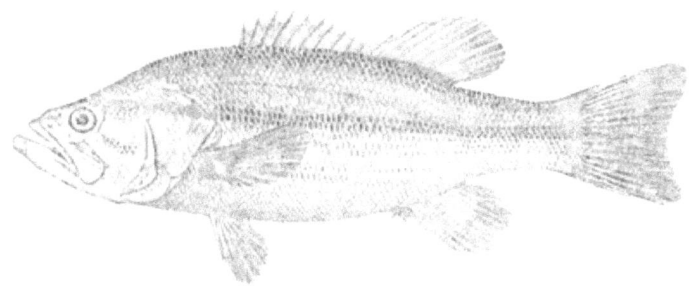

Figure 66.   THE LARGE-MOUTHED BLACK BASS.   Page 118.

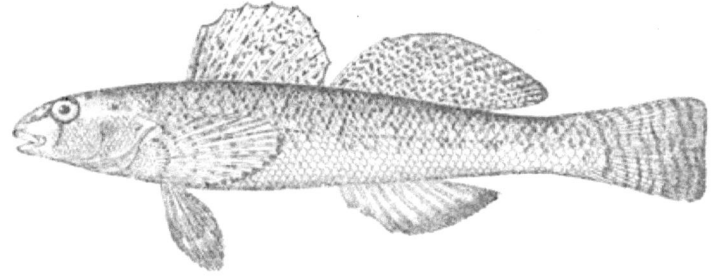

Figure 67.   THE TESSELLATED DARTER.   Page 120.

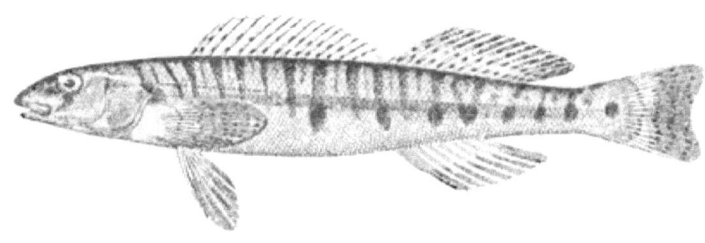

Figure 68.   THE LOG PERCH.   Page 122.

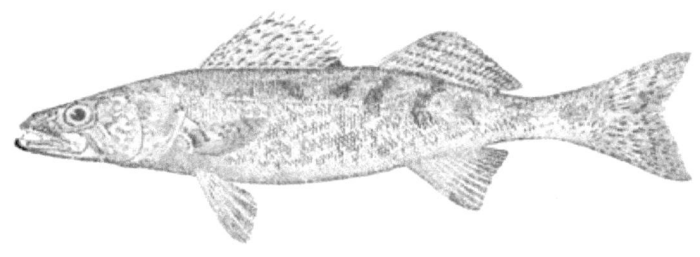

Figure 69.   THE BLUE PIKE.   Page 129.

FISHES OF PENNSYLVANIA – BEAN. PLATE 34.

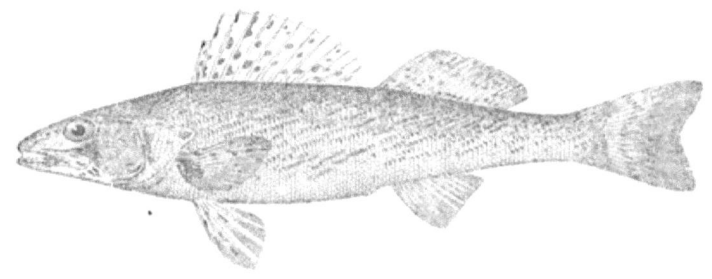

Figure 70.   THE SAUGER.   Page 130.

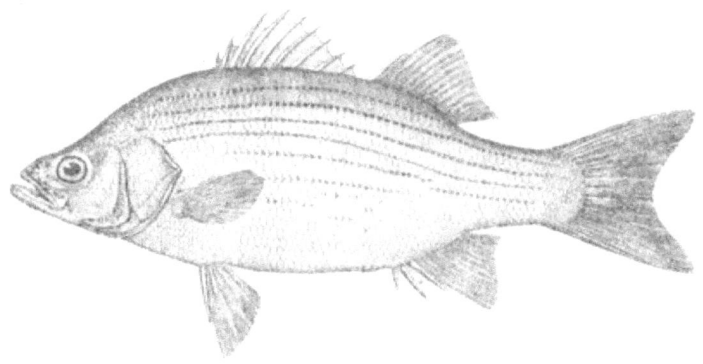

Figure 71.   THE WHITE BASS.   Page 132.

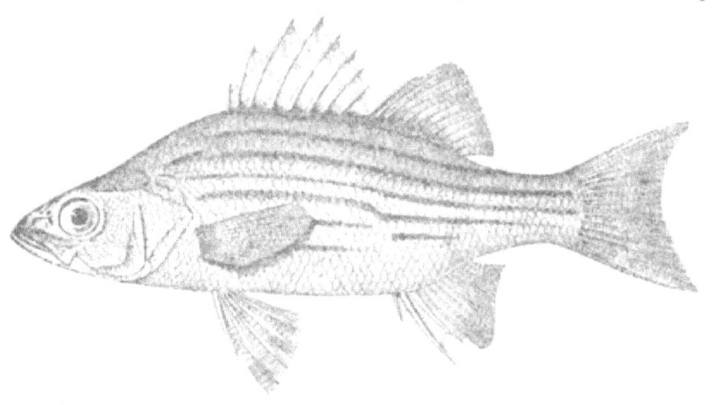

Figure 72.   THE YELLOW BASS.   Page 134.

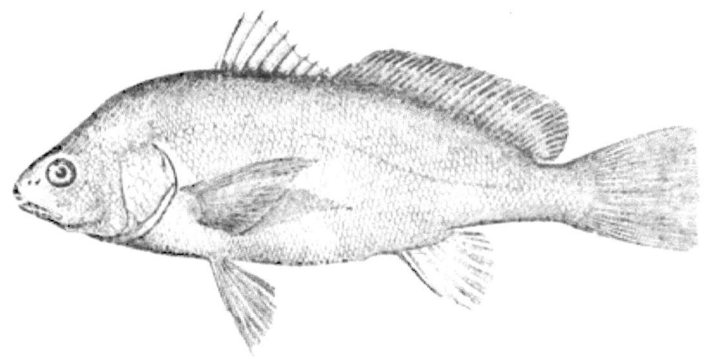

Figure 73.   THE FRESH WATER DRUM   Page 135.

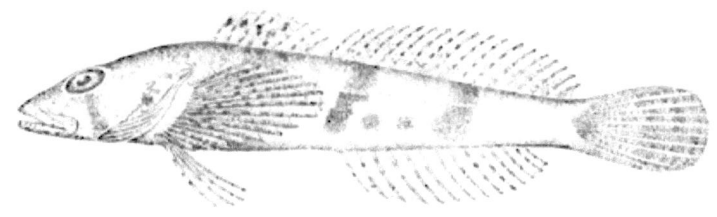

Figure 74.   THE MILLERS THUMB   Page 136.

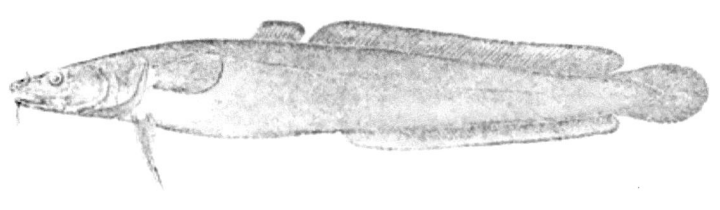

Figure 75.   THE BURBOT.   Page 137.

INDEX OF COMMON AND SCIENTIFIC NAMES.

A.

Acantharchus, 107
Acantharchus pomotis, 107
Acanthopteri, 101
Achigan, 117
Acipenser, 5, 6
Acipenser brevirostrum, 7
Acipenser rubicundus, 8
Acipenser sturio, 6
Acipenseridæ, 5
Alburnellus rubrifrons, 44
Aleby trout, 138
Alewife, 58
Alewife, branch, 59
Alligator, 10
Allosomus, 66
Ambloplites, 105
Ambloplites rupestris, 105
Amia, 11
Amia calva, 11
Amiidæ, 11
Amiurus, 13
Amiurus albidus, 14
Amiurus marmoratus, 16
Amiurus melas, 16, 18
Amiurus natalis, 15
Amiurus nebulosus, 15, 16, 18
Amiurus nigricans, 13
Amiurus ponderosus, 13
Amiurus vulgaris, 15
Ammocœtes, 1
Ammocœtes branchialis, 1
Ammocœtes niger, 1
Anguilla, 95
Anguilla rostrata, 95
Anguillidæ, 95
Apeltes, 99
Apeltes quadracus, 99
Aphredoderidæ, 101
Aphredoderus, 101
Aphredoderus sayanus, 101
Aplodinotus, 135
Aplodinotus grunniens, 133, 135
Apodes, 95
Argentinidæ, 64
Argyrosomus, 66
Atherinidæ, 100

B.

Bachelor, 103
Bachforelle, 78
Bar fish, 102
Bass, banklick, 102
Bass, bayou, 118
Bass, big, 117
Bass, big-fin, 102
Bass, black, 117
Bass, brown, 117
Bass, calico, 102
Bass, dark, 117
Bass fry, 85
Bass, gold, 117
Bass, grass, 102
Bass, green, 118
Bass, hog, 117
Bass, lake, 102, 105, 117
Bass, Lake Erie, 102
Bass, large-mouthed black, 118
Bass, little, 117
Bass, minny, 117
Bass, moss, 118
Bass mummy, 85
Bass, Oswego, 118
Bass, Otsego, 67
Bass, river, 118
Bass, rock, 105
Bass, silver, 57, 102, 132
Bass, small-mouthed black, 116
Bass, spotted, 117
Bass, strawberry, 102
Bass, streaked, 131
Bass, striped, 130, 132
Bass, white, 132
Bass, yellow, 117, 134
Belonidæ, 97
Bill-fish, 4, 10, 97
Bitter head, 102
Black-head, 35
Black horse, 24
Blob, 136
Blue Johnny, 125
Blunt jaw, 34
Boleosoma æsopus, 121
Boleosoma effulgens, 121
Boleosoma nigrum, 120, 121

(141)

Bony fish, 63
Bow-fins, 11
Bream, 54, 113, 116
Bream, blue, 112
Bream, copper-nosed, 112
Bream, red-bellied, 113, 114, 115
Bream, red-head, 113
Bream, red-tailed, 113
Brevoortia, 63
Brevoortia tyrannus, 63
Brochet, 92
Bronze backer, 117
Brook trout, 80
Buffalo, black, 21
Buffalo, brown, 21
Buffalo, high-backed, 21
Buffalo, mongrel, 21
Buffalo, small-mouthed, 21
Buffalo-fish, 10
Buffalo fish, big-mouthed, 21
Buffalo fish, red-mouthed, 21
Buffalo fishes, 21
Bug-fish, 63
Bull-head, 16, 136
Bull-pout, 16
Bunker, 63
Burbot, 137
Burn stickle, 99

C.

Calico bass, 102
Campbellite, 104
Campostoma, 32
Campostoma anomalum, 32
Carassius, 54
Carp, 24, 55
Carp, river, 23
Carp sucker, 23, 24
Carp sucker, silvery, 24
Carpe blanche, 26
Cat, big-mouthed, 14
Cat, blue, 12
Cat, channel, 12
Cat, chubby, 15
Cat, duck-billed, 4
Cat, flannel-mouthed, 13
Cat, flat-head, 18
Cat, Florida, 13
Cat, great blue, 13
Cat, great fork-tailed, 13
Cat, Mississippi, 13
Cat, mud, 18
Cat, Russian, 18
Cat, Schuylkill, 14
Cat, silver, 12
Cat, spotted, 12
Cat, white, 12
Cat, yellow, 18
Cat, yellow stone, 19
Catfish, brown, 17
Catfish, cave, 17
Catfish, channel, 14
Catfish, common, 16
Catfish, great, 13
Catfish, long-jawed, 15
Catfish, margined stone, 19
Catfish, mud, 18
Catfish, small black, 16
Catfish, spotted, 12
Catfish, stone, 18
Catfish, tadpole stone, 20
Catfish, white, 14
Catfish, yellow, 15
Cat-fishes, 12
Catostomidæ, 21
Catostomus, 25
Catostomus catostomus, 25
Catostomus nigricans, 26
Catostomus teres, 25
Cayuga Lake shad, 58
Centrarchidæ, 102
Ceratophyllum, 22
Chain-side, 111
Chivey, 66
Chog-mummy, 87
Chouicha, 72
Chrosomus, 32
Chrosomus erythrogaster, 32
Chub, 36, 37, 51, 118
Chub, big-eyed, 49
Chub, butter, 37
Chub, common, 51
Chub, creek, 51
Chub, day, 37
Chub, horned, 49, 51
Chub, nigger, 37, 50
Chub, river, 50
Chub, silver, 49
Chub-eel, 138
Cisco, 69
Clinostomus margarita, 53
Clupea, 58, 60
Clupea chrysochloris, 59
Clupea sapidissima, 60
Clupea vernalis, 58
Clupeidæ, 58
Cobbler, 87
Cod, fresh-water, 138
Coregonidæ, 65
Coregonus, 65, 66
Coregonus artedi, 14, 66, 68, 69
Coregonus clupeiformis, 66, 67
Coregonus quadrilateralis, 66

Coregonus richardsoni, 67
Coregonus tullibee, 66, 70
Cottidæ, 136
Crappie, 103
Crawl-a-bottom, 27, 122
Creek fish 27
Croaker, 135
Crocus, 135
Croppie, black, 102
Croppie, lake, 102
Croppie, timber, 104
Croppie, white, 104
Cusk, lake, 138
Cut-lips, 36, 37
Cyclas, 136
Cycleptus, 24
Cycleptus elongatus, 24
Cyclops, 4, 62, 117
Cyclostomi, 1
Cylindrosteus, 10
Cyprinidæ, 32
Cyprinodontidæ, 84
Cyprinus, 55
Cyprinus carpio, 55

D.

Dace, 40, 50
Dace, black-nosed, 47, 48
Dace, black-striped, 52
Dace, horned, 50, 51, 52
Dace, long-nosed, 46, 47
Dace, red-bellied, 32, 33
Dace, rosy, 53
Dace, silver-mouthed, 45
Daphnia, 62, 117
Darter, black-sided, 123
Darter, blenny, 124
Darter, blue, 125
Darter, fan-tail, 125
Darter, green-sided, 121
Darter, Johnny, 120
Darter, long-headed, 122
Darter, rainbow, 125
Darter, sand, 119
Darter, shielded, 123
Darter, spotted, 121
Darter, tessellated, 120
Darter, trout, 125
Darter, variegated, 124
Darter, zoned, 124
Dog-fish, 11, 88, 138
Dollardee, 112
Doré, 128
Dorosoma, 60, 63
Dorosoma cepedianum, 63
Drum, fresh-water, 135

E.

Eel, 95
Eel, lamprey, 2
Eelpout, 138
Ellwhop, 58
Ellwife, 58
Enneacanthus, 108
Enneacanthus obesus, 108
Enneacanthus simulans, 108
Entomostraca, 24
Ericymba, 45
Ericymba buccata, 45
Erimyzon, 27
Erimyzon oblongus, 27
Erimyzon sucetta, 27
Esocidæ, 89
Esox, 89, 91
Esox americanus, 89
Esox immaculatus, 93
Esox lucius, 91
Esox nobilior, 93
Esox reticulatus, 90
Esox vermiculatus, 90
Etheostoma, 119
Etheostoma æsopus, 121
Etheostoma aspro, 123
Etheostoma blennioides, 121
Etheostoma caprodes, 122
Etheostoma cœruleum, 125
Etheostoma flabellare, 125
Etheostoma macrocephalum, 122
Etheostoma maculatum, 125
Etheostoma nigrum, 120
Etheostoma olmstedi, 120
Etheostoma pellucida, 119
Etheostoma peltatum, 123
Etheostoma variatum, 124
Etheostoma zonale, 124
Eucalia, 98
Eucalia inconstans, 98
Eventognathi, 24
Exoglossum, 36
Exoglossum maxillingua, 36

F.

Fall fish, 50
Fall fish, smaller, 51
Fario, 74
Fat-head, 35
Frost fish, 66
Fundulus, 84
Fundulus diaphanus, 85
Fundulus grandis, 87
Fundulus heteroclitus, 86
Fundulus majalis, 84
Fundulus menona, 86

G.

Gadidæ, 137
Gar, alligator, 10
Gar, bony, 10
Gar fishes, 9
Gar, short-nosed, 10
Gar, silver, 97
Gar, soft, 97
Gar pike, 9
Gar pike, common, 10
Gar pike, long-nosed, 10
Gar pike, short-nosed, 10
Gars, bony, 9
Gaspagie, 135
Gaspereau, 58
Gaspergou, 135
Gasterosteidæ, 98
Gasterosteus, 98
Gasterosteus aculeatus, 98
Gasterosteus cataphractus, 99
Ginglymodi, 9
Glaniostomi, 5
Glass-eye, 128
Goggle-eye, 102, 104, 105
Gold fish, 54
Goujon, 18
Gray-back, 58
Grayling, 71
Grayling, Alaskan, 71
Grayling, Michigan, 71
Grayling, Rocky Mountain, 71
Green head, 131
Grindle, 11
Gronias, 17
Gronias nigrilabris, 17
Growler, 117
Gudgeon, 39
Gudgeon, New York, 85
Gudgeon, Niagara, 47

H.

Hairy back, 64
Halecomorphi, 11
Hammer head, 27
Haplomi, 84
Hecht, 92
Hemibranchii, 98
Herring, branch, 58
Herring, big-eyed, 58
Herring, lake, 69
Herring, river, 58
Herring, spring, 58
Herring, thread, 64
Herring, toothed, 57
Herring, wall-eyed, 58
Herrings, 58

Hiodon, 56
Hiodon alosoides, 57
Hiodon tergisus, 57
Hiodontidæ, 56
Hog fish, 122
Hog molly, 27, 122
Hog mullet, 27
Horn-fish, 128
Horn-pout, 16
Horny-head, 50
Horse fish, 130
Hybognathus, 33
Hybognathus nuchalis, 33, 35
Hybognathus regius, 33, 34
Hybopsis, 48
Hybopsis amblops, 49
Hybopsis bifrenatus, 37
Hybopsis chalybæus, 41
Hybopsis dissimilis, 48
Hybopsis kentuckiensis, 49
Hyperoartia, 1

I.

Ichthyomyzon, 3
Ictalurus, 12
Ictalurus punctatus, 12
Ictiobus, 21
Ictiobus bubalus, 21
Ictiobus carpio, 22
Ictiobus cyprinus, 24
Ictiobus difformis, 22
Ictiobus urus, 21
Ictiobus velifer, 23
Isospondyli, 56

J.

Jack, 91, 128
Jerker, 50
Jewel-head, 135
John-a-grindle, 11
John demon, 104
Jumper, 117, 118

K.

Killifish, barred, 85, 86
Killifish, common, 86
Killifish, striped, 84, 85

L.

Labidesthes, 100
Labidesthes sicculus, 100
Lake cusk, 138
Lamp-lighter, 102
Lamprey, brook, 1
Lamprey, mud, 1
Lamprey, sea, 2

Lamprey, silver, 3
Lamprey, small black, 1
Lamprey eel, 2
Lampreys, 1
Lawyer, 11, 138
Lepisosteidæ, 9
Lepisosteus, 9
Lepisosteus osseus, 9
Lepisosteus platystomus, 10
Lepomis, 110
Lepomis auritus, 113
Lepomis cyanellus, 110
Lepomis gibbosus, 115
Lepomis macrochirus, 111
Lepomis megalotis, 114
Lepomis pallidus, 112
Leptops, 18
Leptops olivaris, 18
Limnæa, 8
Ling, 138
Log perch, 122
Losh, 138
Lota, 137
Lota maculosa, 137
Luccio, 92
Lunge, 82

M.

Mackinaw, 82
Marthy, 138
Mascalonge, 93
Mascalongus, 93
Maskinonge, 94
May fish, 85
Melantho, 8
Menhaden, 63
Menidia, 100
Menidia beryllina, 100
Menidia peninsulæ, 100
Menobranchus, 68
Mesogonistius, 109
Mesogonistius chætodon, 109
Methy, 138
Micropterus, 116
Micropterus dolomieu, 116
Micropterus salmoides, 118
Miller's thumb, 136
Miller's thumb, slender, 137
Miller's thumb, slippery, 137
Minister, 16
Minnow, blunt-nosed, 36
Minnow, bridled, 37
Minnow, emerald, 44
Minnow, fat-head, 35
Minnow, hungry, 41
Minnow, mud, 88
Minnow, pearl, 53

Minnow, pigmy, 41
Minnow, red-bellied, 33
Minnow, red-sided, 52
Minnow, rosy-faced, 44
Minnow, salt-water, 86
Minnow, silvery, 33, 34, 39
Minnow, smelt, 34
Minnow, steel-back, 32
Minnow, sucker, 46
Minnow, toothed, 86
Minnows, 32
Minytrema, 28
Minytrema melanops, 28
Moon-eye, 57
Moon-eye, northern, 57
Moon-eyes, 56
Morone, 132
Morone americana, 132
Morone interrupta, 134
Moss bunker, 63
Mother-of-eels, 138
Moxostoma, 28
Moxostoma anisurum, 28
Moxostoma aureolum, 30
Moxostoma crassilabre, 30
Moxostoma duquesnei, 29
Moxostoma macrolepidotum, 29
Mud-dace, 88
Mud-fish, 11, 86
Mud-minnow, 88
Mud-minnow, striped, 88
Muffle-jaws, 136
Mullet, 27, 29
Mullet, carp, 29
Mullet, lake, 30
Mummichog, 86
Mummichog, banded, 85
Mummichog, spring, 86
Mummichog, striped, 85
Mummy, 87
Mummy, bass, 85
Muscalonge, 94
Muskallunge, 94
Muskellunge, 94
Myzonts, 1

N.

Namaycush, 82
Needle fish, 97
Nematognathi, 12
Newlight, 104
Notemigonus, 53
Notemigonus chrysoleucus, 53
Notropis, 37
Notropis amarus, 38, 39
Notropis ardens, 42
Notropis atherinoides, 44

10 FISHES.

Notropis bifrenatus, 37
Notropis chalybaeus, 41
Notropis dilectus, 44
Notropis dinemus, 45
Notropis hudsonius, 34, 38, 39
Notropis jejunus, 41
Notropis megalops, 40
Notropis photogenis, 43
Notropis procne, 37
Notropis scabriceps, 42
Notropis whipplei, 39
Noturus, 15, 18
Noturus flavus, 18
Noturus gyrinus, 20
Noturus insignis, 19
Noturus marginatus, 20

O.

Okow, 128
Oncorhynchus, 72
Oncorhynchus chouicha, 72
Osmerus, 64
Osmerus mordax, 64

P.

Paddle-fish, 3, 4
Paddle-fishes, 3
Painted tail, 117
Paludina, 136
Pearch, black, 117
Pearch, trout, 117
Perca, 126
Perca flavescens, 126
Percesoces, 100
Perch, 113
Perch, black, 117
Perch, bridge, 104, 117
Perch, chinquapin, 102, 104
Perch, goggle-eyed, 102
Perch, log, 122
Perch pike, 127
Perch, pirate, 101
Perch, red-bellied, 113
Perch, red-eyed, 105
Perch, ringed, 126
Perch, sand, 102
Perch, silver, 102
Perch, speckled, 104
Perch, strawberry, 102, 104
Perch, striped, 126
Perch, sun, 113
Perch, tin, 104
Perch, trout, 84, 117
Perch, white, 132, 135
Perch, yellow, 117, 126
Percidae, 119

Percopsidae, 84
Percopsis, 84
Percopsis guttatus, 84
Petromyzon, 1, 2
Petromyzon concolor, 3, 9
Petromyzon marinus, 2
Petromyzontidae, 1
Phenacobius, 46
Phenacobius teretulus, 46
Phoxinus, 52
Phoxinus elongatus, 52
Phoxinus funduloides, 52
Phoxinus margaritus, 53
Physa, 8
Picarel, 128
Pickerel, 92, 128, 130
Pickerel, banded, 89
Pickerel, chain, 90
Pickerel, eastern, 91
Pickerel, great northern, 92
Pickerel, little, 90
Pickering, 130
Picorellus, 89
Pike, 91
Pike, blue, 94, 128, 129
Pike, bony, 10
Pike, federation, 91
Pike, grass, 92, 128
Pike, gray, 130
Pike, great, 94
Pike, green, 91, 128, 130
Pike, lake, 92
Pike, mackerel, 89
Pike perch, 127
Pike, sand, 130
Pike, wall-eyed, 128
Pike, yellow, 128
Pilot-fish, 66
Pimelodus lemniscatus, 20
Pimelodus livrée, 20
Pimephales, 35
Pimephales notatus, 36
Pimephales promelas, 35
Pirate perch, 101
Pisces, 3
Placopharynx, 31
Placopharynx carinatus, 31
Planorbis, 8
Poecilichthys, 121
Polyodon, 3
Polyodon spathula, 3
Polyodontidae, 3
Pomoxys, 102
Pomoxys annularis, 103
Pomoxys sparoides, 102
Prosopium, 66
Pumpkin seed, 116

Q.

Quill-back, 23, 24

R.

Razor-back, 102
Red breast, 113
Red-eye, 105, 111
Red-fin, 40, 42, 43
Red horse, 29
Red horse, golden, 30
Red horse, lake, 30
Red horse, long-tailed, 29, 30
Red horse, small-mouthed, 29
Rhinichthys, 46
Rhinichthys atronasus, 47
Rhinichthys cataractæ, 46
Rhinichthys obtusus, 48
Roach, 53, 54
Rock, 131
Rockfish, 48, 122, 131
Roccus, 130
Roccus chrysops, 132
Roccus lineatus, 130
Rough head 40
Round-fish, 66

S.

Sac-a-lait, 102, 103
Sail fish, 23, 24
Salmo, 74
Salmo fario, 78
Salmo irideus, 77
Salmo salar, 74
Salmon, 4
Salmon, Atlantic, 74
Salmon, black, 82
Salmon, California, 72
Salmon, Chinnook, 72
Salmon, Columbia, 72
Salmon, jack, 128
Salmon killer, 99
Salmon, king, 72
Salmon, land-locked, 75
Salmon, quinnat, 72
Salmon, Sacramento, 72
Salmon, Sebago, 75
Salmon, spring, 72
Salmon, Susquehanna, 128
Salmon, Takou, 72
Salmon, white, 128, 129
Salmonidæ, 72
Salvelinus, 80
Salvelinus fontinalis, 80
Salvelinus namaycush, 82
Saprolegnia, 73

Sauger, 130
Saw-belly, 58
Scaphirhynchus, 5
Scaphirhynchus platyrhynchus, 5
Sciænidæ, 135
Selachostomi, 3
Semotilus, 50
Semotilus atromaculatus, 51
Semotilus bullaris, 50, 52
Serranidæ, 130
Shad, 60, 104
Shad, Cayuga Lake, 58
Shad, gizzard, 61
Shad, golden, 59, 60
Shad, hickory, 64
Shad, little, 58
Shad, mud, 63, 64
Shad, stink, 64
Shad-waiter, 66
Shad, white, 61
Shad, white-eyed, 64
Shad, winter, 64
Sheepshead, 135
Shiner, 37, 54
Shiner, common, 40
Shiner, golden, 54
Shiner, red-sided, 52
Shiner, rough-headed, 42
Shiner, spotted, 48
Shiner, white-eyed, 43
Shoemaker, 27
Shovel-fish, 4
Siluridæ, 12
Silver fin, 39
Silver fish, 54
Silverside, brook, 100
Silverside, river, 100
Skim-back, 23, 24
Skip-jack, 60, 101
Smelt, 39, 64
Soldier fish, 125
Spawn-eater, 38
Spear fish, 23, 24
Sphærium, 23, 24
Spoon-bill, 4
Squid hound, 131
Star-gazer, little, 137
Stickleback, bloody, 99
Stickleback, brook, 98
Stickleback, four-spined, 99
Stickleback, two-spined, 98
Stickleback, Williamson's, 98
Stink shad, 64
Stizostedion, 127
Stizostedion canadense, 130
Stizostedion vitreum, 127
Stizostedion vitreum salmoneum, 129

Stone lugger, 27, 32
Stone roller, 27, 32
Stone toter, 26, 32
Streaked head, 117
Sturgeon, bony, 8
Sturgeon, common, 6
Sturgeon, lake, 8
Sturgeon, Ohio river, 8
Sturgeon, red, 8
Sturgeon, rock, 8
Sturgeon, ruddy, 8
Sturgeon, sharp-nosed, 6
Sturgeon, short-nosed, 7
Sturgeon, shovel-nosed, 5
Sturgeon, spoon-billed, 4
Sturgeon, white, 6
Sturgeons, 5
Sucker, banded, 27
Sucker, big-jawed, 31
Sucker, black, 27
Sucker, black-nosed, 28
Sucker, brook, 26
Sucker, carp, 22, 23
Sucker, chub, 27
Sucker, common, 25
Sucker, deformed carp, 22
Sucker, golden, 30
Sucker, grey, 26
Sucker, gourd-seed, 24
Sucker, hog, 27
Sucker, large-scaled, 27, 29
Sucker, long-nosed, 25
Sucker, Missouri, 24
Sucker, mud, 27
Sucker, northern, 25
Sucker, olive, 22
Sucker, pale, 26
Sucker, red-sided, 25
Sucker, rounded, 27
Sucker, sailing, 23
Sucker, sand, 28
Sucker, soft, 28
Sucker, striped, 28
Sucker, sweet, 27
Sucker, white, 26, 29
Sucker, white-nosed, 28
Suckerel, 25
Suckers, 21
Sunfish, banded, 108
Sunfish, bass, 107
Sunfish, black-banded, 109
Sunfish, blue, 112
Sunfish, blue-spotted, 108, 111
Sunfish, chain-sided, 111
Sunfish, common, 115
Sunfish, green, 110, 111
Sunfish, long-eared, 113, 115

Sunfish, mud, 107
Sunfish, pond, 116
Sunny, 116
Susquehanna salmon, 128
Sword-fish, 10
Synentognathi, 97

T.

Teleostomi, 3
Thorn back, 99
Thunder pumper, 135
Thymallus, 71
Thymallus ontariensis, 71
Thymallus ontariensis cis-montanus 71
Thymallus signifer, 71
Tin month, 102
Tobacco box, 116
Togue, 82
Top minnow, black-sided, 87
Top minnow, striped, 87, 88
Trota, 78
Trout, 118
Trout, aleby, 138
Trout, brook, 77, 78, 80, 81
Trout, brown, 78, 117
Trout, California mountain, 77
Trout, golden, 77
Trout, gray, 82
Trout, lake, 82
Trout, mountain, 117
Trout perch, 84
Trout, rainbow, 77
Trout, red, 82
Trout, salmon, 82
Trout, speckled, 77, 81
Trout, von Behr, 78
Trout, white, 117
Truite, la, 78
Tuladi, 82
Tullibee, 70
Tylosurus, 97
Tylosurus marinus, 97

U.

Umbra, 88
Umbra limi, 88, 89
Umbra pygmaea, 88
Umbridae, 88
Uranidea, 136
Uranidea gracilis, 137
Uranidea meridionalis, 136
Uranidea richardsoni, 136
Uranidea viscosa, 137
Uranidea wilsoni, 136

V.

Valvata, 8

W.

Welshman, 118
White fish, 61, 67
White fish, Menomonee, 66
White fish, mongrel, 70
White fish, round, 66
White fishes, 65

Y.

Yellow tail, 85

Z.

Zygonectes, 87
Zygonectes dispar, 87
Zygonectes notatus, 87

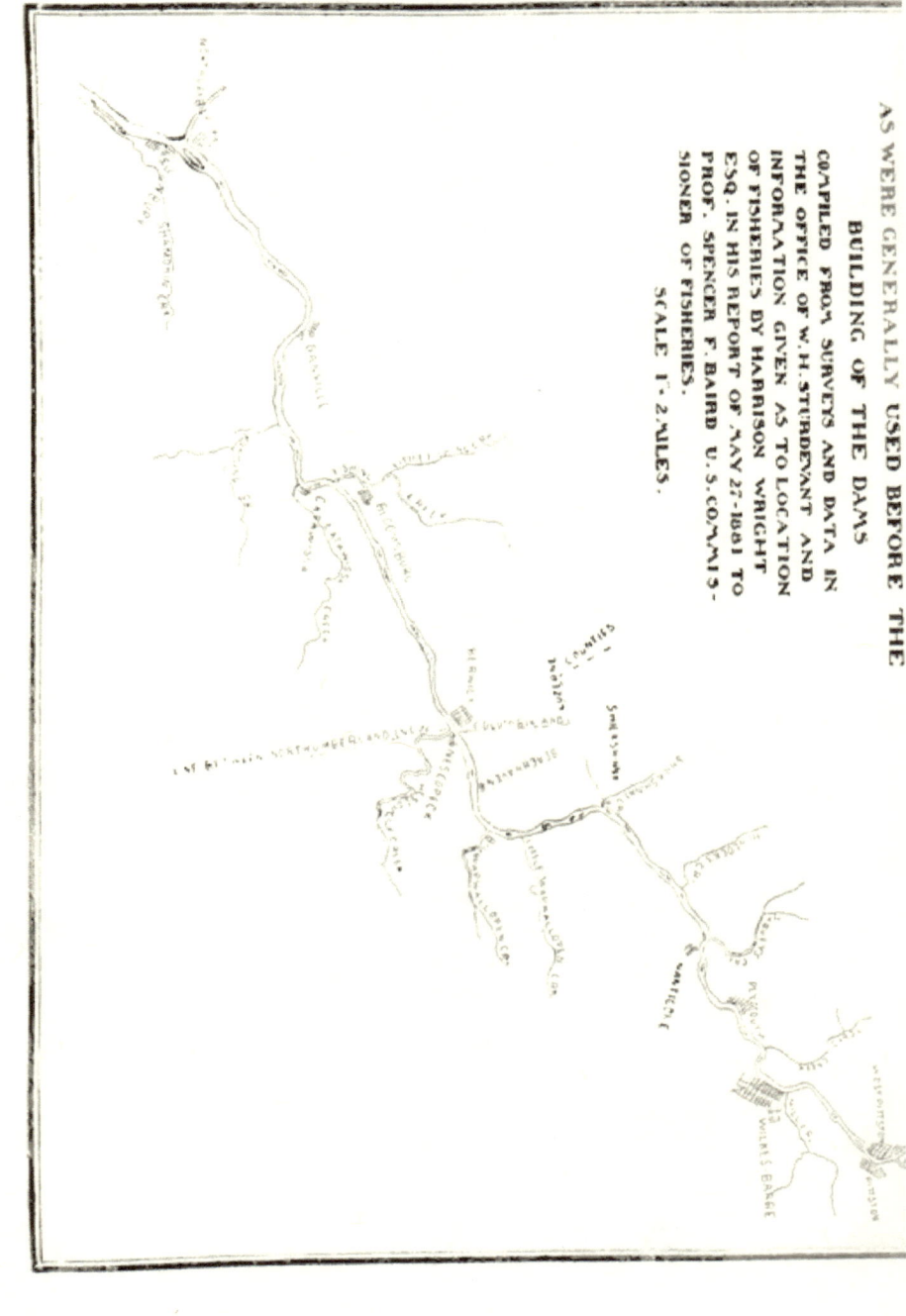

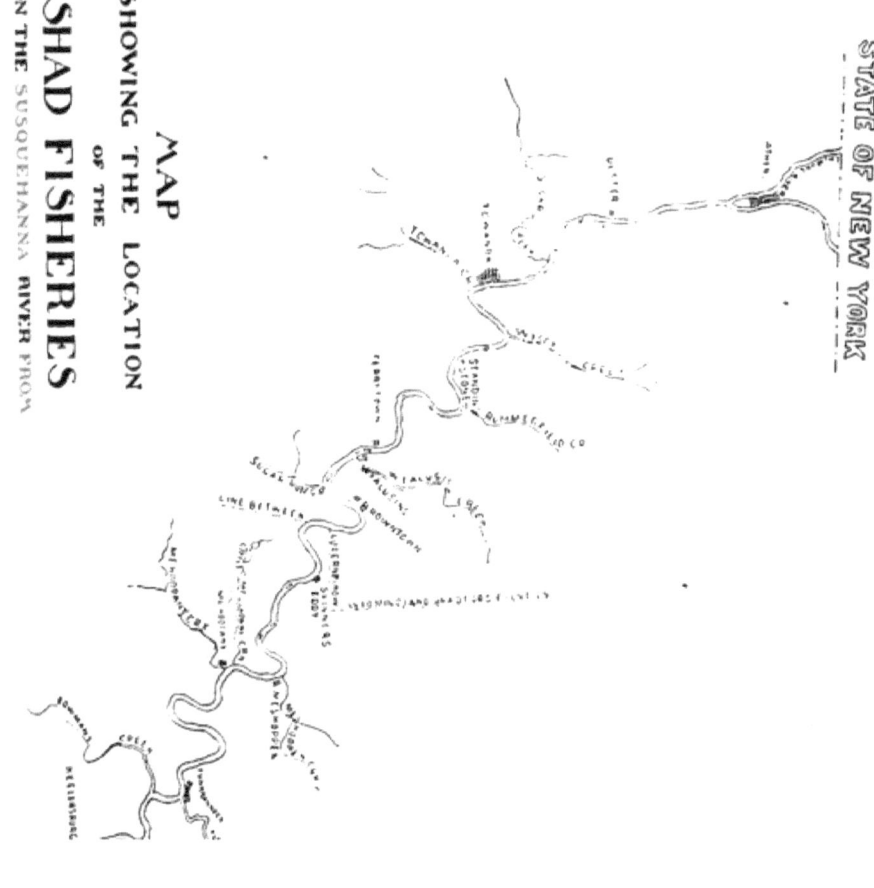

MAP SHOWING THE LOCATION OF THE SHAD FISHERIES ON THE SUSQUEHANNA RIVER FROM

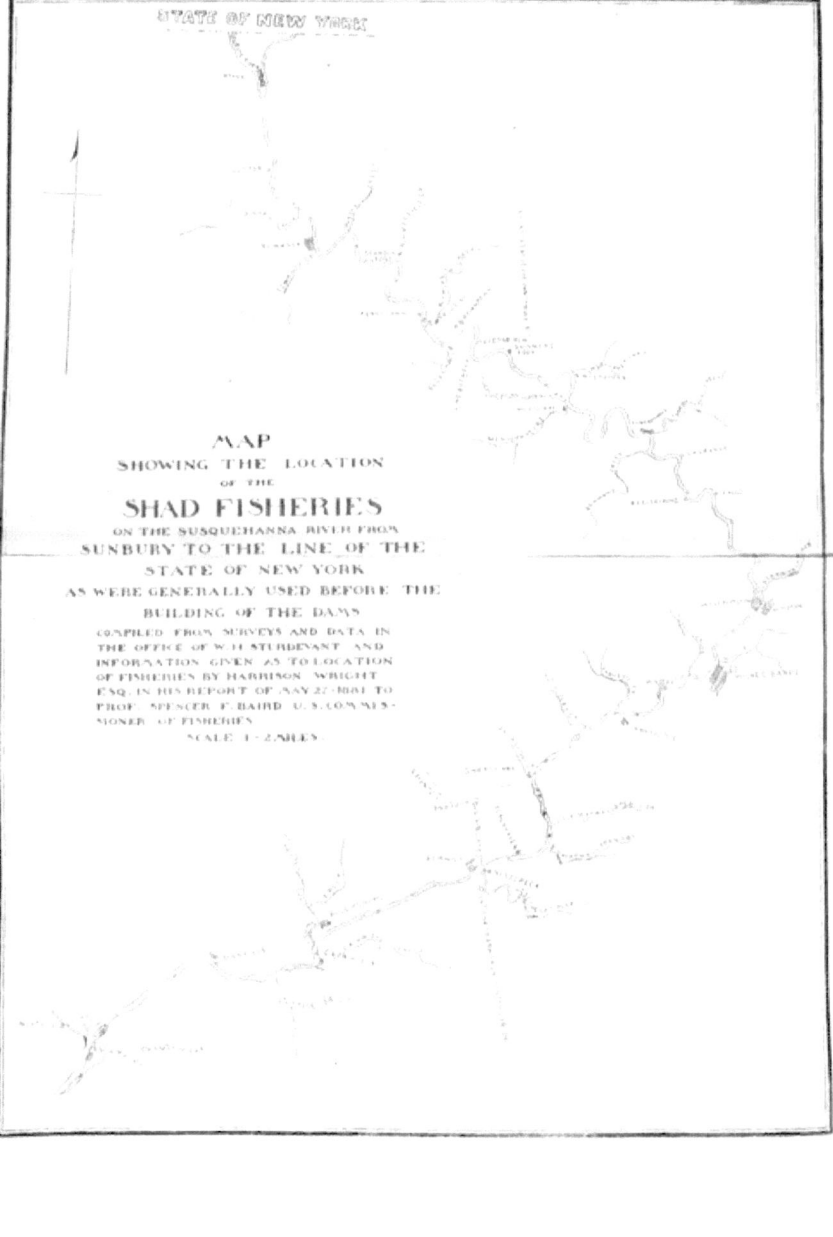

www.ingramcontent.com/pod-product-compliance
Lightning Source LLC
Chambersburg PA
CBHW021815230426
43669CB00008B/763